D1602329

The Super-Rich

Also by Stephen Haseler

THE GAITSKELLITES

THE DEATH OF BRITISH DEMOCRACY

THE TRAGEDY OF LABOUR

EUROCOMMUNISM

ANTI-AMERICANISM

THE BATTLE FOR BRITAIN: Thatcher and the New Liberals

THE POLITICS OF GIVING

THE END OF THE HOUSE OF WINDSOR

THE ENGLISH TRIBE

The Super-Rich

The Unjust New World of Global Capitalism

Stephen Haseler

First published in Great Britain 2000 by
MACMILLAN PRESS LTD
Houndmills, Basingstoke, Hampshire RG21 6XS and London
Companies and representatives throughout the world

A catalogue record for this book is available from the British Library.

ISBN 0–333–76428–5 hardcover
ISBN 0–333–76429–3 paperback

First published in the United States of America 2000 by
ST. MARTIN'S PRESS, INC.,
Scholarly and Reference Division,
175 Fifth Avenue, New York, N.Y. 10010

ISBN 0–312–23005–2

Library of Congress Cataloging-in-Publication Data
Haseler, Stephen, 1942–
The super-rich : the unjust new world of global capitalism / Stephen Haseler.
    p.   cm.
Includes bibliographical references and index.
ISBN 0–312–23005–2
1. Wealth.   2. Rich people.   3. Capitalism.   4. Income distribution.
5. International trade.   I. Title

HC79.W4 H375   1999

99–052035

This book is printed on paper suitable for recycling and made from fully managed and sustained
forest sources.

10   9   8   7   6   5   4   3   2
09   08   07   06   05   04   03   02   01

Printed & bound by Antony Rowe Ltd, Eastbourne

Dedicated to the memory of my mentor, **Tony Crosland**

Contents

Preface

The idea that the 1990s, following the collapse of the Cold War, represents the beginning of a new epoch in world history is now commonplace. So, too, is the view that we are faced with a new era of economics, based upon a new type of capitalism. This new capitalism– which has broken the borders of nations, and seems to be sweeping all before it–has already secured a whole genre of critical literature dedicated to explaining it. It has been called 'raw capitalism', 'turbo-capitalism', 'manic capitalism', 'casino capitalism', the 'global trap', or, more sedately, simply 'global capitalism.'

There is an insistent, nagging, question about this new capitalism. Is it a new dawn, or, as many serious writers are beginning to suggest, a new nightmare? In this book I often call this new world economic system 'Super-Rich Capitalism,' a term I hope will capture the flavour of what I believe to be its deadly serious social consequences, particularly the emergence of sharp inequalities within the domestic societies of the West. When some estimates calculate that the world's three richest people possess 'assets worth more than the combined gross domestic product of all the least-developed countries', and others point out that the wealthiest 500 people own as much wealth as half the population of the globe, and 500 hundred or so transnational corporations account for 80 per cent of world trade (and over 70 per cent of investment), then we certainly have a severe problem, if not exactly a nightmare, on our hands.[1]

In Chapter 1, I outline the contours of this new generation of super-rich and what are now their egregious, breath-taking, fortunes. New global capitalism is giving birth to nothing less than a new global aristocracy–a largely family-based class, or caste–which, through a variety of mechanisms, controls the huge accumulations of private capital – increasingly through inheritance. This class may or may not be as rigidly entrenched as were the old aristocracies, access is not nearly as restricted (particularly over the generations), and its numbers are growing; even so, the new global super-rich (together with the corporations they work through) are now largely unconstrained, indeed triumphant – so much so that they are even re-ordering the world according to their needs.

The great argument for old-style welfare capitalism used to be that, unequal though it was, it created a 'rising tide for *all* ships'. New global capitalism is no such 'rising tide.' As I attempt to describe in Chapter 3, the majority of us are beginning to feel decidedly insecure, and some of our ships are actually 'sinking'. Most people – middle America, middle England – need jobs. After all, a job is all that most people will ever have, and remains the key to a financially adequate life. Yet this bed rock of the western middle class is now under threat. In the new global capitalist system, work is becoming devalued, with the rewards for employment going sharply down and, crucially, the rewards for capital and inheritance going up.

Of course, globalists point to the much-touted 'US economic model' as creating large numbers of new jobs. But so many of them, as in the sister globalist economy, the UK, are low-paying, chronically insecure, and increasingly part-time with limited or no benefits. Sceptics, not unreasonably, describe them as 'McJobs', and their recipients as the 'working poor.' Indeed the new working poor in the Anglo-American world can be very poor indeed – at a recent count the lowest paid 10 per cent of European workers earn a staggering 44 per cent more than their US equivalents – many of whom possess a standard of living much lower than those out of work in Euroland.[2]

It is a huge irony – and a seriously bad omen – that in the new capitalism there are more risks attendant on working for a living than there are for owning capital. In reality, there is no 'flexible' capital market to equal the 'flexible labour market'. The basic right to capital (*as opposed to a job*) remains inviolate; and, in the real world, the owners of capital will only, at the very worst, lose but a portion of their 'possession' whereas the owner of a job can lose everything – and at regular intervals during a lifetime! It also augurs badly for the future that, in today's global capitalism, rewards often tend to be higher for doing nothing, or next to nothing – accruing and using capital through inheritance – than for the hard work of securing skills in order to work for a living.

As mobile capital seeks share 'performance' and lower and lower costs (particularly the social costs which pay for community services), and with the emergence into the world labour market of new economic super-powers, China and India, the western middle class is facing a future of deadly competition – low wages, low welfare and insecure work. In the name of global 'competitiveness' governments will compete with each other to bid down – and down – wages and welfare. It is, theoretically at least, difficult to see where and when this frightening downwards dynamic will end. It is not unreasonable to ask supporters of new global capitalism: 'when does the bidding down stop?'

As Christopher Whalen has argued, it was 'arrogant' for us in the west during the Bretton Woods era to believe that we could develop the industrial capacity of poor nations and believe that we would never have to compete with them, and that what we are now essentially doing is 'redistributing capital to certain poor countries at the expense of industrial workers in the advanced world. So we have to lower our standards of living for the middle class.' It is the central thesis of this book that there is now a divergence of interest between the mass of the western world's peoples and the global super rich – as they work the global system, what French economist Alain Parguez calls the 'international rentier economy. . . a regime which places the concerns of wealth holders ahead of other economic interests'.[3]

There is every sign that this new global capitalist system is still carrying all before it. Even after the Asian crises of 1997 and 1998 a United Nations analysis could still report that the global flow of capital (foreign direct investment) was rising, with only small falls in that directed to the developing countries. In fact the new capitalist system is such that these 'crises' can often give globalisation a fillip, by making the assets and labour costs in developing markets cheaper. Thus, looking to the future, we need to face the fact that, as things stand now, the new global capitalism – nothing if not dynamic – will forge, year after year, remorselessly, a brave new world of minimal government, lower and lower welfare, weaker and weaker state regulation.

This brave new world is all about economics. The new global system – big capital and the super-rich – is, literally, recreating the world: building a regime tailor-made to its needs in which even the realm of culture and ideology bends to its demands. I try to argue in Chapter 5, that the new capitalism and its market sovereignty is also destroying the realm of politics-that it is doing so by eroding the sense of political community, weakening the institutions of politics (primarily the nation-state), and discrediting politicians, and even the calling of the political and public life. Today's heroes are businessmen, not statesmen.

This deadly new global capitalism cannot be overthrown. The realistic goal must be to limit and constrain its reach, to civilise it, and calm it down. Supporters of global capitalism certainly possesses a sense of triumph, and a clear view that there is no alternative. I believe this to be wrong. What is needed now is a revived social democracy which is not fearful of the judicious use of state involvement, which seeks the vital – though unexciting task – of re-establishing the balance between the state and the market, the public and the private.

Unfortunately, at century's turn, the so-called 'left of centre' governments in Anglo-America, the parties of the 'third way' pioneered by Clinton and Blair, cannot, certainly as of writing, properly be described as seeking to restore the balance. The truth is that they, like their political opponents on the right, accept all the primary assumptions of the new capitalism, of globalisation, and of 'competitiveness.' They do not seek an enhanced state, or public sector, which can negotiate with mobile capital; rather, they advocate a handmaiden state – whose primary function is to provide skills to service capital.

If the 'third way' turns out not to be a new way at all, then the temptation amongst opponents of global capitalism will grow to revert to the kind of 1970s socialism which gave the left such a bad name – and, indeed, contributed to its historic defeat. The key to renewing the politics of the centre-left is not the need to return to command economy which threatened the pluralism inherent in the mixed economy, rather it is to renew faith in the judicious, strategic, use of power of the state, or the political community. A government's control over its internal market is the only lever the political community has left in negotiating with global capital – primarily the transnational corporations, but also with foreign exchange speculators. As I suggest in the final chapter, it should use it.

The central problem, though, is the increasing weakness of that erstwhile standard-bearer of the political community – the nation-state. Even most sizeable nation-states are simply no longer in a position to negotiate equally and seriously with mobile capital and global corporations – and there is also no immediate prospect of a global government arising to take the place of national governments. A world economic government – to parallel and to regulate global capitalism – will remain an aspiration only.

Difficult though it remains for many people to accept, the logic points in only one direction: that the only states that can properly negotiate with global capital and corporations are large 'regional' governments, the, often embryonic, regional super-states. As I argue in my final chapter, the prototype, of course, is the European Union and Euroland, where the union, its rich internal market, and its new single currency, the euro, can now bring serious political weight to bear upon global capital. There is, of course, another 'regional super-state' – one more mature than Europe, with all the necessary tools already at its disposal. It is, of course, the federal government of the USA. Washington, like

Brussels, is potentially immensely powerful, easily able should it possess the will to do so, to bring some balance to the global economy. That it cannot yet do so, that it is hobbled in negotiating with transnational capital, is testimony to the huge cultural hold of free-market ideology on the Americans.

What, then, are the real chances of containing and civilising global capitalism? William Greider has suggested that 'the elites of media, business, academia and politics...have already made up their mind on these questions. They are committed to promoting the global economic system- and to defending it from occasional attacks from angry, injured citizens.'[4] I'm not so sure. Already we can see the beginnings of a serious intellectual revolt against global capitalism. It is being fuelled by serious second thoughts from many who have been at the centre of global finance. Financiers George Soros and James Goldsmith have both written books warning about the dangers posed by the new global capitalism. Soros has gone as far as arguing that 'market fundamentalism is a greater threat to an open society than any totalitarian ideology'.[5] Felix Rohatyn, another serious financial practioner, and latterly US ambassador to France, takes the deficiencies of new global capitalism so seriously that he suggests that 'if we are to prevail in the arguments to come, we must make clear that we do not believe that open markets mean the end of government and the sacifice of social protection'.[6]

This reassessment is now being joined by writers as diverse as Kevin Phillips, Edward Luttwak, Michael Lind, William Greider and Lester Thurow, and in Europe, again from a wide variety of political backgrounds, by, amoungst others, John Gray, Will Hutton, Anthony Giddens, Hans-Peter Martin and Harald Schumann and Harry Shutt. Although, as of writing, this group is small beer compared with the still dominant pro-globalist outpourings of the mass media, such revisionism, even though it is against the grain, can, as long as it contains the kernel of a real truth, grow very, very, quickly.

In my mind much depends on Europe, more particularly the European Union, and more particularly still, Euroland. I argue in this book that a great world drama may be about to unfold – as the social market culture of Euroland (together with the social democratic governments of Germany and France) begins to look as though it could cohere into a political critical mass which may at last begin to confront the imperatives of global capitalism.

Such a confrontation will probably not be driven by ideology or political predilictions, but rather by events and pressures. Total immersion in the global capitalist world will, inevitably, demand ever more 'competitiveness' – and, with China and India joining the world labour market, Europe will need to compete by lowering wages, casualising employment, eroding the welfare state, and the public sector, and effectively ending the 'social partnership' between unions and business. Yet, even though the pressure is growing on the 'sclerotic' Europeans to so 'reform', and obey the imperatives of globalism, such a course, irrespective of its dubious merits, may, in democracies, simply not be politically possible to achieve.

As of writing, Europe seems to be coping relatively well with the global financial crisis which began to afflict the economy in 1997. The Euro – the most important global economic project since post-war reconstruction – has been launched, and the European Union remains the world's largest single market. Although the 'reforms' advocated by the globalists are being introduced at the margin of European life, the Union remains shielded from the new capitalism's worst excesses, and the fundamental structure of social democracy, or social market capitalism, remains securely intact.

As even that great modern monitor of popular moods, *Time* magazine, has argued, Europeans may indeed be able to 'chart their own course' separate from the 'flexible but relatively ruthless capitalism of the United States'.[7] Of course, as a leading commentator has suggested, the notion that 'the much maligned welfare states of Europe' could become 'a zone of relative currency stability and a source of growth is a big economic change that official Washington is having trouble taking on board. It contradicts much of the conventional wisdom that developed about the global economy in the 1990s.'[8]

How official Washington responds to this new Europe – to the idea that global free-market economics may have serious, potentially devastating, social consequences, and that there is an alternative, less destructive, social democratic economic model for the future – will determine the course of world economic history well into the new century.

In writing this book I am conscious that, as a political scientist, I bring the instincts and preferences of politics to bear upon the world of economics. I make no apology for this, as my own view is that the whole debate about globalisation and global capitalism is too narrowly defined, and often takes little account of its political, social and indeed cultural consequences. One of the great things about the arrival of the Euro on the world scene is that it is as much a political act –

indeed one of the great political acts of the twentieth-century – as it is an economic one.

The book is also an attempt to reassert, and place in a contemporary context, some of the postulates of pre-globalist social democracy. For this reason I have dedicated the book to the memory of my intellectual mentor, the British social democrat Tony Crosland. Re-reading his works again, after so many years, and now that the ravages of unconstrained market capitalism are all about us, I can see the force in his argument for balance, and for civilising capitalism. During the 1970s we lost this sense of balance as western societies careened towards an over-mighty state; yet, during the 1980s and 1990s, as a reaction to the failings of socialism, we have careened again – this time to a rapacious, raw capitalism.

In this environment the social democratic – or social market – legacy has taken a considerable battering at the hands of the free-market right in the last two decades. However, in my view, social democracy still stands as a realistic, credible, view of the world. To seek a productive capitalism, but only in the context of a strong political community which can constrain its excesses, is no pipe-dream. To stress political principle and human values – in Crosland's case the imperative of equality – amidst the insistent dry materialism of market economics may be an essential basis for making life in the twenty-first century tolerable. In the coming millennium it surely cannot be above the wit of humankind to so civilise the rawness and 'mania' of the global capitalist machine.

I would like to thank my colleagues at London Guildhall University, particularly my friend and colleague in the Euro Research Forum, Jacques Reland, and my research assistant, Robert Silver. Officials at the US Department of Labor, and at the Federal Reserve Board in Washington, DC, were extremely helpful. Among others who helped me arrive at my thoughts here – who listened, corrected, provided insights – were Jon Temple, Roger Fox, Dick Taverne, Dick Leonard, John Stevens, John Sheldrake, David Carlton and David Reisman, and in the United States Michael Lind and Mark Falcoff. Of course the views expressed here are mine and mine alone.

London
STEPHEN HASELER

Notes

1 Quotation from *International Herald Tribune* report of 1999 UN Human Development Report, 14 July 1999. The other figures are drawn from

Nawal el Saadawi, 'Sounding the Century' series on 28 February 1998, BBC Radio 3. Printed in *The Observer*, 22 February 1998.

2 Cited in David Smith, *Will Europe Work?* (London: 1999) p. 13.

3 Both quotations cited in William Greider, *One World, Ready or Not* (New York: 1997) p. 287.

4 William Greider, *Who will Tell the People* (New York: 1993) p. 393.

5 George Soros, *The Crisis of Global Capitalism* (London: 1998), p. xxii. See also James Goldsmith, *The Trap* (Basingstoke: 1993).

6 Felix Rohatyn, 'Markets with Protection, and America with Europe', *International Herald Tribune*, 15 October 1998.

7 'The Right Track', *Time*, 8 December 1997.

8 Jim Hoagland, 'Needed, a Cooperation Agenda for America, Europe and Japan', *International Herald Tribune*, 12 October 1998.

1
The New World

The super-rich

The end of the forty years of Cold War was more than the political triumph of the West over the Soviet Union. It was also more than the victory of freedom and pluralism over command communism. When the Berlin Wall cracked open and the iron curtain fell a new form of capitalism came into its own – global capitalism – and with it new global elite, a new class.

This new class already commands wealth beyond the imagination of ordinary working citizens. It is potentially wealthier than any super-rich class in history (including the robber barons, those 'malefactors of great wealth' criticised by Teddy Roosevelt, and the nineteenth-century capitalists who inspired the opposition of a century of Marxists). The new class of super-rich are also assuming the proportions of overlordship, of an overclass – as powerful, majestic and antidemocratic as the awesome, uncompromising imperial governing classes at the height of the European empires.

The awesome new dimension of today's super-rich – one which separates them sharply from earlier super rich – is that they owe no loyalty to community or nation. The wealthy used to be bounded within their nations and societies – a constraint that kept aggregations of wealth within reason and the rich socially responsible. Now, though, the rich are free: free to move their money around the world. In the new global economy super-rich wealth (capital) can now move their capital to the most productive (or high profit, low cost) haven, and with the end of the Cold War – and the entry into global economy of China, Russia, Eastern Europe and India – these opportunities have multiplied. The super-rich are also free to move themselves. Although still less mobile than their money, they too are becoming less rooted, moving easily between many different locations.

Millionaires

Mobility is made possible by the lack of a need to work – a 'lifestyle' normally fixed in one nation or location for many years at a time. It is this escape from the world of work which effectively defines the super-rich. The lowest-ranking dollar *millionaire* household can, depending upon the interest and inflation rate, secure an *unearned* annual income of, say, $60 000 per year, which is almost double that of the median annual income of American families and four times that of the median income of British households.[1]

These millionaires are by no means lavishly well-off, particularly if they are in three- or four-people families or households. However they are financially independent – as one commentary put it, they can 'maintain their lifestyle for years and years without earning even one month's pay'.[2] It has been estimated that in 1996 there were as many as six million dollar millionaires in the world, up from two million at the end of the Cold War.[3] Over half of these – estimates claim about 3.5 – are to be found in the United States.[4]

Multimillionaires

However these dollar millionaires find themselves at the *very* lower reaches of the world of the super-rich. Their homes and pensions are included in the calculations that make them millionaires, they often work – if not for a living, then for extras – and their lifestyles are often not particularly extravagant or sumptuous. They are, in fact, poor cousins in comparison with the more seriously rich families and individuals who are now emerging in the global economy. Official US statistics report that around a million US households – the top 1 per cent of total US households – possess a *minimum* net worth of over $2.4 million each and an average of $7 million each. In Britain the top 1 per cent have an average of around $1.4 million each.

The top half a per cent of US households, about half a million people, are staggeringly rich. This group has a *minimum* net worth of $4.7 million and an *average* of over $10 million each, which could produce an unearned annual income of over $600 000. In Britain the top half a per cent, around 48 000 households, have on average something like $2 million each – a fortune that can produce, again depending on interest and inflation rates, an unearned annual income of around $120 000 before tax and without working.[5]

These households are the truly super-rich, whose net worth, much of it inherited, is the source of considerable economic power and produces an income (mainly unlinked to work) that allows, even by affluent Western standards, extraordinarily sumptuous lifestyles. Estimates vary about the world-wide number of such super-rich families and individuals, but over two million in the plus $2.5 million category and over one million in the over $4.7 million (average $10 million) category would seem reasonable.[6]

Although huge amounts of the money of these multimillionaires are held outside the United States, in Europe, Asia and Latin America, this tells us nothing about the nationality of the holders.[7] In a sense these super-rich multimillionaires are the world's true global citizens – owing loyalty to themselves, their families and their money, rather than to communities and territorial boundaries – but reasonable estimates suggest that over half of them are American, and that most of the rest are European, with – certainly until the 1998 crash in Asia – a growing contingent from Asia.[8]

Their money is highly mobile, and so are they themselves, moving between their various homes around the world – in London, Paris and New York; large houses in the Hamptons in the United States, in the English and French countryside, and in gated communities in sun-belt America, particularly Florida, southern California and Arizona, and for the global super-rich the literal mobility of yachts in tropical paradises not scarred by local poverty.

Mega-rich and billionaires

Amongst multimillionaires there is a sharpish distinction to be made between those at the lower end – say the $20 million net worth households – and those at the higher end – say the $500 million plus households. The distinction is one of power, not lifestyle. From most perspectives the income from $20 million (say $1 million) – about 70 000 US households in 1994 – can, at least on the face of it, produce the same kind of lifestyle as income from the net worth of the more serious multimillionaires (there is arguably a limit to the number of homes, yachts and cars that can be enjoyed and consumed in a lifetime).[9] $50 million in net worth, however, simply does not command as much economic power – over employment, over small businesses – than do the resources of the big time multimillionaires, much of whose money is tied up in big transnational corporations.

At the very top of this mega-rich world are the dollar billionaires, those who command over $1000 million in net worth, a fortune that can secure an unearned annual income, depending on inflation and interest rates, of $50 million a year before tax – staggeringly well over 1000 times more than the average US income. In 1997 estimates of the number of these ultra-super-rich individuals varied from 358 to 447 world-wide, and the number is growing fast, virtually doubling during the few years of the post Cold War era.[10]

Who are the billionaires?

The 400 or so billionaires in the world are a varied lot. In one sense they are like the rest of us (and like those who will read this book). They are overwhelmingly Western, primarily American or European, and male, but they represent no single ethnic group, no single social background, and certainly possess no single business or financial secret for acquiring these awesome fortunes.

Many of the billionaires, though, would not be in the mega-rich category without an inheritance – which remains the most well-trodden route to great multimillion dollar wealth. Of the top 400 wealthiest people in the United States, 39 made the list through inheritance alone and many of the others had some inheritance to help get them started.[11] The British queen, Elizabeth Windsor, is perhaps the most famous example of such massive unearned wealth. In 1997 Phillip Beresford (*The Sunday Times'* 'Rich List', (*Sunday Times* 6 April 1997) put her net worth at a staggering $10.4 thousand million in 1992 (double the 1997 figure for top-listed Joseph Lewis). However, after she took a rival 'rich list' to the Press Complaints Commission over its valuation of her assets, *The Sunday Times'* Wealth Register excluded from its calculations the royal art collection, which, had it been included, would have given her a $16 billion figure, making her the world's wealthiest woman and the second wealthiest person in the world, with half the net worth of the Sultan of Brunei but more than the Walton family.[12]

In contrast to the inheritors, there are some 400 'self-made' mega-rich men (there are no women). Yet even these men of merit have not necessarily made their inordinate fortunes through extraordinary amounts of work and talent – certainly not its continuous application. Many of the self-made mega-rich are certainly talented and creative (and often ruthless), but many of them have become mega-rich through one-off bursts of insight or risk or luck.

William (Bill) Gates is seen as 'self-made', very much the American entrepreneurial hero. His vast resources – *Newsweek* calls him 'the Croesus of our age' – have been built upon the meritorious image of having run a successful company which provides a real service, a real addition to human understanding and communication. His huge net worth – he was listed in 1997 by *Forbes* magazine as the richest American at $36.4 billion – is based upon the value of his shares in his company Microsoft. It was Gates' original burst of imagination that created his fortune – the initial stock offering in 1986 of 100 Microsoft shares cost $2100 but by the first trading day in August 1997 this had risen to 3600 shares at $138.50 each! Gates' personal share of the company rose from $234 million to $37.8 billion in the same period.[13] Certainly Gates has managed the company and taken many crucial decisions. Yet as Microsoft grew he needed the more 'routine' skills of thousands of major company directors – such as managerial aptitude and the ability to stave off competition. As with all established businesses, less and less risk and less and less creativity was needed (and a junior hospital doctor probably put in more hours).

Paul Raymond is a different type of self-made billionaire. Described by academic John Hills as Britain's richest man – in 1995 he placed him ahead of Joseph Lewis – Raymond's fortune is thought to be well over £1.65 billion. Having founded Raymond's revue bar in the Soho district of London, with topless dancers, he made his money by investing in soft pornography and property.[14] Like Gates he had the talent to spot a coming market – albeit one that was less elevating and educational. And also like Gates, and the other mega-rich, once the original burst of inventiveness (perhaps amounting only to the one great insight) was over the rest of his working life has consisted of simply managing his empire and watching his money grow.

Intriguingly, no person whose talent has been put to continuous use throughout his or her career or vocation – such people as writers, sportsmen and women, professionals such as accountants, architects, professors, teachers, engineers, even distinguished physicians and pop stars – makes it to the higher reaches of the mega-rich. Even the pop star Paul McCartney of the Beatles, with a mere £400 million, is only the thirty-seventh richest Briton.

The truth is that the key to entering the world of the mega-rich, and certainly the billionaire class, is not work or talent or risk taking (millions have those attributes in abundance). Rather it is capital. To the mega-rich it is capital – not even their own product or service – which counts. It is capital by which they measure themselves and their worth.

Perhaps the most perfect exemplar of such capitalism – finance capitalism – is Joseph Lewis. By 1997 he had arguably become Britain's richest person, overtaking both the queen and David Sainsbury and family, and he was approaching the foothills of America's 'top twenty' mega-rich. His lifestyle conforms to the popular image of the global capitalist, virtually a parody of the genre. He lives in a Bahamas villa and owns a 62 metre yacht that is four storeys high. He plays the exchange markets in front of a bank of computer screens. Whereas fellow finance capitalist Jimmy Goldsmith built an estate in South America, Lewis has bought a whole village. He has invested in British football and in the auctioneers Christies (which, along with fellow auctioneers Sotheby's probably own the most impressive intelligence records on the world's high-net-worth individuals).

Born in the East End of London, Joseph Lewis made his fortune in foreign exchange dealings. Starting out as a London caterer laying on medieval banquets for rich tourists (with a sideline in cashmere shops) Lewis only made real money when he went into foreign exchange dealing. He, as well as other mega-rich dealers such as George Soros and the Barclay brothers, use relatively small amounts of money to move markets, and profit from the changes. This is often condemned as 'speculation' or worse (the prime minister of Malaysia called Soros 'a devil'). Yet 'speculation' conjures up the idea of considerable risk. The reality, however, is very different. It normally takes rather small amounts of money – particularly if the big players cooperate – to start the ball rolling (that is, create a selling spree in a marginal market) in an overvalued currency. In this 'Canute Play' the super-rich currency players find a central bank that is 'playing Canute' – trying against all the odds to bolster an ailing currency – and then target its home economy. When the process gets going devaluation becomes inevitable; and in such an environment it takes very little intelligence (or risk), though considerable capital, to make huge profits. And in these 'Canute Plays' the capital often comes not from the individual himself but from huge lines of credit made available by foreign currency trading banks. (One estimate has it that credit lines of up to £6 billion are available for Joseph Lewis's currency operations.) Britain fell to this 'Canute Play' in 1992 when the British government handed £5 billion to 'the market' in an attempt to shore up the unshoreable.

Lewis's fortune is certainly the result of great talent. For all self-made, mega-rich people, capital needs to be earned, and often their own work and talent (together with considerable luck) help to create the precious capital in the first place. However, once an initial amount of capital has been acquired, life suddenly becomes much easier. Moving further up the line from super-rich to mega-rich to billionaire – hardly requires extraordinary talent, hard work or even risk (certainly no more talent, hard work or risk than that offered and encountered by millions of the non-wealthy). As a fortune builds it can often assume a dynamic all of its own, with the owner of the original wealth simply being carried along as the fortune grows and grows. In a relatively stable economy it is very difficult to lose a fortune.

Comparisons

This group of late twentieth-century billionaires not only dwarf their 'ordinary' super-rich contemporaries but also the earlier race of mega-rich 'robber barons' who were so identified with the burgeoning capit-alism of the early twentieth-century. In terms of resources at their personal command, in 1997 William Gates, was three times richer than John D. Rockefeller (Standard Oil) was in 1918, Warren Buffet was over ten times richer than Andrew Carnegie (Steel) was in 1918, and it was estimated that in 1992 the British queen was ten times richer than Henry Ford (automobiles) was in 1918, although some of these early-twentieth-century super-rich probably commanded a greater percentage of their nations' resources.[15]

The resources at the disposal of these super-rich families – a huge pool of the globe's wealth – are truly astounding, beyond the wildest imaginings of most of the affluent Western middle classes. These high net worth individuals (HNWI's, as they are depicted in the financial services sector that serves them) accounted for almost $17 trillion in assets in 1996.

The power – that is, command over resources – of the world's super-rich is normally expressed in raw monetary figures, but the sheer, egre-gious extent of these private accumulations of wealth can also be given some meaning by making comparisons. For instance, even though it not comparing like with like, it is still an astounding statistic – showing the enormity of the issue – that the combined wealth of the world's dollar millionaires is more than twice the entire gross national product of the United States and equal to the combined GNP of the 'Group of Seven' countries – the US, Japan, Germany, France, Britain, Italy and Canada.[16] John Gray, drawing on figures from the 1998 United Nations Human Development Report, has reported that 'the world's three richest individuals are worth more than the combined assets of 48 of the world's poorest countries. Eighty four of the world's richest people have a combined worth greater than that of China.'[17] So the wealth of just one of these super-rich individuals is equal to that of about 12.5 million of his fellow humans.

Just as awe-inspiring is the fact that the total wealth of the world's few hundred billionaires equals the combined income of 45 per cent of the planet's population.[18] It is also somewhat sobering to realise that the *individual* wealth of the world's billionaires can exceed the gross national product of whole nations.[19] The world's ten richest billionaires all individually possess more in wealth than the GNP of many nation-states. The world's richest individual, the Sultan of Brunei, weighing in at over $45 billion, commands more resources than the combined GNP of 40 nation-states. To give his wealth some form of reality, it is larger than the GNP of the Czech republic (population 10.3 million); while William Gates commands more resources than the GNP of Africa's oil-rich giant, Nigeria (with a population of 111.3 million); the Walton family commands over $27.6 billion, more than the GNP of Vietnam (peopled by 73.5 million); Paul Sacher and the Hoffmann family command over $13 billion, more than the GNP of Bulgaria (population 8.4 million); Karl and Theo Albrecht command over $8 billion, more than the GNP of Panama (with its 2.6 million inhabitants); Joseph Lewis, the highest ranking mega-rich British citizen, commands just under $5 billion, which gives him more control over resources than his country of residence, the Bahamas.[20]

Another way of grasping the huge personal agglomerations of wealth in the modern global economy is to compare income levels. On 1997 interest-rate figures, and assuming that all assets are not income producing, the Sultan of Brunei could easily receive from his assets something in the region of $3 billion a year as income – compared with an average of $430 per person in the 49 lowest-income nation-states, $2030 per person in the 40 middle-income nation-states, $4260 in the 16 upper-middle income states and $24 930 in the 25 highest income economies. (The sultan's $3 billion a year is an extreme case, but the standard billionaire's $50 million a year and the standard millionaire's $120 000 a year are also powerful reminders of astounding economic inequalities.)

Get the world's top three mega-rich (dollar billionaire) people into one room and you would have assembled command over more resources than the GNP of Israel; the top four and you would tie with Poland, the top ten and you would beat Norway and South Africa. Europe's richest 20 families command around $113 billion, a little more than the whole Polish economy; America's richest 10 ($158 billion) and Britain's richest 1000 families ($156 billion) together command more resources than the GNP of the entire Russian Federation.[21]

If the top 200 or so billionaires could ever be assembled together then the command over assets, in that one room, would outrank the GNP of each of Australia, the Netherlands, Belgium, possibly even Brazil; and with 400 or so billionaires the one gathering would outrank Britain and almost overtake France!

It is these kinds of statistic that bring into sharp focus the economic power limitations of elected presidents and prime ministers (and other public sector officials) – who also have to share their economic power with cabinets and parliaments – compared with the economic power of the unelected mega-rich, whose only accountability is to the market. Such economic power was on display when the American media billionaire Ted Turner decided to donate $1 billion to the United Nations and 'to put on notice...every rich person in the world...that they're going to be hearing from me about giving money'.[22] For a Western politician to move a billion dollars in the direction of the UN would have involved months and months of negotiating and a bruising campaign.

All of our four categories of the world's super-rich (the 'ordinary' millionaires with up to $2.5 million, those with $2.5–5 million, those with $5–1000 million, and the billionaires with over $1000 million) have a combined net worth of $17 trillion, more than double the GNP of the United States.[23]

Just as awe-inspiring is the proportion of national wealth of the Western nations held by their own passport-holding super-rich.[24] In 1995 in the US the amount of wealth (total net worth) held by 90 per cent of American households – everyone under the top 10 per cent – came to only 31.5 per cent, whereas the top 10 per cent of American households own 69.5 per cent of the US. More striking still, the top 1 per cent of Americans hold 35.1 per cent of US wealth, and the top half a per cent of households (500 000 households), those with a minimum net worth of $4.7 million, own 27.5 per cent of the US.

In Britain too the super-rich also own a huge proportion of the net worth of their country.[25] In 1992 the top 10 per cent of Britons owned half of the country's marketable wealth (for the top US 10 per cent the 1995 figure was a whopping 69.5 per cent). The wealthiest 5 per cent of Britons owned around 37 per cent of Britain's marketable wealth. The top 1000 super-rich families in Britain own about $160 billion worth of wealth, about the same average (0.16 billion each) as the top half a per cent in the US; Britain's top 100 command $89 billion, its top 50 own $69 billion and the top 20 own $42 billion.[26]

Among the 1997 British 'top twenty' Joseph Lewis (finance) was estimated to have a net worth of $4.8 thousand million; Hans Rausing (food packaging) came just behind with $4.72 thousand million; David Sainsbury (retailing) and Garfield Weston and family (food production) third with $4 thousand million each; Richard Branson (airline, retailing and entertainment), Sir Adrian and John Swire (shipping and aviation) and the Duke of Westminster (landownership) all joint fifth with $2.72 thousand million each; Lakshimi and Usha Mittal (steel) eighth with $2.4 thousand million; and Joe and Sir Anthony Bamford (construction equipment) and Viscount Rothermere (newspapers) joint ninth with $1.92 thousand million.

A particular feature of the British super-rich scene is the concentration in very few hands of land ownership. Britain – or rather the land area known as the United Kingdom – is, quite literally, owned by a very small caste; as is the capital city, London. It remains a poignant commentary on wealth concentration that large tracts of London are owned by just a few individuals. The Duke of Westminster, through the Grosvenor Estate, owns around 200 acres of Belgravia and 100 acres of Mayfair – a dynastic inheritance created by the seventeen-century marriage of Cheshire baronet Thomas Grosvenor to Mary Davies, the '12 year old heiress to a London manor that at the time included 200 acres of Pimlico'. Viscount Portman owns 110 acres north of Oxford Street. Lord Howard de Walden's four daughters, through a holding company, own 90 acres of Marylebone. Elizabeth Windsor, the queen, remains the 'official' owner of 150 acres of 'crown estates' in central London, as the eight crown estates commissioners address their annual report to her. Andrew Lycett has argued that although 'millions of pounds are exchanged every week in leasehold property deals... London still has no sizeable new land-owners' with the exception of the Sultan of Brunei and Paul Raymond.[27]

Richer still, yet richer

And the super rich are getting richer. The former vice chairman of the US Federal Reserve Board said in 1997 that 'I think when historians look back at the last quarter of the twentieth century the shift from labour to capital, the almost unprecedented shift of money and power up the income pyramid, is going to be their number one focus.'[28] The figures are indeed dramatic. In the US the top half a per cent rose from 23 per cent to 27.5 per cent between 1989 and 1995. The next half a per cent rose from 7.3 per cent to 7.6 per cent in same period. However the next 9 per cent fell from 37.1 per cent 33.2 per cent, while the lowest 90 per cent fell from 32.5 per cent to 31.5 per cent. As the most reliable and scholarly analysis put it, the evidence shows 'a statistically significant increase in the share of household net worth held by the wealthiest half a percent of [US] households from 1992 to 1995'.[29]

There are no figures available for the British top half a per cent, but tax authority figures – which do not include the considerable amounts of offshore money held by the British-passport-holding rich – suggest that whereas the top 1 per cent of the population were losing ground between 1950 and 1980, during the Thatcherite, globalising 1980s and 1990s their share of the wealth of Britain stabilised.[30]

And the assets held by the world-wide super-rich (the HNWIs) are expected to continue to grow. One assessment portrays them as more than doubling (from $7.2 trillion in 1986 to $15.1 trillion in 1995), and they are projected to grow from the 1996 level of $17 trillion to $25 trillion (up by more than 50 per cent) by the new millennium.

On present trends, this growth will be world-wide. Intriguingly the 1996 super-rich 'market' grew more rapidly in Latin America than anywhere else – perhaps a function of the ease with which millionaires can be created where a traditionally stratified social structure is melded with global capitalism. Yet it is in Asia where the most consistent growth in the new millionaire super-rich has taken place – an incredible 15 per cent annual growth rate in the HNWI market over a decade up to 1996. And it was estimated, before the Asian markets collapsed in early 1998, that 'Asia will outstrip North America as the second largest private banking market in the world (after Europe) by the year 2000.'[31]

Getting greedier?

Yet perhaps the most interesting of all the recent trends in the economics of the super-rich is not the in growing number (or their geographic diversification) but rather their changing behaviour. The super-rich are simply becoming more demanding. Whereas 'old wealth', bounded by nation and social responsibility, tended to want preservation of capital and a long (sometimes life-long) relationship with their bankers, 'new wealth' – particularly that generated in the post Cold War era – is concerned with investment performance. In an era of low inflation (where there are small returns from deposit markets) the performance-driven super-rich seek out securities, futures and options. In a stable political and inflation environment they are therefore more prone to take risks than their forebears, they diversify more easily, and buy and sell more readily.

Above all they are driven by profit, and it is this search for return and profit that makes them global in their reach and interests. The 'offshore' assets of the super-rich (the HNWI market) proves the point. According to one estimate, between 1989 and 1996 they helped fuel a growth in offshore assets from $2.3 trillion to $6.6 trillion.

And this new need for performance (mainly of profits) is in turn causing the growing private banking market – well-known names such as Goldman Sachs, Credit Suisse, UBS, JP Morgan, Merrill Lynch – to cater to the new millionaires by diversifying their investments across both asset classes and the globe. Also, 'the range and style of services [by private banks] will differ greatly, for instance, between banks focusing on serving the mega-wealthy and those serving the merely affluent'.[32]

Anyone for noblesse oblige?

Yet when 'the performance' has been a success and the profits are made, can we expect our new global wealthy to develop *on a world scale* the social obligation that infused the more traditional upper classes and helped to create the social cohesion and welfare states of modern continental Europe?

It is unlikely. Traditional capitalism's essential individualism and cultural egalitarianism always placed great limits on the feudal instinct of *noblesse oblige*, but the new global capitalism will expunge it. Not only is modern global capital less rooted in social background, but now it is also less rooted in nation. Also, and crucially, the new global capitalism exists at a time when, at least in the societies of the West (where most of the super-rich still live), the decline of religion has eroded the idea of philanthropy. Robber barons with a social conscience – the creators of the great American foundations – have become an historical curiosity.

It certainly used to be more difficult for 'the rich man to get into heaven than for a camel to enter the eye of a needle', but no longer. For many in the secular West, riches are not only the measure of success but also the highest good. A ruling-class sensibility – so democratically unappealing – did produce a sense of common endeavour. Now, though, the new super-rich have little in common: they have no common religion and no common government. All that is left is millions of competing individuals with a shared ideology of individualism.

Where is the money?

Apart from the sheer size of the wealth of the super-rich and their changing economic behaviour, one of the most intriguing aspects of super-rich life is the way in which they hold their wealth. What they do with their money is no idle speculation. In the new global economy their decisions about how to deploy their portfolios can move economic mountains, change governments, even regimes. Intriguingly, the super-rich hold their wealth in very different ways from the average middle-income American and British household.

In total amounts the American-domiciled super-rich – the top half a per cent – possess more 'other real estate', more stocks, more bonds, more in trusts, more in personal businesses than the bottom 90 per cent, the mass of Americans.

This mass (the bottom 90 per cent) of Americans have a large proportion of their net worth (a huge 78 per cent) in their principal residences and in cars (13 per cent), and of course their debt levels, or liabilities (43 per cent of net worth) are high, with principal residence debt amounting to almost half of their principal residence assets (over a quarter of their assets). By comparison only 7 per cent of super-rich net worth is in principal residences, a miniscule half a per cent in cars. As for debt, the super-rich do not like it and do not have to have it – it amounts to only 4 per cent of their net worth. Unlike the broad mass of the population (who have only 8 per cent of their net worth in stocks and shares) the super-rich are conspicuous for their love of the stock market – employing virtually a quarter of their total net worth. And as would be expected they also invest much more heavily (a massive 42 per cent) than do the mass of Americans (only 4 per cent) in personal businesses; and it is striking that between 1992 and 1995 the top half a per cent saw their share 'notably increase…almost entirely at the expense of the group between the 90th and the 99th percentiles'.[33]

In Britain much the same pattern of distinction between the rich and the rest exists. Shares remain the big divider. In Britain the top 1 per cent of wealth holders possess more shares than all the rest put together (with the majority of Britons not owning one between them). The bulk of the top 1 per cent's financial assets are held in the form of shares whereas Middle England's wealth is overwhelmingly held in the form of residential property – their own homes.[34]

Families and corporations

It is not surprising that super-rich individuals and families hold a considerable part of their wealth in and through corporations. Some sociologists, though, point to a subtle though crucial difference in shareholding between the mega-rich and the super-rich. At the very top of the globe's social pyramid the mega-rich – probably amounting to no more than a few hundred families – own sizeable, mainly minority interests in large enterprises, and effectively control them.

However, because of the growth and dispersal of shareholdings – held by pension funds, banks, even universities – even the mega-rich do not tend to have outright control of large corporations. One expert has suggested that 'it is doubtful whether family holdings of less than five per cent can signify "control"', and there are few examples of such concentration. In 1980, of the 252 largest US enterprises only 32 were controlled by families (only two through a majority of shares); and amongst the major shareholders in Union Pacific in 1980 were the Harriman family, the Rothschild family, the Kirby family and the Kemper family, yet not one of these families possessed more than 2 per cent of the total shareholdings, a pattern that had hardly changed since 1938.[35]

Alongside these large enterprise stockholders there are a group of investors – many of them just as mega-rich – who come nowhere near to controlling companies because they diversify their portfolios into a variety of enterprises. The number of these 'rentier shareholders' (essentially big time coupon clippers) has grown dramatically with the rise of stock exchanges and the ability to spread financial risk around the world. These 'rentiers' are described by Edward Luttwak as those

> who live off dividends, bond interest . . . and real-estate rentals, rather than the active conduct of a business or profession. When seen on the golf courses and boat docks of the fenced in and carefully guarded residential enclaves they so greatly favour, from Palm Springs, California to Hilton Head, South Carolina . . . rentiers kitted out in their Ralph Lauren clothes superficially resemble businesspeople or professionals on vacation. But their vacation never ends.[36]

A further strand of the globe's mega-rich – some of them bordering on being only super-rich, some of them, preposterous though it may seem, even believing themselves to be 'middle class' – are the salaried executives or directors of some of the large corporations. To these super-executives need to be added the new race of those who hold multiple part-time directorships and executive positions in a variety of enterprises (what the Marxists call 'finance capitalists').[37] The salaries of these executives are so huge that they themselves can build up considerable shareholdings or pension funds, receiving almost the kind of income available to the big time owners of capital.

And, of course, some of these mega-rich people can have multiple identities. 'A rentier capitalist may also be a finance capitalist . . . the daughter of a rentier capitalist may marry an entrepreneurial capitalist, and an executive capitalist may regularly play golf with a finance capitalist.'[38]

And what has been called 'kinecon groups' build up over the generations. These are sets of 'interrelated kin who control the corporation through their combined ownership interests and strategic representation in management'.[39]

Below these mega-rich individuals and families there exist the majority of the top 1 per cent of wealthy Americans. These super-rich folk also hold a large proportion of their wealth in businesses, but in small and medium-sized businesses (often their own) which are dependent for their future upon the large corporations and the mega-rich. Of the assets held by the top 1 per cent of Americans – the super-rich – just under half are listed as held in 'businesses' (whereas well under a quarter are held in stocks and bonds).[40]

Family inheritance

Yet this issue tends to obscure just as important a question: how do they raise it in the first place? And what are the processes of accumulation in the global economy?

Money is made – and capital accumulated – every day of the year. Profits are the key to it, and these profits are the source of both corporate capital and individual accumulation. Yet for the super-rich – those who have the money 'to play' and therefore to grow – where does it all start? How do they get it in the first place?

The Western media tend to concentrate upon the large, often inordinate salaries of corporate executives, pockets of wealth that can often lead to significant capital accumulation. Outlandish corporate pay remains a public issue. Even the market-oriented British Labour Party campaigned against 'excessive' and 'exorbitant' top corporate salaries in the run-up to the British general election of 1997, and gas chief Cedric Brown's salary and perks sparked off a national controversy.

As one US academic put it, Stephen Hilbert's $39.6 million from Conseco Inc., Lawrence Coss's $28.9 million from the Green Tree Financial Corporation and James Donald's $25.2 million from the DSC Corporation were 'not exactly painful.'[41] Some spectacular examples of those also feeling no pain were Andrew Grove of Intel, paid a salary of $3 003 000 and $94 587 000 in long-term compensation in 1996, Edward Pfeiffer of Compaq Computers, paid a salary of $4 250 000 and

$23 546 000 in long-term compensation in the same year, and (twenti-eth in one list in 1996) Drew Lewis of Union Pacific, paid a salary of $3 131 000 and $18 320 000 in long-term compensation.[42]

These huge salaries can, over the years, certainly add up to a large capital sum even though they also attract tax. However a more secretive, wholly unearned and much more important route to wealth remains inheritance. The amounts are staggering. The economist Robert Avery of Cornell University argued at the beginning of the 1990s that 'we will soon be seeing the largest transfer of income in the history of the world' as the older generation leave wealth to the baby boomers.[43] Some guest-imates place inheritance at 6 per cent of US GDP each year![44] Apart from straight gifts during the lifetime of the giver, there is also the mammoth transfer of unearned wealth – including whole businesses – upon the death (or retirement) of the super-rich giver.

And this inheritance culture will continue to grow. Two dynamics will see to that. First, the present generation is more wealthy than any before. Second, this coincides (or is the cause of) the increasing financial pressures on the young. Hence, as the political scientist Kevin Phillips has argued,

> for young Americans, those under thirty or thirty-five, two decades of polarisation had brought a special, though widely unappreciated, irony: not only were they (and those younger) in danger of being the first generation of Americans to suffer a lower standard of living than their parents, but they would be the first generation to receive – or not receive – much of their economic opportunity from family inheritance, not personal achievement.[45]

A very troublesome feature of inheritance is the growth in the number of recipients of unearned cash income – the use of inherited money to consume and live on. There are a considerable number of people within super-rich families whose unearned annual income is not derived from their own net worth, but rather from their parents' or grandparents' net worth. One estimate suggests that 46 per cent of the US 'affluent' give at least $15 000 a year to their adult children or grandchildren.[46] But partly because it is often shrouded in mystery some of the egregious sums involved are, unlike huge salaries, rarely exposed to public view.

Also, the sting is taken out of super-rich inheritance as a political issue because many middle income families and individuals inherit money themselves, (albeit fairly small amounts.) This creates a considerable constituency for inheritance, indeed helps to create an inheritance culture. Western politicians either accept inheritance as untouchable – except at the margins – or even support it ideologically as creating 'islands of independence' from the state. During the Thatcherite years British Conservatives saw wealth as 'cascading down the generations' and as a bulwark against socialism. Yet, ironically, what has now begun to emerge is a capitalist version of the much derided state welfare 'dependency culture'. Dependency upon the family has been substituted for dependency on the state.

A ruling class?

These super-rich families and individuals possess huge personal wealth and command considerable influence over resources. They have control of or influence over the great corporations, and they hand their extraordinary wealth down through the generations. But, do they amount to a new ruling class?

Certainly the new regime is very different from the old class model. Today's mega-rich are not like the 'old style capitalists' who owned great businesses outright and could – and did – personally direct huge resources and thousands of workers. These traditional 'mogul' capitalists (the popular image derived from nineteenth-century capitalism) still exist, but are now called 'entrepreneurial capitalists' and run their own shows (people such as the late James Goldsmith, Alan Sugar, the founder of Amstrad, and Anita Roddick of Bodyshop are good examples). Yet the wealth of the world's richest people is no longer held in this way – rather it is held 'impersonally', primarily in the form of stocks and bonds.

The nineteenth-century Marxian notion of 'a class' of capitalists – based upon highly concentrated capitalism – is also now redundant. A modern socialist argument that the control of corporations is still highly concentrated in 'knots of financial power' by small numbers of financial capitalists operating interlocking directorships and cross-shareholding – in other words, concentrated shareholder power – has taken its place. However in today's huge and diverse global economy, such traditional concentration simply does not exist. The emergence of the modern globalised corporate culture has dispersed shareholdings and separated ownership from control.[47]

But do the super-rich amount to a new *global* upper class on the traditional pattern? Formerly highly divided societies with a super-rich upper class – such as imperial Britain, the home of modern capitalism – have produced a cohesive, self-conscious, self-confident, socially exclusive, super-rich upper class possessed of a community of feeling.

The new global super-rich, only amount to 'a class' in the sense that they now tend to *share* a dependence on impersonal capital (primarily shares and bonds). But the super-rich are too numerous, too fragmented nationally, ethnically and geographically, and too divided into different types to be an old-fashioned class.

Also, capitalism is rather bad at rulership. Even traditional, preglobal, capitalism was too individualistic and pluralistic to create a cohesive upper class. There is some evidence to suggest that a US 'business establishment' existed even into the 1980s. The American mega-rich who held multiple directorships and 'key positions in the intercor-porate network' tended to be drawn from a more integrated social background – exclusive boarding schools, a listing in the social register ('the crucial indicator of social exclusivity'), membership of exclusive big city clubs – than those with a directorship in a single enterprise.[48]

And of course in Britain – with cohesion amongst the super-rich secured by public schooling and the shared experience of land owner-ship – in France and amongst the Japanese zaibatsu, the sense of class or caste was always pronounced, and this was reflected in their postwar business culture as well.

However in the US, with the rise of Dallas, Chicago, San Francisco and Los Angeles, the American business establishment, historically grouped along the eastern seaboard, became even less cohesive – certainly in geographical terms. And with new generations coming on stream, cap-ital inheritance can often mean dispersal. As well as disputes over money – which may sour fellow 'class feeling' – the average size of individual holdings within the inheriting family group falls, and 'dynas-tic families dissipate into myriad rentier families'.[49]

In the most systematic and sophisticated analysis of postwar capital-ism, John Scott argues that this more dispersed shareholding has led to 'a consequent reduction in – though not a disappearance of – family control and influence'. He suggests that those with less than 5 per cent of the shares of a company have little purchase on decision making, and those with 5–10 per cent have only a 'potential for control'. Very few super-rich have such a concentration of shares – in fact they usually disperse their shareholdings among a variety of enterprises.

Of course the dispersal of share ownership developed apace with the huge growth of pension funds during the 1970s, 1980s and 1990s. In reality, modern global corporations are now controlled by 'constella-tions of interests' – families, banks, pension funds.[50]

So the big question remains: who drives these great corporations? For if corporations run the world and shape our lives, then those who run the corporations are truly a new ruling class. For a time a new 'managerialist' theory emerged which argued that shareholders no longer controlled corporations; rather there was a separation of ownership and control, and the decisions of these great corporate behemoths were now taken by a new managerial class – 'captains of industry' such as Britain's Sir Peter Walters of BP, Sir Denys Henderson of ICI, and Ian Vallance of BT. Such managers or 'executive capitalists' can virtually determine their own huge incomes, but can only enter the ranks of the super-rich by transferring their huge income payments into shares and bonds. These executives are in capitalist locations that enable them to operate the system for high personal reward. And the super-rich trust them.

James Burnham, in his famous book *The Managerial Revolution*, argued that this growth of managerialism was bringing family capitalism to an end. And in 1963 A. A. Berle argued that 'the transformation of property from an active role to passive wealth has so operated that the wealthy stratum no longer has power'.[51]

However, the new global capitalist order has rendered this debate somewhat redundant. Whether the power to direct the affairs of the corporation resides amongst the 'capitalists' or the 'managers' hardly matters anymore. It is the logic of the market – and increasingly the global market – which dictates. And both capitalists and managers have to dance to this new tune.[52] The great decisions of the corporations are informed and determined by market profitability, not by the particular preferences or tastes of individuals or families or managers! There used to be room for these preferences – many of them reflecting a social or moral concern. Those days are now over.

The truth is that the new assertive market in the new global capitalism causes both shareholders and managers to demand performance and profitability. Because of the new business environment shareholders now feel free to demand profitability – and managers, in order to keep their jobs, feel the need to deliver it. Whether they take part in corporate life or not, whether they own or control the great corporations or not, the shareholders – led by the global super-rich – will always reap the rewards.

An overclass?

If the new global super-rich do not amount to an old-style ruling class, they are certainly becoming an overclass: the mirror image of the more publicised urban underclass – separated from the rest of us, with distinct interests that differ from those of the mass of the peoples of Western societies.

In a very real sense the new super-rich are becoming removed from their societies. This is happening physically. The higher levels of the super-rich have always lived apart: within their walled estates or in wealthy ghettos in the centre of Manhattan, London and other cities. They have always owned possessions that have singled them out. Today, of course, mere diamonds, helicopters and expensive cars no longer signify the apex of great wealth. Now it is the luxury yacht (normally personally designed by John Banneman), the personal aeroplane – the Sultan of Brunei has a Boeing 747 – (normally supplied by Grumanns), and one or two of the highest valued paintings that signify someone has reached the top.

Although the ordinary super-rich – including simple dollar million-aires – cannot afford this mega-rich lifestyle, they too are increasingly becoming separated, removing into wealth enclaves. Some estimates suggest that by 1997 there were 30 000 gated communities and that in parts of the US a third of all new homes were being built behind walls. These gated communities are home to as many as eight million Americans, and thus have become a normal aspect of the lifestyle of the vast majority of the top 10 per cent of US wealth holders and their families.[53]

These gated communities have their own security forces and amenity centres and their own codes of what is acceptable – ranging from the colour of doors and the planting of shrubs to rules against political posters – which residents accept as part of the local social contract. It amounts to an embryonic privatised local government, an epochal development that will inevitably lead those inside the gated communities to demand deep cuts in local taxes and services. Schooling still exists outside the gated communities, although the demand for private schooling within the walls can be expected to grow.

Such a separated existence finds its extreme form in capitalist Russia, where the new super-rich are not only separated by money but are also essentially above the law.

Critics may argue that we should 'never trust a country where the rich live behind high walls and tinted windows. That is a place that is not prospering as one country.' They may also suggest that such 'fragmentation undermines the very concept of civitas-organised com-munity life' and 'the basic ethic of mutuality which is the notion behind the US',[54] yet such separatism is increasingly the reality. And if the perceptible growth of inequality within Western societies continues then the world outside the ghettos of the wealthy will become even more unattractive to them.

Of course one test of loyalty to a society is a willingness to pay its taxes, particularly if they are not onerous. Yet increasingly the super-rich are dodging the taxes of their countries of origin. In 1997 the *New York Times* reported that

> nearly 2,400 of the Americans with the highest incomes paid no federal taxes in 1993, up from just 85 individuals and couples in 1977. While the number of Americans who make $200,000 or more grew more than 15 fold from 1977 to 1993, the number of people in that category who paid no income taxes grew 28 fold or nearly twice as fast, according to a quarterly statistical bulletin issued by the IRS.[55]

So difficult was it for the US authorities to collect taxes from the super-rich that Congress introduced a new tax altogether – the Alternative Minimum Tax – to catch them.[56] With the American 'middle classes' – the middle income groups – paying a larger percentage of their earnings in taxes (including sales taxes, property taxes and social security payroll taxes), tax evasion and avoidance is becoming a growing cause of economic inequality and social fracture.

In Britain the super-rich also escape paying their fair tax share. The queen – who until 1994 was allowed by her government to pay no taxes at all, and since then has only had to pay some of them – is literally above the law as far as tax is concerned and remains a role model for tax dodging. As does her son, the heir to the British throne, Charles Windsor, who has also been placed above the law by British governments as he is specifically exempt from paying corporation tax, capital gains tax and death duties. The Duchy of Cornwall, the territory owned by Charles and run as a company, has not been liable for tax since 1921.[57]

Other British super-rich, who unlike the royals are not 'above the law', nonetheless manage to avoid their share of taxes. Lloyd's 'names' are a striking example. 'According to Robson Rhodes, the accountants, the most striking advantage is that Names are treated like businesses...so losses incurred in the market can be offset against other earnings...they enjoy business property relief for inheritance tax purposes on their deposits and funds which support their underwriting.'[58] Dodging taxes – even in this highly friendly tax environment – is final proof, should it be needed, of the lack of even a residual loyalty to nation and home society on the part of many super-rich families.

Companies – huge, large and medium-sized – are also well into the tax dodging game. One scam, now well used, is 'transfer pricing', which allows companies to pay tax where they want, which naturally is the country or haven with the lowest tax regime. They can do this by doing much of their spending in the high-tax countries, thus cutting their tax obligations, and making most of their profits – using subsidiaries with little more than a front office with a few staff – in low-tax countries.

For super-rich tax dodgers a helpful dynamic often sets in. Home governments, in order to keep what money they can within their borders, make even more strenuous attempts to keep money at home by lowering even further the tax burden on rich people. The idea, not always fanciful, grew that more tax money could be attracted by taxing less. In Britain the top rate of tax was reduced from 98 per cent to 40 per cent during the country's move to market capitalism, and in the US, even after a decade and a half of falling taxes for the upper income groups, by the late 1990s the authorities were still struggling manfully to lower the burden even further by even lower capital gains taxes.

This timidity of national governments in their relations with the super-rich takes many forms. For instance capital flight is conducted primarily via computers – cash in suitcases smuggled on board aircraft bound for exotic places are now fantasies from the past – and national governments can therefore, if they really want to, get at records stored on hard-disks in headquarters in New York, London, Paris and Frankfurt. But the threat by banks and financial institutions to relocate in the event of such an oppressive intrusion into their 'secrecy' keeps local governments from doing anything more than administering the occasional slap on the wrist.

In this environment it is hardly surprising that the amount of 'off-shore' money is growing rapidly. The IMF reported that a staggering $2000 billion is located beyond the reach of the countries in which the money was made – in the growing number of safe-haven tax shelters, ranging from the Cayman Islands, through the Channel Islands and Lichtenstein to Singapore. German commentators estimate that 100 000 tax-evading rich people have transferred many of their assets to a new favourite safe haven: the rock of Gibraltar.[59] 'Trickle down' – the 1980s public relations term for the idea that wealth trickles down to the masses from those who make and own large chunks of it – has now been replaced by 'gush up and out'.

Another sign of the detachment of the super-rich from their domestic societies is their decreasing involvement in those societies. Potential economic and social changes in their countries of origin and residence used to be of great concern to the wealthy. They saw their destinies as linked to their countries of birth, and they spent considerable amounts of money (and willingly acquiesced to relatively high tax regimes) in order to stabilise and ameliorate social changes that might otherwise threaten their interests. This strategy was at the root of much of the progressive, centrist politics of the Western world in the twentieth century.

Now, though, domestic – that is, national – social and economic changes are no longer of such urgent concern. Should a local environment turn hostile to them – not just because of a government's economic policy, but also, say, because of its law and order or policing strategy – then they can simply up sticks and leave, both financially and in person. And often the mere threat, or assumption of a threat, to withdraw their assets and patronage is enough to persuade the domestic politicians to secure a friendly environment. Such threats are now regularly made, either implicitly by corporations (who take jobs with them) or explicitly by high-profile, super-rich individuals, as was the case before the 1997 British general election with the musical entrepreneur Andrew Lloyd Webber, the actor Michael Caine and the boxer Frank Bruno.

Of course emotional ties to the land of their birth are bound to remain; and there will doubtless be a certain discomfort in being forever on the lookout or potentially always on the run – not, like the Jews, because of persecution, but because of the possibility of advantage and gain. However the arrival of global communications – particularly satellite television for entertainment and the internet for financial transactions – and the increasing number of locations that are overclass friendly, has made mobility, even expatriation, much easier to handle.

This overclass of the twenty-first century will be built upon a fundamental divergence of interest between the super-rich – both members and aspirants – and the rest of us. Simply, there will be those whose interests are tied to the performance of the global economy and those, the majority of people in the West, dependent upon jobs and welfare, who, bounded within their communities and nations, will continue to depend upon the success or failure of their own countries, regions or cities. George Orwell's aphorism that 'the poor are the only true patriots' may take on real meaning, but will need to be amended to include large sections of the Western middle class.

Whereas 'the locals' will need skills in order to be employed and avoid the minimal (or worse) welfare systems, the new global overclass, many of them not needing to work, will need financial advice, and will be catered to by professionals, some of whom themselves will make it into the overclass.

And there is a further frightening twist. The dread prospect exists that for those who need jobs – those who have only their labour to fall back on – even this haven will be removed. Old-style capitalism, as Eric Hobsbawm and others from a Marxist perspective have argued, may have exploited the masses, but it also, crucially, included them. Now that global capitalism, and its need for 'performance', demands that technology replace jobs, such inclusion may be over. Workers – the largely capital-less – may no longer be exploited and thus will create no surplus, so will be needed by no one! And in the market system, little or no demand for labour means low or no wages for labour. And all this potential pauperisation in an era when the pressure on the welfare systems of the West will become acute.

'The world is in the hands of these guys'

The emergence of this global overclass not only raises the question of equality – or inequality – but also of power. Supporters of this new 'free market' global capitalism tend to celebrate it as a force for pluralism and freedom; yet so far these egregious aggregations of assets and money have placed in very few hands enormous power and influence over the lives of others. Through this accumulation of assets and money the super-rich control or heavily influence companies and their economic policies, consumer fashions, media mores, political parties and candidates, culture and art.

What is more the resources at the disposal of many of these super-rich individuals and families represent power over resources unattained by even the most influential of the big time state politicians and officials – 'the panjamdrums of the corporate state' who populated the earlier, more social democratic era, and who became targets of the new capitalist right's criticism of the abuse of political power.

In the new capitalist dispensation it is the global super-rich who are 'lords of humankind', or 'lords of the Earth' like Sherman McCoy in Tom Wolfe's all too apt social satire on Wall Street, *Bonfire of the Vanities*, weilding power like old-fashioned imperial pro-consuls. The new global super-rich have now got themselves into a position where they not only have a 'free market' at their disposal, and not only is this market now global, but they can also command the support of the world's major governments.

No single event has shown up the raw power of these global super-rich speculators than the 'bail out' of super-rich investors in Mexico in early 1995, when, with the US Congress baulking at using taxpayers' money, half a dozen public sector officials – including Clinton and Camdessus – put together a $50 billion package (the largest credit aid programme since Marshall Aid) to bail out those global super-rich who were in trouble. In the face of criticism of this use of huge amounts of public money to support private 'risk takers', all Michael Camdessus (who as chief executive of the International Monetary Fund was no mean man of power himself) could say was that 'the world is in the hands of these guys'.[60] The extent to which 'these guys' were bailed out, yet again, by the Western taxpayer following the early 1998 Asian market collapse is not yet known.

Of course the earlier preglobal era saw huge disparities in income and wealth. Yet these existed within established societies and polities from which the earlier super-rich, their assets and income could not easily move. Now, though, mobility, and mobility over an increasingly boundless area, is the name of the game.

Onward and upward

The new super-rich global overclass seems to be possessed of one crucial attribute: a sense of ultimate triumph. As globalisation has proceeded all the bulwarks of social democracy that stood in their way, the cultures that acted as a balancing force and succeeded in civilising, and to some extent domesticating, raw capitalism have fallen. The primary casualty has been the nation-state and its associated public sector and regulated markets. The global economy has also helped to remove that other crucial balancing power available in the Western world – trade unions – which for the most part acted to check unbridled business power and ensure some basic rights to employees, often at the expense of rises in short-term money incomes.

Finally, the end of the Cold War was a seminal moment and played a fateful role as midwife. At one fell swoop the end of command communism (in Eastern Europe, in Russia and, in the economic field, in China) made footloose capital both possible and highly attractive by adding a large number of low-cost production and service centres and new markets to the economy. It also removed the need for the Western super-rich to be 'patriotic' (or pro-Western). It also made redundant the instinct of social appeasement held by many Western capitalists and induced by the need, in the age of Soviet communism, to keep Western publics from flirting with an alternative economic model.

The stark truth is that not one of these obstacles – not the public sector, not the trade unions, not an alternative economic and social model – is ever likely to be reerected. In the short to medium term, without a change in the political climate of the Western world there is nothing to stop further globalisation, higher and higher profits, more and more millionaires. For the new overclass it is onward and upward.

2
The Super-Rich Game

The up-escalator to Brazil

The new global financial system, which provides the framework for the operations of the new, mobile, super-rich elite, is now in place and appears to be increasingly stable and sustainable. It is driven by a powerful economic logic – the imperatives of free-market capitalism; and its ideology – international freedom and pluralism – underpins its support amongst opinion formers. It also has a growing constituency amongst the more bounded, less affluent – who, although not directly involved in the global economy are, like millions of Western pensioners, increasingly dependent upon its success.

For the rest of the world's population the reality of this new order is much less enticing. Now that the smoke of early battle is lifting a clear outline of the future is appearing. Critics of new global capitalism present the depressing social profile of Brazil as an image for the coming world – an image brought into even sharper relief following its financial crisis of early 1999. Mikhail Gorbachev, during a trip to San Francisco, asked 'will the whole world turn into one big Brazil, into countries with complete inequality and ghettoes for the rich elite?'[1]

It is a good question. The brutal social extremes of Brazil – which is the world's second largest market for corporate jets but at least one quarter of its people go to bed hungry every night – are indeed the product of the same global capitalist dynamic: weak governments, great global corporations investing 'competitively', a low-waged poor with an inadequate welfare state side by side with a super-rich elite.

The key to the whole system (the global game) is the free movement of capital around a world that is no longer divided between hostile nations and ideologies. To invest in this global system is to place your assets on an up escalator to a new and higher level of operations that are both more profitable and more stable than the lower-level domestic societies and economies.

Millions of Western individuals and families have placed at least a portion of their assets at this higher level of economic operations (with mobile assets but immobile houses and jobs – although the financial rewards from houses and jobs can be removed from the domestic economy and placed on the up escalator). But the super-rich (or mega-rich, or overclass) are, for all intents and purposes, *fully* internationalised or globalised.

Access to global capital movement is typically and primarily bought through shares and bonds which since the end of the Cold War have become the main conduit for capital mobility. By investing in shares – particularly those of multinational companies – the new super-rich are entering the great arteries of the world-wide system, which transmits their money to the promised land of global profits, wherever in the world it can produce a high return.

The spectacular growth in the operations of the great stock markets of New York, Frankfurt, Paris and the leading markets in Asia show how millions upon millions are now taking this shareholding 'up escalator' to the global level. The percentage of net worth of all Americans held in stocks and bonds rose from 11 per cent to 18 per cent between 1989 and 1995, and amongst the super-rich top half a million it rose from 17 per cent to 24 per cent. In Britain the rise was just as pronounced.[2]

'Performance' or high-return profit is increasingly likely to be found in low-cost areas where the wage levels are much lower than in the Western societies from which the money originally came.[3] It is obvious that producing goods with any sizeable labour content in low-cost areas will provide much greater profits for the shareholders of the companies involved. One major global capitalist put it this way:

> In most developed nations, the cost to an average manufacturing company of paying its workforce is an amount equal to between 25% and 30% of sales. If such a company decides to maintain in its home country only its head office and sales force, while transferring its production to a low cost area, it will save about 20% of sales volume. Thus a company with sales of $500 million will increase its pre-tax profits by up to $100 million every year.[4]

Lower social costs – the taxes on business and capital that governments force corporations to pay in order to finance various aspects of the welfare state – are a key gateway to profitability, and thus share perform-ance. As long as countries can provide a secure political framework (democratic or undemocratic) and a pool of relatively skilled workers, then shareholders will increasingly demand investment in low-social-cost areas – Asia, Russia and Eastern Europe and those Western locations where costs and taxes are competitive by Western standards. The Thatcherite model for Britain included low social costs as a strategy to compete with Britain's European neighbours. In 1994 British social security as part of indirect labour costs was well under half that of France and Sweden and just over half that of Germany, the Netherlands and Portugal.[5]

Capital unbound (globalisation)

The compulsion amongst more and more rich people to make more and more money – to seek performance from shares and investments – feeds a global strategy. For only by 'going global', by taking as much advant-age as possible of lower costs, can such a performance be improved and really big profits secured. This is the dynamic behind globalisation – the new transnational, global order – and is the reason why it cannot, or certainly not for the time being, be stopped.

Commentators are still divided over the full extent of this new world. Two German journalists, Hans-Peter Martin and Harald Schumann, are stark in their assessment, and their warnings. They argue that 'the world race to achieve maximum efficiency and minimum wages is opening wide the gates to irrationality', and that if 'the powers of the transna-tional economy are not successfully brought under control [we] may be on the road to military clashes'.[6] William Greider, in his powerful pioneering polemic *One World, Ready Or Not*, also describes the reality of a new world order – a capitalism acting like 'a machine that reaps as it destroys', throwing off 'enormous mows of wealth and bounty while it leaves behind great furrows of wreckage'.[7]

Of course in theory a fully globalised world would see the complete integration of markets for workers, products and capital. Obviously we are a considerable time away from such a new world, and a single global market for workers is probably little more than a pipedream. As for products, one measure of product market integration is the ratio of trade to output, and although this ratio has risen sharply since the 1950s, 'Britain and France are only slightly more open to trade today than they were in 1913'.[8] Another test is price convergence across the globe, and by the late 1990s there was no sign that this had occurred.

Thus, as the magazine *The Economist* argued in 1997, 'product markets are still nowhere integrated across borders as they are within nations'.[9]

But it is the super-rich and the pension funds, not the working population or their products or services, who are leading us into the new world. It is the global market for capital, newly unbound capital, the working material of the super-rich, which is increasingly integrated. The figures are impressive. Foreign direct investment – that is, the movement of capital from locations in one country to locations in another – continues to grow. It has been estimated that as much as one trillion US dollars is transferred across political boundaries from one country to another *every day*.[10] In the decade from 1983 foreign direct investment outflows increased at an unprecedented compound annual rate of 29 per cent, three times faster than the growth of exports (9.4 per cent) and four times the growth of world output (7.8 per cent).[11]

Critics point out that much of this capital mobility is simply between Western countries. Robert Taylor argues that 'as much as 81% of the world's foreign direct investment is located in the affluent industrialised nations of the US, Britain, Germany and Canada'.[12] Linda Weiss has also discovered that the globally oriented Anglo-American economies account for more foreign direct investment than pre-collapse Asia.[13] Critics also point out that the bulk of capital mobility is accounted for by mergers, acquisitions and privatisations – purely a switch of ownership rather than new production or services.[14] Of course these mergers and acquisitions, and often privatisations too, reduce costs and involve the laying off of domestic labour or employing new labour at lower rates. The golden rule of economic globalism – that mobile capital should move to lower-cost areas irrespective of national or social loyalty – is upheld.

Of course much of the big money traded on financial markets every day is hardly a reflection of the globalisation of finance or trade. Much of it is the result of free movement *within* regional groupings such as the European Union, the North American Free Trade Area or the Japanese-led Pacific Rim trading bloc.[15]

As Paul Hirst and Grahame Thompson have pointed out, investment has not exactly gushed away from the West – certainly not in the 1980s. In fact during the 1980s, according to some estimates, the share of FDI outflows going to non-Western countries dropped from 25 per cent to 17 per cent and the ownership and control of businesses across national borders only equalled a very small percentage of the total domestic investment of the rich economies – although since 1990 and the end of the Cold War FDI has picked up dramatically.[16] And the net outflow of capital (or the current account surplus) from advanced countries, even Japan, was still in single figures in 1997. This led Ankie Hoogvelt, in one of the most impressive critiques of the globalisation process, to argue that far from a globalisation of capital we are seeing an 'implosion' of capitalism, – 'an intensification of trade and capital linkages within the core of the capitalist system, and a relative, selective, withdrawal of such linkages from the periphery'.[17]

However, since 1990 and the end of the Cold War, foreign direct investment has picked up dramatically. The proportion of FDI going to low-cost areas in non-Western countries rose to 27 per cent in 1991 and 40 per cent in 1993, and remained at or around this record level for some time (35 per cent in 1995).[18] Capital (FDI) inflows into all developing countries rose from $31.9 billion in 1995 to $38.5 billion in 1996, falling back marginally to $37.2 billion in 1997.[19] And most of this increase went to a handful of countries – the bulk of total Third World FD investment ended up in China, Singapore, Malaysia, Thailand, India, Hong Kong, Taiwan, Mexico, Brazil, Argentina and Egypt. China is the biggest player in this league. In 1993 it was the second largest recipient of FDI after the US, and it accounted for 37 per cent of the total foreign-derived Third World investment.[20]

Even after the financial crises in the Asian nations in 1997–8 the flow of capital to the region – but to a cheaper area where the costs were even lower – was not necessarily expected to fall in any significant way. The UN predicted that world-wide foreign direct investment would rise to $430 billion during 1998, compared with $414 billion in 1997 (with with FDI inflow into China only expected to fall from $45 billion to $40 billion), and this may not, depending on the political situation, prove to be wildly off when the dust settles.[21]

You ain't seen nothin' yet

The raw figures of foreign direct investment may not – even in the 1990s – be overly exciting, but the truth is that these are very early days. Of course globalisation, particularly the globalisation of finance, has been developing for some decades now. Financial capital found ways to evade the capital and exchange controls imposed during the Bretton Woods era, and offshore financial markets, which were beyond the control of nation-states, started to grow in the 1960s and developed rapidly in the 1970s and 1980s. Yet if the twenty-first century is to be the global century, then we will look back on the turn of the millenium as very early days. The likelihood is that we are only at the very beginning of the new global order, living perhaps in the equivalent of the 1840s before the huge burst of Victorian capitalist activity.

All the portents are that the logic of the market will ultimately force a fully global order. Even though inertia always plays a role, it will only be a question of time before those decision makers – be they shareholders or managers – who do not perform well are demoted or sacked. Should their costs be uncompetitive they will simply lose their jobs, like millions of workers before them.

At the behest of the shareholders, global performance will be needed across the sectors. The first burst of post-Cold War mobile capital was invested in the production of goods with a high labour content, for example cars. For some time Western governments consoled themselves with the view that such mobility – with its consequent job losses in the West – would be restricted to goods rather than services, and the idea was floated that the best Western economies would enjoy a comparative cost advantage in the service sector. There was, thankfully for the West, a limit to the ability of the Asian 'tigers' (and the East Europeans) to attract capital. Their limited population was one crucial factor. However by the third decade of the twenty-first century the global labour force will have grown by as much as six billion people as China, India, Bangladesh and others join the former countries of the Soviet Union in the labour market. (In 1997 Britain's GNP per capita was 30 times higher and the US's 40 times higher than that of the Peoples Republic of China.)[22]

And crucially, the complacent notion that these great new economic civilisations will not be able to skill up their workforce for both the goods and the services sector is highly fanciful. In truth, we 'ain't seen nothing yet'.

Fear and blackmail: 'the Faustian pact'

Although the new globalised world of the super-rich is being built upon mobile capital, debates about its numerical value are not the real issue. The reality is that Western economies are influenced not just by the amount of capital flight but also by its *possibility* – indeed its increasing probability in the new, more open, deregulated global economy.

Western governments are faced with a kind of blackmail: if capital (corporations and super-rich individuals) does not get its way in the Western economies – if wages or the social costs to business are too high, or if skills are not appropriate – then capital will move to more accommodating areas. As James Carville, President Clinton's feisty

Cajun campaign guru, is reported as saying, 'I wanted to come back as the president or the pope. But now I want to be the bond market: you can intimidate everybody.' This kind of blackmail is often public. The Swedish government is a case in point, having been successfully publicly intimidated by Peter Wallenberg of Scania Lorries – Wallenberg threatened to move his headquarters unless the government brought down the budget deficit – and by Bjorn Wollrath of the insurance company Scandia, who threatened to boycott Swedish government bonds.[23]

More often, though, such threats are not articulated – they do not need to be as the effect is the same. As *Newsweek* magazine has argued, governments are induced into what it calls 'a Faustian pact': they can have access to global capital as long as they obey the imperatives of corporations and the super-rich with respect to low costs.[24]

Have we been here before?

Some critics maintain that the new global order is nothing new. They point to an earlier 'globalisation' in the 50 years before the First World War, when there were large cross-border flows of goods and massive international movements of money, trade and people – all of which which helped rather than harmed overall living standards in the West.

This previous 'globalisation', however, was in a wholly different league from today's version. In the late nineteenth century few manufacturing or service centres appeared outside the industrialised countries, and there was no threat to relocate them. Also, this previous bout of international economics amounted not to a globalisation process but to a 'Westernisation' process. The opportunity to make profits from dramatically lower costs by laying off workers in Britain and hiring lower-cost workers in the US was simply not available – certainly not in the numbers and the time-scale that operate today. And crucially, this great westward capital flight, from Europe to the US, took place in a general economic climate in which labour was still needed and not, as today, increasingly surplus to requirements.

Also, during this earlier 'globalisation' – during the age of the nation-state – companies were grounded in one country with outposts abroad, and most of their profits were repatriated. Today, though, the old corporate structure – radiating out and back to the home base – has been replaced by Robert Reich's corporate 'webs'. And the technology available to these new corporate webs is of a different order from that in late-nineteenth-century Europe; 'any activity that can be conducted on a screen or over the telephone, from writing software to selling airline tickets, can be carried out anywhere in the world. . . . Even medical advice or education can be sold at a distance over telecoms networks.'[25]

Size and suddenness

However the key difference between the earlier globalisation and that taking place today is the sheer scale of change – and its suddenness. The size and speed of the development of today's global economy has no historical precedent. This time there is the 'China factor' and the 'India factor' – the 'six billion factor'. The very heart of the globalisation thesis rests upon the vision of China and India as up and coming economic superpowers. At the turn of the millenium the world economy is embracing an additional 4–6.5 billion people, a quantum leap not seen before in economic history. In comparison the previous bursts of globalism, of capital moving beyond the confines of its home in North-West Europe (through Western colonialism and the paced migration into North America) look paltry.

The populations and economies of India and China, as well as those of mini economic superpowers such as Pakistan, are no longer separated from the rest of the world by politics, information, technology or capital. These new economic societies will challenge the West not only in the industrial sector but also in the service industries, and only the prejudiced will continue to believe that the people of these countries will never be skilled enough to compete with those in the West. The American political thinker Michael Lind has argued, in a passage the import of which deserves quotation at length, that

> Within a generation, the burgeoning third world population will contain not only billions of unskilled workers, but hundreds of millions of scientists, engineers, architects, and other professionals willing and able to do world class work for a fraction of the payment their American counterparts expect. The free trade liberals hope that a high wage, high skilled America need fear nothing from a low wage, low skill Third World. They have no answer, however, to the prospect – indeed, the probability – of ever increasing low wage, high skill competition from abroad. In these circumstances, neither better worker training nor investment in US infrastructure will suffice. . . . It is difficult to resist the conclusion that civilised social market capitalism and unrestricted global free trade are inherently incompatible.[26]

And this revolutionary change will happen within a very short time-span, in a few decades only. We are in the very early stages of this revolution, merely at its foothills. In the late 1990s the Western populations were already experiencing some very real ripple effects from Asia, either from the competitive challenge or from its financial problems, which, through devaluations, could lead to bigger economic challenges!

If this addition to the global economy were smaller in terms of numbers or the transitional phase longer, then the necessary adjustments, perhaps, would be almost manageable, or so some free trade theorists argue. But the magnitude and suddenness of this quantum leap in the dimensions of the global economy mean that dramatic and unstable changes can hardly be avoided. Massive underemployment and unemployment in the West, caused primarily by capital moving to low-cost areas, cannot now be easily discounted.

Also, this awesome quantum leap in the world's labour market is going hand in hand with a more performance-oriented Western capitalism that is determined to secure share performance and profit maximisation. This is a fatal combination. The pressure on corporate decision makers is now to lower costs in order to boost performance, and if they have not yet taken advantage of low-cost areas, in the absence of political change they will soon get around to it in a big way. Indeed if they do not, then replacement decision makers can be expected to do it for them.

China

China looks in great shape for the twenty-first century. One observer argues that 'a larger pool of cheap well-trained workers, tamed inflation and a stable exchange-rate should add to the attraction for foreign investors of a country that is successfully managing political transition'.[27]

China's competitiveness is likely to be sharpened by the remarkable reform of its state sector, particularly its state-owned economic enterprises – steel, chemicals, heavy engineering, shipbuilding, textiles and banking. Another potentially rich vein of reform and privatisation exists in the country's military sector, as the People's Liberation Army owns a variety of manufacturing and service operations, ranging from technology to hotels. Add these sectors to China's huge local–state sector and the township and village collective enterprises, which are already serving as subcontractors for manufacturing firms in Hong Kong and Taiwan, and via these the US and Europe, and you have the makings of the much prophesied economic colossus of the new century.

Of course any resulting unemployment – particularly in the urban areas – would further depress labour costs and thus maintain China's huge competitive edge over both the West and its Asian neighbours (even after the devaluations of the Asian currencies that took place in 1998), as would a decision by China to retain its authoritarian political system whilst marketising and globalising its economy. Jeffrey Henderson has suggested that China may indeed mutate into 'market Stalinism' – 'a more thoroughly capitalist, but still authoritarian, economic and political form, rather like South Korea between the early 1960's and mid 1980's'.[28] John Gray thinks it more likely that China will develop into what he describes as a 'modern neo-authoritarian state', which would develop an enduring political legitimacy and be 'an exemplar of indigenous modernisation on a par with Japan'.[29]

Such an authoritarian political system would be that much more able to restrain wages and other costs and perhaps organise a skill base, thus ensuring that the Peoples Republic remains attractive to mobile investment and firmly on the path to becoming the world's dominant economic power.

Alternatively China could take the route towards political modernisation and democracy, becoming, over time, a Westernised, if not Western, nation. A liberal-democratic, free-market China could, though, pose an even greater challenge to the West. If it no longer constituted a geopolitical or ideological problem, no Western political action could be taken to place constraints upon capital movements.

Technology

Some scholars see technology, not mobile global capital or trade, as the motor of change and the cause of the West's increasing social problems. Robert Lawrence, in his scholarly defence of free trade, makes the powerful argument that 'technological changes and changes in management practices, rather than trade, are the source of growing inequality'.[30]

Of course technological advance tends to have a life of its own, irrespective of the social organisation in which it is set. Yet the combination of technological change and global markets is combustible. Technology, like capital, is now mobile. Although the advanced technology base and infrastructure of the Western nations means that for some transnational companies there will remain an incentive – in terms of profit – to keep jobs in the West, technology, particularly high technology, is becoming as mobile as capital, and China and India have the economic base with which to establish competitive infrastructures, particularly transportation.

Also, crucially, global capitalism's culture of share performance dictates that technology should be used primarily to engineer lower costs, even if this leads to a massive shedding of labour. In the new, technologically sophisticated global system, labour is becoming increasingly redundant. As Martin and Schumann suggest, we may be entering a 20:80 global society in which a staggering 80 per cent of the world's population are unemployed, but pacified by a 'diet of 'tittytainment' – the modern equivalent of bread and circuses.[31]

Without the pressures of the new globalism, technological advances could be managed. The West's social problems could be mitigated by a series of radical and creative measures to maintain overall living standards, such as job sharing or non-profit infrastructural work, as well as increased leisure. This was very much the hot topic amongst social democratic theorists in the West in the 1950s and 1960s.[32] Yet, of course, in a climate in which increasing share performance and profits are demanded the pressures are all the other way: technology opens up a world in which more people will join the league of the super-rich and the existing super-rich will grow even wealthier.

Corporate unbound: space stations circling the Earth

The free movement of capital – out of the domestic economies and into the global system – is largely made possible by the great arteries of the system carrying the life-blood of big mobile money. These arteries are the corporations – what used to be called multinationals but are now more accurately termed transnationals.

These modern corporations are great political power centres in their own right. Even in the early 1950s the chairman of the editorial board of *Fortune* magazine was arguing that corporations had become so powerful that the president of the United States had a dependence on them that was, 'not unlike that of King John on the landed barons at Runnymede, where [the] Magna Carta was born'.[33] Columnist Joe Rogaly in the *Financial Times* speaks for a growing number of opinion formers when he says that the corporations now 'matter more than ever' and 'are heading for dominance over the lives of most advanced countries'.[34]

The sheer size of these transnationals is awesome. According to UNCTAD (United Nations Conference on Trade and Development) about one third of all private productive assets in the world are under the 'common governance' of transnational corporations, and many, many more are linked to and reliant upon them. It has also been calculated that the sales of each of the top ten transnational corporations amounted to more than the GDP of 87 countries. General Motors, Ford and IBM almost out-rank Britain in terms of GDP (and, of course, when calculating the GDP of Britain the productivity of British-based transnationals is counted in!)[35]

Staggeringly, of the 100 largest economies in the world, more than half are corporations, not countries. General Motors' sales figures are higher than the GNP of Denmark. Ford's are higher than the GNP of South Africa. Toyota's are higher than the GNP of Norway. 'The top 200 firms' sales add up to more than a quarter of the world's economic activity.... The dominance of the top 200 firms over our world economy is growing steadily. In 1982 their sales were the equivalent of 24.2% of world GNP. They now [1996] equal 28.3%.... Corporate profits are soaring, jumping 75% from 1990 to 1995.'[36]

These transnationals are no longer simply domestic commercial operations that increasingly operate abroad, as did many British corporations during the empire or the great American corporations during the period of the Cold War. In truth the modern transnationals should no longer be viewed – as they have been since the inception of capitalism – as commercial entities owing a loyalty to, and even deriving an identity from nations, as 'American corporations' or 'British corporations' or 'German multinational corporations'.

Robert Reich, in his path-breaking book *The Work of Nations*, has argued that to think that the big transnationals are loyal to their countries of origin – are patriotic – is 'charming vestigial thinking'. He suggests that 'the new organisational webs of high-value enterprise, which are replacing the old core pyramids of high volume enterprise' are reaching across the globe in such a manner that there will soon be no such organisation as an ' "American" (or British or French or Japanese or West German) corporation, nor any finished good called an "American" product'.[37]

Nowhere is such 'charming vestigial thinking' more prevalent than in Western popular journalism, where the big corporations are still treated as national businesses. Even when it is clear that great icons of Britishness are owned by foreigners (Rover and Rolls Royce are owned by BMW, HP Sauce and Lee and Perrins Worcestershire Sauce are owned by Danon, Jaguar is owned by Ford of the US, the Essex and Suffolk Water Company is owned by Companie des Eaux, France, and Rowntree Chocolate is owned by Nestlé) it takes time for the public to see the corporations in a new light.

Can you get more British than the ocean liner *Queen Elizabeth II* (in the 1990s owned by Norwegians) or *The Times* of London (owned by Rupert Murdoch, formerly an Australian but now a US citizen)? Can you get more American than foreign-owned Doubleday, RCA, Giant Foods, Pillsbury or Goodyear? Or more American than General Electric, Proctor and Gamble or IBM, all of which are now essentially stateless, with highly decentralised 'corporate webs' spreading around the globe with foreign profit centres and employees?

Robert Reich has given life to all this by drawing a vivid picture of what – and from where – consumers are actually buying when they deal with one of the big cosmopolitan corporations:

> When an American buys a Pontiac Le Mans from General Motors . . . he or she engages unwittingly in an international transaction. Of the $10,000 paid to GM, about $3,000 goes to South Korea for routine labour and assembly operations, $1,750 to Japan for advanced components (engines, electronics), $750 to West Germany for styling and design engineering, $400 to Taiwan, Singapore and Japan for small components, $250 to Britain for advertising and marketing services and about $50 to Ireland and Barbados for data processing. The rest – less than $4,000 – goes to strategists in Detroit, lawyers and bankers in New York, lobbyists in Washington . . . and General Motors shareholders – most of whom live in the United States, but an increasing number of whom are foreign nationals.[38]

This depiction, written at the beginning of the 1990s, is now somewhat underdrawn. So diverse (and, in terms of nationality, often unknown) is their ownership that almost the only certain link between a transnational corporation and its supposed nationality is the city of its headquarters. Both in their ownership and their activities transnational corporations are now wholly independent world actors. Instead of being a part of a nation they are increasingly nations themselves – in competition with nations for resources. In their tactical operations they may live within the laws of nations, but strategically they operate on a global basis. They float above the domestic economies as majesterially as spacecrafts circling the Earth.

They need 'the Earth' – the domestic economies – for skills, and for consumers of their services and products. But they are now autonomous beings, able to rise above their national base, bargain with their erstwhile 'host' nation as well as other nations, and shift resources from one nation to another.

Corporations and free trade

The modern global corporation is now like an old-fashioned nation itself, a political cum legal entity and a community of interest that informs, even determines, the lives of those within it. This revolutionary development makes redundant not only the traditional idea of international relations, but also the great economic backbone of international relations – free trade.

The basic theory of free trade – pioneered by David Ricardo – retains its residual charm. The theory of comparative advantage dictates that two countries forming a trading partnership (that is, a single market without trade restrictions) should specialise in the production of goods and services in which they have an absolute or comparative advantage, and that together they are more productive than they are separately. Yet the burden of the free trade argument has always rested on the proposition that companies are part of a country's economy – that is, capital is essentially national, rooted in place. As John Gray reports, 'in the classical theory of free trade capital is immobile', and he quotes David Ricardo as arguing that 'every man ... has a disinclination to quit the country of his birth ... [and this] checks the emigration of capital'.[39]

Now, however, globalism, the workings of the transnational corporation and footloose capital have led theorists to puncture this logic, for the new realities of the global economy, with its large amounts of mobile capital, make such a model redundant. Gray himself is one of a number of theoreticians who believe that 'both in theory and practice the effect of global capital mobility is to nullify the Ricardian doctrine of comparative advantage', and according to Martin and Schuman, 'Ricardo's basic postulate [comparative cost advantage] ... is now completely out of date'.[40]

In today's new global capitalism David Ricardo's famous example of the universal benefits of comparative advantage – of Britain specialising in textiles and Portugal in wine (even though Portugal only has a comparative advantage in wine) – is utterly negated if the rewards of free trade no longer go to the respective countries' populations. In the preglobal world, and presumably in Ricardo's mind, both the British and the Portuguese people – rooted as they were, and largely are, in their native soil – would have been better off because their capitalist elites were likewise rooted in their native soil and the profits accruing to them would, one way or another, have found their way into the general society.

This is no longer happening. Profits are now being creamed off by the transnational corporations, who owe no loyalty and pay few taxes to any local or national society, and the profits are going disproportionately to the owners of companies not the employees, to shareholders not into wage packets. Indeed, even some proponents of free trade now concede that it may 'hurt wages in both the short-term and the long run', that although it may make a nation better off, it may still harm those primarily dependent upon wages.[41]

Of course free-trade will continue to be the ruling orthodoxy of globalisers, free marketeers and companies that support mobile capital. Free trade will allow Western societies to continue to import low-cost products from global companies based in low-cost centres, and often these same companies will continue to export high-tech products from high-cost centres. This process will enrich the companies and those who own them, but, as has been argued, not necessarily *the people* in the countries where these companies are seemingly located.

The sad fact is that high-tech exports do not create a large number of jobs. For instance in the late 1990s a $2.1 billion contract signed by the French with South Korea for high-tech fast French trains produced only 800 jobs in France, and following the transfer of much of the technology to South Korea, the Asian market can confidently expect at some time in the future to buy fast trains directly from South Korea.[42] As many businesses temporarily based in Western OECD countries turn to exporting services, then the domestic economies will lose out because services tend to pay lower wages than the manufacturing industry.

Hostages to the system: pensions

If corporations were the only group with a vested interest in the new global capitalist regime, then by now a head of steam might have built up against globalisation. However pension funds are as mobile and footloose as other capital. It is the pension funds that give overclass capital its democratic face, for pension funds represent the savings of millions of ordinary people, who indirectly (and unknowingly) take part in the stock markets. 'When the Cold War ended in 1989 there were less than one hundred million people in the world economy who owned shares through pensions. If present trends continue, then in twenty-five years time this number could expand to 2 billion.'[43] In Britain in 1957, pension funds owned 3.9 per cent of beneficial shares in British enterprises; by 1993 this had risen to 34.2 per cent.[44]

Pension funds are truly enormous. In Switzerland, Denmark, Holland, the United States, Britain and other Anglophone countries private pension programmes have assets that equal 50–100 per cent of GDP. And pension funds are set to grow. Demographic changes already mean that two thirds of all people who have lived to the age of 65 are still alive today.[45]

Pension funds are also in the vanguard of the internationalisation of money, of enhancing globalisation. They – or rather pension fund managers – do so by 'encouraging corporations to promote a higher return on capital for their shareholders', a process that reinforces the search for low-cost production and service centres. They have considerable power in the stock markets of the world. Take the US mutual fund industry. One reason why it has grown from $1.1 trillion in 1990 to $3.4 trillion today is the growth of defined-contribution retirement savings programmes which now account for about one third of all mutual fund assets (for the giant Fidelity group, 65 per cent of its assets in 1997). As David Hale argues, 'Instead of the Japanese and Anglo-Saxon forms of capitalism encouraging different investment agendas, pension fund trustees will require managements everywhere to focus on maximising the return to corporate shareholders, not stakeholders such as corporate suppliers, main banks or employees.'[46]

Thus the desire for performance, for profits as the key economic need, can no longer simply be dismissed as the product of the greed of the super-rich; it is now emanating from those who act for the ordinary man and woman – the pensioner and future pensioner. Should pensioners ever be asked, they would obviously want – maybe even demand – that their fund manager invest their pennies in the most profitable manner, and therefore globally.

Yet in a very real sense this pension money is a hostage. Although globalisation – as this book argues – increases divisions in the West and, potentially at any rate, threatens the living standards of vast swathes of the West's population, responsible politicians (those who agree with this analysis) can do little to limit its effects. The living standards of pensioners and future pensioners – the very living standards that the political critics of globalisation tend to worry about most – would, paradoxically, be put at risk if the pension industry could no longer invest globally to secure the biggest immediate return. It creates a very hard choice.

As long as the financial fate of the West's pensioners is linked umbilically – through shares and corporations – to the global market, then globalisation will retain, on top of its super-rich supporters, a powerful constituency in the West.

3
The Rest of Us (or the End of the Western Dream)

That sinking feeling

Postwar capitalism – that mix of private and public, social and market that operated from the 1950s to the late 1970s – was a great Western success story. It created that most historically elusive of outcomes: rising profits and a rise in the income and living standards of almost everyone. Inequality was not banished, but it was a political economy in which 'a rising tide lifted all ships'. Socially it saw the emergence of a mass Western middle class and the dream of mass prosperity. In such an optimistic environment only extreme egalitarians worried overly about inequalities and the riches of the wealthy.

Unfortunately, in today's new, rawer, global capitalism the metaphor of the rising tide that lifts all ships no longer holds. A more suitable metaphor would now be a superliner (where those who can scramble aboard are safe, secure and become increasingly wealthy) surrounded by little ships in trouble, with many sinking. This 'sinking' was confirmed by the most powerful economic player in the US government in the late 1990s, US Federal Reserve chairman Alan Greenspan, who conceded that the 1990s had witnessed an absolute decline – sometimes quite steeply – in the living standards of millions of US individuals and families; a similar worrying decline to that which had occurred in that other highly global-friendly nation, Britain.[1]

Inequality

In today's capitalism there are real signs of social division – between a growing super-rich class and the rest, including a middle class that is, no longer confident and secure but is fragmenting, with many 'sinking'.

The sad truth is that those economies that are most exposed to globalisation and conform to its dictates with free-market strategies – the US, Britain and New Zealand amongst them – are taking a leading role in the story of this rising inequality.

During the 1980s there were increases in the measure of inequality for all leading Western nations, with the intriguing exception of France. In the US the Gini index rose from 31 to 34 (compared with 27 to 31 for Britain, 25 to 27 for the Netherlands and 23 to 23.5 for Belgium).[2] OECD figures also show that the US had the highest percentage of low-income persons of any of the OECD countries.[3] And in the 1990s – as globalisation grew apace – an in-depth OECD study of inequality in the leading Western nations, published in 1995, showed that the US was leading the world in terms of inequality, with Canada second, Australia third, Britain fourth and New Zealand and France joint fifth. Interestingly, most of the continental European nations – those shielded from the full impact of globalisation by a social market or social democratic tradition – came well down the field, and Norway, the Netherlands, Belgium, Finland and Sweden would have had to more than double their inequality ratios to match the US.[4]

In the US, as in the other globalised Western economies, the number of super-rich people continues to grow. In 1993 over one million people had incomes of $200 000 or more, a number that had risen consistently every year: in 1980 it was less than 200 000, in 1985 about 300 000 and in 1989 about 800 000 – a steep rise even allowing for inflation.[5] Yet this good news coincided with increasing social division, and with millions experiencing a fall in real income. In the US the standard inequality index showed an upward trend in inequality during the 1970s, and this upward trend continued in the 1980s. New Zealand witnessed a sharp upward trend after 1985. Not surprisingly Britain also witnessed a sharp rise in inequality, particularly when compared with the other EU countries.[6]

The UK under Thatcherism adjusted to the emerging global economy more fully than any other Western nation. This process of painful change began in 1976 when, under pressure from the International Monetary Fund, the country dramatically changed its economic course, dumping the social democracy of the Labour government and later adopting, decisively and ruthlessly, the Thatcherite globalist model. The fact that Margaret Thatcher was able to depict the British left's alternative programme (of a *national* solution involving a siege economy) as unreal – based upon illusions about 'opting out' of the world economy, of Britain being able on its own to withstand global economic forces – helped to make her new globalisation course more pronounced. 'There is no alternative' to globalisation, she successfully argued. But her victory was bought at a price: a new era of growing inequality.

Before 1976 and Britain's revolutionary 'adjustment' to global economics, life in the country had been becoming more and more equal in terms of both income and wealth. After thirty years of social democracy Britain was probably a more equal society than it had ever been before, and may ever be again. According to John Hills, the index for income after direct taxes in Britain stood at 47–59 in 1913 (the precise figure elusive for that time), 43 in 1938, 35 in 1949, 36.6 in 1964 and 32 in 1974–5. From the mid 1970s, as the social effects of globalisation began to take hold, the inequality index rose dramatically and by 1984–5 it had reached 36.2. According to Hills, 'the rise in inequality after 1978 . . . is more than large enough to offset all of the decline in inequality between 1949 and 1976–7 – and almost large enough to take it back to 1938'.[7]

Similar trends towards inequality have been reported for New Zealand, another 'free market' country made defenceless against globalisation in the 1980s. Between 1981 and 1989 the New Zealand equality index (Gini coefficient) rose by almost three points – from 26.7 to 29.5, a larger percentage rise than that of the US in the 1980s.[8]

In the US itself, the primary host to global capitalism, inequality also rose sharply in the 1980s and 1990s, a trend made more remarkable by the fact that it had also risen during the 1970s. In 1994 the Council of Economic Advisors reported that 'starting some time in the late 1970's income inequalities widened alarmingly in America'.[9] In the 1980s the average income of the poorest fifth of American families actually declined by about 7 per cent whilst the richest fifth became about 15 per cent wealthier (a stark statistic which left, in 1990, the poorest fifth with only 3.7 per cent of the nation's income and the richest fifth with a little over half!) Among all advanced countries where data for the 1980s are available, the US showed the most dramatic expansion of inequality, a social division that one American scholar argued was 'lethal to our middle class way of life'.[10]

By 1994 the share of the US income cake held by the poorest fifth of Americans had declined to 3.4 per cent. Between 1992 and 1996 American families in all the lowest income groups – those earning less than $10 000 a year through to those in the $50–$75 000 category – received a smaller share of the nation's total pretax income whereas those in the higher categories – $75 000 to $200 000 or more, received an increase.[11] The political scientist Kevin Phillips, in a provocative account of social division in the US, argued that a sure sign of increasing inequality was the 'converging income shares of the middle quintile and the top 1 per cent of the US population'. He pointed out that between 1987 and 1989 the income share of the middle quintile fell from 16.3 per cent to 14.7 per cent whereas that of the top 1 per cent rose dramatically, from 8.3 per cent to 13 per cent.[12] By 1998 the middle quintile was predicted to drop to 14.3 per cent and the top 1 per cent to rise even further, to 13.5 per cent.[13]

Robert Reich designed an important graphical representation of income distribution in the US: the sagging, elongated wave, where a 'symmetrical wave' described how the rich were getting richer as the poor got poorer, with the middle beginning to sag. He suggested that

> throughout the 1950's and 1960's . . . most Americans were bunching up in the middle, enjoying medium incomes. . . . But beginning in the mid 1970's, and accelerating sharply in the 1980's, the crest of the wave began to move toward the poorer end. More Americans were poor. The middle began to sag, as the portion of middle-income Americans dropped. And the end representing the richest Americans began to elongate, as the rich became much, much, richer.[14]

Although there was a slight upturn in bottom incomes in the US during 1997, because of the tight labour market, Reich's wave effect was still operating a decade later.[15]

Wealth

Of course income inequality is only one measure of the social division in Western nations. Wealth also counts, and the story of wealth distribution in the US and Britain since the late 1970s is a striking one. The super-rich are taking a bigger and bigger share of the wealth of these Western nations.

The extent of wealth inequality in the US during the 1990s is illustrated by the fact that in 1995 the mega-wealthy (the top half a per cent, or 500 000 families) controlled 24.2 per cent of assets and 27.5 per cent of net worth, the top 1 per cent of American households (about one million) possessed 31 per cent of assets and 35.1 per cent of net worth, the next 9 per cent (the affluent) possessed 31 per cent of assets and 33.2 per cent of net worth, and all the rest (over 89 million households) only possessed 37.9 per cent of assets and 31.5 per cent of net worth.[16]

Between 1989 and 1995 there is evidence that the super-rich were pulling away from the merely affluent. Federal Reserve figures show that during these years the US mega-rich (the top 500000 households) increased their share of total assets from 21.4 per cent to 24.2 per cent. The next 500000 also increased their takings, from 6.5 per cent to 6.9 per cent. Below them, the share of the next nine million (the 90–99 percentiles) fell quite substantially, from 35 per cent to 31 per cent. On a take of 'net worth' the same pattern applies, with the top 500000 (the mega-rich, with an average net worth of $11.3 million per household) rising from 23 per cent to 27.5 per cent, the next 500000 (average net worth of $3.1 million) up from 30.3 per cent to 35.1 per cent, whereas the merely affluent (just under nine million households with an average net worth of about $720000) fell from 37 per cent to 33.2 per cent! The Federal Reserve also reported that this worrying trend had accelerated in the 1990s.[17]

The sheer extent of super-rich wealth concentration is highlighted by their command of assets. The top million US households have a staggering 42.2 per cent of all stocks (up from 39.3 per cent in 1989), 55 per cent of all bonds (up from 45.4 per cent in 1989) and over 70 per cent of business (up from 55.8 per cent). Intriguingly, during the 1990s this rise in super-rich businesses has been at the expense of the American business middle class, whose share of businesses fell starkly from 35.3 per cent in 1989 to only 20.8 per cent in 1995.

The rise in super-rich net worth is partly accounted for by a fall in their liabilities. But whilst the super-rich are reducing their liabilities for the mass of Americans they are rising – alarmingly so.[18] The high and rising mortgage debt of ordinary Americans – a frightening rise of 56 per cent between 1989 and 1995 – is yet another discordant aspect of the supposed boom years of the 1990s.[19]

Not surprisingly Britain resembles the US in this 'wealth gap'. In the early 1990s the British super-rich – the top 1 per cent of the population, with an average wealth of $1.3 million each – owned a huge 18 per cent of the country's marketable wealth and the top 5 per cent owned a staggering 37 per cent of all wealth.[20]

This unhealthy concentration of wealth is not new. Back in the 1930s the top 1 per cent owned as much 58 per cent of all the country's wealth. The mass of Britans were capital-less and propertyless. As R. H. Tawney poignantly argued, Britans who fought during the First World War on the Somme and at Passchendaele 'probably do not own wealth to the value of the kit they took into battle'. Yet for the first seven decades of the twentieth century things were slowly improving with the top 1 per cent's stake declining from 68 per cent in 1911 (for England and Wales) to 20 per cent in 1976 (for the UK as a whole). This half-century long spreading of wealth, primarily the product of progressive tax policies, amounted to what Charles Feinstein has called 'a major economic and social revolution'.[21]

However this wealth 'revolution' stalled as the British economy became more globalised. During the 1980s and 1990s wealth distribution remained static. Britain, like the US, remained a country with vast wealth inequalities. By the end of the 1980s – after a decade of Thatcherite market radicalism – the top 10 per cent of adults owned 45 per cent of the wealth, and 30 per cent of adults still had less than £5000 in assets.[22] Even after Thatcher's entrepreneurial and popular capitalist revolution, wealth and land still tended to go hand in hand. John Scott, in the most sophisticated analysis available, described the 'top twenty' of the British league of wealth as 'a mixture of urban and rural rentier landowners and entrepreneurial capitalists'. Scott argues that because research into this very murky area can only concentrate on relatively visible sources of wealth, and is often unable to penetrate into the anonymity of most shareholdings and bank accounts, rentiers, whose assets are concentrated in such anonymous investment portfolios, are normally underrepresented in any hierarchy of wealth holders. Even so, he argues that land and entrepreneurial capital remained the major sources of really large fortunes in the 1980s, and that 'the wealthiest landowners are the long established landowning families of Cadogan, Grosvenor, and Portman, most of whom own substantial urban estates as well as their country acres'.[23]

The pattern of land ownership in Britain provides a very interesting glimpse into the continuing, and stubborn, maldistribution of wealth, and into the contours of the British section of the global super-rich overclass. In what is still the most up-to-date account of landowning in a highly underresearched field, a 1970s study concluded that whereas the British state (both central and local) only owned 19 per cent of the land in overpopulated areas, the private sector owned the rest, and 'impersonal capital' (financial institutions and the like) owned over 54 per cent.[24]

Tolerating inequality

The growing social divisions in Western countries – particularly the startling, egregious concentrations of wealth amongst the super-rich – are beginning to disturb a wide variety of people. Many establishment figures worry about inequality in purely prudential terms – about the point at which inequality will lead to social upheaval, for example race riots in the US, class-based upheaval in Europe. However there is a growing moral, even aesthetic dimension. Even systematic free market globalists find such huge disparities seriously troubling. Arthur Seldon calls them 'disturbing and offensive',[25] and Jeff Gates believes that we need a reassessment 'now that these accumulations have reached what anyone would agree has no conceivable purpose other than to preclude others from the modest accumulations essential to economic self-sufficiency'.[26]

The question for the new super-rich – 'how much is enough?' – is becoming insistent. Questioning egregious, outlandish inequalities is a normal human response to excesses. It is certainly a question of taste, but also of basic social justice and an innate sense of fairness and proportion. Even Americans, who tend to ask fewer questions than people from other cultures about disproportionate financial rewards, 'have a normative value set with which they judge a person's earnings as either fair, too high, or too low'.[27] The question of fairness – of proportion – in terms of the sharp divisions now emerging in the domestic societies of the global economy is leading to a revival of the equality debate.

In a sense the history of Western capitalism is also the history of growing equality. With the abandonment of slavery and serfdom the notion of equality of worth took hold. Political equality – 'one man one vote' and later 'one person one vote' – and legal equality – all are equal before the law – became fundamental precepts of Western society during the twentieth century.

The problem for those who support free-market capitalism, and indeed for others, is the issue of economic equality. 'Inequality, it is said, is the price to be paid for economic efficiency... attempts to divide the pie more equally simply shrink it... [and] without the incentives offered by inequality, either as a reward or punishment, a capitalist economy simply loses its dynamism.'[28] The belief that inefficiency is caused by economic equality dominated the Anglo-American postwar intellectual landscape, so much so that a pretty firm consensus was formed.

Since then a few brave souls have directly challenged this belief. These iconoclasts argue that wealth generation may be social in nature, that, as Will Hutton argues, as well as the link between the individual (that is, individual rewards and punishments) and the economy, there may be also a crucial relationship between social cohesion and wealth generation.[29] American economist Ravi Batra has produced a startling argument that inequality can trigger a serious economic downturn, even a depression. This argument is based upon the banking system. It asserts that great wealth disparity leads to two concurrent dynamics. At the poorer end the borrowing needs of the poor grow, yet at the same time the banks become awash with deposits from the super-rich. The banks cannot afford to pay interest on the deposits without lending them out, thus as the concentration of wealth increases the number of banks with less creditworthy loans rises. This low creditworthy environment can result in panic and a rush on the banks. Only great concentrations of wealth – the existence of a super-rich caste that can afford to take heady risks – can cause this unstable financial situation. 'Batra's work shows the rate of wealth concentration steepening abruptly just before the onset of the Great Depression', and 'if his theory is correct it is important to monitor wealth accumulation with as much up to date data as possible' concludes American social critic Denny Braun.[30]

Not all the arguments against economic equality are about efficiency – some rest upon moral propositions. Robert Nozicke, echoing John Locke, believed that rights to property are so important that they should not be violated in the name of equality, as long, that is, that these rights are 'justly' acquired in the first place (but, as is usual with economic liberals, the question of whether, say, inheritance, is a 'just' method of acquiring property or capital rights, is left unanswered).[31] Another 'moral' argument against economic inequality rests upon the proposition that inequality is fairer – this is the meritocratic view that it is unjust for talent and hard work to go unrewarded, the inevitable outcome in a strictly egalitarian system.

However, even during the fairly benign phase of Western capitalism in the postwar period, a minority believed there should be greater economic equality than was the norm at the time. A social democratic approach during this era was a 'presumption in favour of equality', with 'inequalities being justified if, and only if, differential rewards work to the benefit of the community as a whole and we can assume that access to jobs which command differential rewards would be on the basis of genuine equality of opportunity'.[32] Of course many egalitarians were aware that the 'equality of opportunity' in which they believed might be little more than rhetoric because 'an equal start in the race of life' was and still is impossible in most Western societies.

Now that global capitalism has replaced national capitalisms, a new egalitarian issue has raised its head. When the state was a serious player alongside the private sector then inequalities of wealth and income were less important, because many people of talent, ability and creativity could gain some purchase upon power and influence through public and political work (in parties, local and central government, and national and regional bodies). However in the era of global capitalism, when the state has been weakened and politics reduced, then those with wealth are the only ones with power. And this raises the spectre of serious inequalities of *power* – in a sense, political inequality, a much more favourable target for egalitarians.

Even so a presumption in favour of equality has not yet caught on amongst the broad mass of the Western middle class. A vague desire for social justice (rejection of the unfairness, the wrongfulness of huge gulfs in living standards and life chances) may remain, but it will not lead to serious criticism of the new globalism or to movements pledged to real measures of redistribution.

It seems reasonable to believe that a passion for equality and the policies of redistribution will only appear when the belief that modern capitalism is the only way to deliver general prosperity is broken, when median income is falling and a large number of 'ships' are not rising but sinking. If this is allied to a widespread view that disproportionate wealth and income is increasingly *unearned*, that upward mobility is not possible because of deep structural obstacles, then a backlash against the inequities of global capitalism may begin.

The end of the middle class

Growing economic inequality is, in itself, only likely to annoy intellectuals – and only some intellectuals at that. The days of public-sector leftists dominating opinion are over. With the main Western media outlets – newspapers, magazines and television – now firmly in the private sector, those in the contemporary opinion-forming class (largely composed of popular journalists) are likely to follow the lead of their employers and take a relaxed attitude towards inequality. As will most people. A popular backlash against global capitalism is unlikely to be triggered by measuring the increasing differences between people, or even by sharp inequalities rearing their head at either end of the social spectrum – amongst the underclass or the super-rich. What, though, may cause serious concern, even rebellion, would be growing popular fear about the durability of the way of life of the Western middle classes.

The most impressive creation of preglobal capitalism was the large, stable, prosperous middle class, which built itself up by stages, and through fits and starts, to the point in the 1950s when it took off and millions, the majority, were beginning to live the kind of life depicted by the term 'the American dream'. This was the 'diamond-shaped' society, at the bottom and top points of which were a relatively small underclass in the inner cities and a tiny, almost invisible class of the very rich. Crucially, the stability of this society was guaranteed by wave after wave of blue-collar workers and their families 'improving themselves' through mass consumerism and identifying with the system – even, in the days of Thatcher and Reagan, with the right wing of the system.

This 'dream' was the end-product of an astounding historical fact: that in the hundred years between 1870 and 1970 'each successive generation lived twice as well as its predecessor'. Robert Lawrence records the extraordinary fact that for a century beginning in 1870 average real wages in the US increased by around 2 per cent a year, meaning that 'real wages doubled every thirty-five years, making the American dream a reality'.[33]

It is the potential end of this dream that is devastating news for global capitalism. There is no longer a widespread expectation that the coming generations will live better than the present ones. Indeed the opposite is true. Many will have a lower living standard and increasing insecurity at work – in other words they will be sinking ships in a society where all ships are supposed rise with the tide.

Sinking ships: lower living standards

In the two Western societies most integrated into the global economy – the US and Britain – there is now very clear evidence of declining living standards for a large number of their peoples.

The argument about lower standards is based upon an array of figures that show falls in average hourly income. Of course a household's income can show a rise, but if that is based upon one or more family members having two or three jobs, of 'working until they drop', then in truth living standards are falling. One startling statistic shows a long-term (20 year) downward trend: in 1997 the average hourly earnings in the US were below those in 1977![34] According to some calculations the average hourly earnings of production workers in private industry in the US fell in real terms between 1987 and 1996 by as much as 7 per cent (wages rose by 31 per cent but inflation, as measured by the Consumer Prices Index, rose during the same period by 38 per cent).[35] The lower two fifths of the population seem to have been hit particularly hard, with millions of US workers and their families seeing their standard of living fall as a result of the minimum wage being 25 per cent lower in 1997 than it was in 1970.[36]

Furthermore ships were sinking throughout the fleet. Professor Alan Krueger, chief economist of the US Labor Department in the mid 1990s reported income falls across the spectrum:

> from 1979 to 1989, the inflation-adjusted wage rate of the worker in the bottom 10th percentile – someone earning just above the minimum wage – fell by an astounding 16%. The real wage of the median worker fell by 2%. Only higher income workers did well: at the 90th percentile pay increased by 5%. From 1989 to 1997, real wages for workers at the bottom essentially stopped falling and the growth of wages for workers at the top continued at a more moderate pace. *But the wages for workers in the middle – the vast American middle class – continued to erode, with the median workers wage falling 5% since 1989.*[37]

Of course there is a lively debate about such sensitive statistics, and controversy – the 'deflator dispute' – surrounds the assessment of inflation.[38] There is also considerable evidence that in 1998, in the tight US labour market for part-time, temporary, benefitless work, the average hourly rates increased at the lower end of the scale. However, regardless of the technical rows, 'there is little dispute that, no matter how they are measured ... real wages took a different track in the the early 1970s'[39] – they started falling.

Harvard academic Robert Lawrence has set this dramatic fall in wages in the US in its proper historical context. He argues that for a hundred years, between the 1870s and the 1970s, average real wages in the US doubled every thirty-five years, and consequently 'each successive generation lived twice as well as its predecessor'. Now, however, this American dream no longer holds, for Lawrence reports that since 1973 the 'real wage growth in the US has departed sharply from its long term trend. Between 1973 and 1994 real compensation increased by just 8.6% – less than half a percent a year ... it [compensation] lagged considerably behind the 24% rise in output per hour recorded over the same period.'[40]

In Britain there are similar disconcerting trends in wage rates. During the 1980s income inequality certainly increased – as Stephen Jenkins reported, 'income levels rose for most, but were stagnant for the poorest income groups'.[41] However, during the 1990s, as the full force of globalisation hit the British economy, some incomes began to fall, and average real earnings also fell. Weekly pay for the lowest 10 per cent of males and the lowest 25 per cent of females fell between 1989 and 1995. Also the average weekly hours worked by the lowest decile rose, whereas for the highest decile they fell.[42] Real median earnings were £228 per week in the spring of 1993 but had fallen to £225 by the spring of 1996. A spokesman for the British Labour Party, which was in opposition at the time, placed the blame on the 'flexible labour market'. These bleak figures, he argued, were the result of 'well paid full time jobs... over a period being replaced by badly paid part-time jobs'.[43]

Flexible labour (part-time working)

The falls in earned income during the 1990s took place in a changed environment for labour, and for work more generally. As it took hold, the new capitalism was ensuring that labour was both less secure and less valued.

Increasing job insecurity followed naturally from the progressive introduction of the 'flexible labour market' – one of the central pillars of the new globalism, an approach lauded across the Anglo-Saxon political spectrum from Ronald Reagan's conservatives in the 1980s through to Tony Blair's New Labourites in the late 1990s. At the heart of the argument for a flexible labour market was the not unreasonable notion that no one should expect a job for life.

Of course the postwar American dream was never based upon a job for life. However, for most middle-class Americans in the preglobalisation era, relatively secure work was certainly an expectation; as was the ability, if the family was prepared to move to a new location, to find equally well paid or better paid work elsewhere. And umbilically linked to this secure work, an integral part of the job, indeed often a recruiting tool, was a package of benefits, including health care and pension coverage. In Britain, too, relatively secure, adequately paid work, with the back-up of state health and pension benefits, was also an expectation.

The labour market created by the era of global capital certainly brought to an end any complacency on this score. It did so by systematically replacing full-time work by part-time, by the creation of a huge 'contingent' workforce. It has been estimated that in the US during the 1990s temporary worker agencies – such as Kelly Services and Manpower – grew twice as fast as the nation's GNP.[44] It has been estimated that all kinds of 'contingent labour' – contract and temporary workers, involuntary part-timers, employees of subcontractors, and homeworkers – grew by a staggering 120 per cent in the first half of the 1980s.[45]

The US Bureau of Labor Statistics has noted that the number of part-time workers rose to 19.5 per cent of the workforce in 1994, up from 14 per cent in 1968, but according to Susan Houseman of the Upjohn

Institute, such data fails to account for the 'growing number of Americans who hold *two* part time jobs, or a full time and a part time job. They appear instead in the official count as full timers, working a total of more than 35 hours per week.'[46]

In Britain in all types of household part-time work is increasing: 5.9 million worked part-time in December 1992, rising to 6.3 million in September 1996 (five million of these being women).[47] In Britain between 1979 and 1993 full-time work fell dramatically – by a huge 10 per cent.[48] Will Hutton has calculated that between 1975 and 1993 the proportion of the adult population in full-time tenured jobs fell dramatically from 55 per cent to 35 per cent. And many of these, he argues, were not wholly defined by their income, which ranged widely from high to low, but rather by their insecurity.[49]

And in both Britain and the US, as the economic boom of the late 1990s gathered pace – ahead of the inevitable recession – many new jobs were created, but most of these much-touted additions to the job pool were of the part-time, contingent variety. 'Contingent labour' is difficult to define properly – for instance some analysts believe it should include self-employed independent contractors (the kind of worker who is a victim of corporate downsizing). Even so, a 1995 US Bureau of Labor Statistics study, which defines contingent labour as individuals who do not possess an implicit or explicit ongoing contract of work, suggests that 15 per cent of wage and salary workers are contingent.[50]

In any event, the rise of contingent labour has produced a new pattern of corporate employment based upon an inner core and outer periphery of employees. In the summer of 1997 the *New York Times* ran a controversial series of reports from across the country on the effects of downsizing. It reported that

> at many companies, an upper tier of full time core workers enjoys the best combination of pay, benefits, hours and job security that a company can offer. Below them is a second tier of less valued part-time, temporary and contract workers who, in addition to being less expensive, can be discharged more easily, giving corporate managers the flexibility that they say is essential to compete in an increasingly global economy.[51]

Of course this new system of contingent labour (and, more generally, the flexible labour market), which is demanded by the global economy, does in some senses serve the needs of people, of labour as well as of capital. Flexibility and part-time working appeal to many women and some men because it fits in with their family responsibilities. And in principle labour flexibility is a highly appropriate mechanism for an advanced, complex society.

However the 'hire and fire' economy of the Anglo-American globalised system is not essentially a response to changing social needs. Rather it has taken advantage of them in order to save costs. Contingent labour relieves the employer from burdensome social costs such as having to pay expensive health care benefits or pensions. In the US this amounts to a major breach by capital and corporations of an unspoken social contract whereby the middle class, who could expect little or no state support for health, could rely upon their employer to provide health care benefits as part of a relatively secure job contract. In Britain the plug has also been pulled on another social contract – the increasing army of contingent workers used to be able to rely upon a relatively adequate benefit system, but now see it progressively eroded.

Flexible labour markets make it easy for capital to respond quickly to changing market conditions by being able to hire and fire easily. However this too often means that employees, rather than the so-called capitalist 'risk takers', bear the risks of the free-market system. What is more there is no evidence whatsoever that the hire and fire economies have done any better than those with more regulated labour markets.

Hidden unemployment

Karl Marx famously coined the idea of a 'reserve army of the unemployed' acting as a weapon that could be used by employers to discipline workers. As the number of core workers has shrunk and that of contingent workers has risen, modern global capitalism now has its own 'reserve army' available – and, in a sense unknown to Marx, on a global scale! Of course many part-time workers, unlike the unemployed of old, are not seeking full-time work and therefore cannot be counted as 'reserve' in the Marxist sense; however, many, many are, and with welfare being pared down, with more income needed in traditional households and with the growth of single parent families and people living alone (who need a proper wage, not a supplementary one), the demand for full-time, benefit-linked work will always be high.

Contingent, part-time work serves another function too. Western governments, in this media age when public relations seems all-important, are fighting a constant battle of presentation. The growth in part-time work serves to hide the extent of unemployment. During the 1970s the unemployment rate began to rise across the OECD world – up from 3 per cent at the beginning of the decade to an average of about 6 per cent at the end. The 1980s saw unemployment rise further, denting the view that unemployment was a passing phase, linked to economic cycles.

In the early 1990s, with the corporate mania for downsizing in full swing, it became obvious that structural factors such as changing technology and footloose global capital in search of low costs were causing high unemployment. Harry Shutt has pointed to technology as being responsible for this higher unemployment, and as a reason for the new phenomenon known as 'jobless growth', particularly in Europe. He argues that 'taking the 1974 to 94 period as a whole, there has been negligible growth in the numbers of employed people in the countries of the European Union at a time when the level of economic activity (GDP) has expanded significantly', and he points to the example of Spain, where employment fell by over 8 per cent during the period whilst the economy virtually doubled in size![52]

In the late 1990s the peak of the Anglo-American boom did create a tightish labour market and an American 'jobs miracle' was proclaimed. But the high employment figures hid the fundamental – and grave – changes that were overwhelming the world of work. For included in the employment numbers were millions and millions of employees who were not in full-time, secure work, were not in adequately paid work and – more harrowing even than that – were not in work that provided proper social benefits. This 'jobs miracle' was a statistical con-game. And at the heart of the myth of late 1990s 'full employment' was the assumption – accepted by most of the Anglo-American media – that high employment meant high living standards. 'A lower jobless rate means little', argued the *New York Times*, 'if a $15 an hour factory worker is fired and earns only half of that in his next job'.[53] Rarely was the question asked: would you prefer to be in work in the US or Britain, or unemployed and on welfare in France or Germany? Millions of those employed in Britain or the US would have answered in favour of the European alternative.

In the late 1990s an extremely serious problem began to emerge: in the event of the boom turning to bust, how to deal – in a society deeply resistant to increased taxation – with the growing numbers needing welfare provision.

Insecurity

But perhaps the most important consequence of the new 'hire and fire' labour flexibility is the widespread and profound insecurity running through the fabric of the working populations of the free-market economies. Insecurity is indefinable, and its extent is not statistically provable. Yet the signs of anxiety are there for everyone to see: employees work longer and longer hours, workers stay late at the office not in order to finish necessary work but to secure their positions, and there is an increase in useless paper work to justify jobs and salaries. Of course job insecurity certainly keeps people on their toes, as well as on other people's toes, but there is no evidence that it produces higher growth rates than was the case in the more regulated and structured labour markets of the 1950s, 1960s and early 1970s. The jury is still out, and may always be out, on whether labour market competition and insecurity or stability and cooperation produce a more efficient economy.

And, anyway, aside from the economics of it all, there is a deep unfairness in the fact that in modern capitalist societies insecurity is unequally spread. Owning capital is simply a more secure way to live than earning a living. Even in a financially turbulent world, even too in a financial meltdown, the risks to capital are far less than the risks to private sector employment. Capital ownership provides many more real choices, and opportunities for diversification and manipulation, than does a job. Investments are highly unlikely to do badly in good times, and even if shares and bonds plummet there is normally some capital left; yet if you lose your job, particularly with few state benefits available, your whole lifestyle will change.

For most people in the West under pensionable age, income from employment is the very foundation of their lifestyle, if not their life. Other sources of income (dividends from shares, interest from bonds, small inheritances, rent) may help out, but tend to be marginal. So if all you really have to your name is a job, then the character of your employment – particularly its security – becomes important. For the employed majority, if not for those who employ them, the new capitalism's destruction of traditional job security is a real set-back.

Arguments against job security, against a job for life, are well understood. On the face of it jobs for life, even jobs for half a life, seem inefficient, and greater flexibility in the labour market may not only be good for employers but for workers too. Yet it remains a mystery why employment and jobs should be singled out as deserving of such flexibility? Arguments are rarely heard about the inequities of 'wealth for life' or 'inheritance for life'. In truth wealth for life and inheritance for life are real things. In normal times large aggregations of wealth are very difficult to lose; and in times of financial instability, although losses can be made, they rarely affect lifestyle as dramatically as does the loss of a job. Often the worst that can happen is a reduction from a lavish to a high living standard – from a large to a small yacht, from three Mercedes to one, from three homes to two.

Standing back from the immediate arguments, however, it is somewhat unedifying and defeatist that at the turn of the twenty-first century our civilisation can still treat its working people as children in need of discipline. We are able to put a man on the moon and produce spectacular technological advances, yet even Western countries are apparently unable to produce a more stable, less anxious working environment and social and personal life for their people.

Flexible, hire and fire labour policies may also cause wider problems in society. Disposable jobs could induce a short-termism that would feed through into normal social values. Richard Sennett, in his fascinating book *The Corrosion of Character, The Personal Consequences of Work in the New Capitalism*, argues that this connection is very real. It appears that 'when people talk in earnest about family values, "No long term" is no way to raise children. We want them, for instance to learn how to be loyal; a management consultant told me he felt stupid talking to his children about commitment, since at work he does not practice it.' He also argues, intriguingly, that hire and fire labour flexibility may undermine the work ethic: 'the classic work ethic was one of delayed gratification: coping with immediate frustration usually requires a sense of sustaining purpose, of long term goals. The flexible work ethic undermines such self discipline; you must seize the moment, delay may prove fatal.'[54]

The devaluation of wages (and work)

The American (and Western) middle class was forged on the work ethic. The capitalist system of the twentieth century, which created this middle class, differed from the old aristocratic system it replaced by exalting productivity and creativity – that is, work – over lineage. The medium and small businesses, the professional classes, even the big corporate culture, all defined themselves by their work – by securing their money the old fashioned way, by earning it!

Yet the new globalised economy, and the new capitalism it is creating, is turning this value system on its head. Work itself is becoming devalued. Earning money, as opposed to making or having money, is becoming more difficult. In the 1990s – before, that is, the financial gyrations of 1998 – earned income (wages and salaries) fell as a percentage of total income. Global capitalism was clear about its priorities: lower rewards from work, higher rewards from investments and inheritance.

Wages versus profits

From 1989–95 US wages were stagnant or declining for the vast majority of the workforce – amounting to 80 per cent of working men and 70 per cent of working women. And this was during a time when profits were at a postwar high. For instance the average after-tax profit rate for non-farm businesses was 7.5 per cent in 1994 compared with an average 3.8 per cent in the 1952–79 period. 'By the close of the second quarter of 1995, the return on equity for Standard and Poor's list of five hundred major blue chip companies was running at an annual rate of 20% – the best ever for corporate America.'[55] Another estimate, reported in the *Wall Street Journal*, was that corporate profit margins in the US rose between 1989 and 1996 from 6 per cent to 9 per cent.[56]

The same trend was observable in Britain. Looking at the same issue from a different vantage point, income from employment (wages) diminished as a ratio of all household disposable income from 90.4 per cent in 1977 to 73.3 per cent in 1994, while income from rents, dividends and interest rose from 10.7 per cent to 13.6 per cent, and that other source of non-earned income, benefits, including state pensions, rose from 6.2 per cent to 12.3 per cent.[57]

One look at the riches and rewards created by investments as opposed to wages and salaries shows the advantages of investing over working. Charles Handy has calculated that 'A £10 million investment, for example, which is made on the expectation that it will recover its costs in ten years time and provide a 20% compound return, will, in the next ten years, if the expectation is met and if things continue the same, earn an extra £26.4 million, and even more in the years following.'[58]

Wages versus inheritance (or the rise of sleeping money)

Of all the income coming into all the households in the British and US economies the share of pay has been going down and the share from interest, dividends and straight gifts (inheritance) has been going up. Of course much of this is concentrated at the top. Take shares for instance. In Britain there is a dramatic distinction between the wealth holdings of the top 1 per cent and the rest – the top 1 per cent hold almost half of their portfolios in shares whereas less wealthy groups hold progressively less and less in shares.[59] Figures show shares as a percentage of total asset values rising from 15.9 per cent to 22.4 per cent in just four years – from 1987–8 to the end of 1991.[60]

Inheritance is also concentrated at the top but is now becoming increasingly widespread. It is very big business, perhaps the biggest business of all in today's global capitalist economy. The British free-market Conservative government in the 1990s talked approvingly of a future economy dominated by inherited wealth as wealth 'cascaded down the generations'. In the US Robert Avery of Cornell University has predicted that 'we will shortly be seeing the largest transfer of income in the history of the world'.[61] And political scientist Kevin Phillips has argued that inheritance is 'about to become a critical component of the younger generation's future, *something America has never before experienced*'.[62]

The working poor

Perhaps the single most powerful illustration of global capitalism's devaluation of work, and of earned income, is the growth on both sides of the Atlantic of the working poor. These are the millions of people who put in a fair day's work but end up without a fair day's pay. In the US the Bureau of Labor Statistics defines the working poor as 'persons who worked (or were looking for work) during twenty-seven weeks of the year, and who lived in families below the official poverty line'.[63] Twelve million workers fell into this category in 1993.

In Britain, where there is no official poverty line or count of the number living in poverty, low pay, in reality 'poverty pay', is also a feature of the employment landscape. In 1991 a staggering 28 per cent of those with *less than half average income* were in households with some kind of income from work, including a third who were self-employed.[64] The low value set for the minimum wage in both the US and Britain tells the whole story of poverty pay.

Of course for some, poverty pay is simply an addition to family income. As Paul Gregg and Jonathan Wadsworth have reported, 'new jobs – often McJobs – are taken disproportionately by those with another household member already at work'.[65] For others low pay is acceptable if it places you on the ladder to higher pay. And for some, work, any work at virtually any pay, will suffice because of the need to be in a working environment. However none of these arguments outweigh the attack that low pay makes upon the work ethic – for if work is underpaid it will be undervalued. Nor do they outweigh arguments about equity – for who can argue that the gap between the ability, creativity and dedication of the working poor and that of the inheriting class (whom we looked at earlier) is large enough to begin to justify the gap between them in income and wealth.

All in all, though, the issue is not only, or even primarily, about the equity of low pay and insecure work in a world of high unearned income and wealth. Rather it is about how the new global economic system is leading to the destruction of the traditional middle-class way of life. The 'American dream' and its British equivalent – the belief that hard work secures major rewards, and that children can look forward to at least as good a standard of living as their parents – is now all but a thing of the past. Whether this 'dream' will slowly turn into a nightmare, in which the economic system, so historically popular, becomes an enemy of the people, remains to be seen.

4
Super-Rich Capitalism: An Audit

What capitalism was

John Gray, in his compelling work *False Dawn*, makes a distinction between 'good' and 'bad' capitalism. He suggests that 'in a global free market there is a variation on Gresham's law: bad capitalism tends to drive out good'. The 'badness' consists of capitalism's new global dimension which, with nations and their political communities weakened, allows market economics to create a 'downward harmonisation'.[1]

When capitalism was national it was also social. In the preglobal era the development of the Western capitalist model provided the best of both worlds. On the one hand a private market sphere encouraged enterprise, capital accumulation and rapid economic growth; but at the same time a serious role for the nation-state allowed the public sector to negotiate on equal terms with the private, providing not only a social dimension to capitalism but also a democratic input, particularly in the the ability to regulate and entrench people's rights at work. For a time this 'social democratic capitalism' amounted to a virtuous circle: economic growth both promoted a growing meritocratic middle class and weakened traditional inequalities.

It was this model of social democratic capitalism which set the tone of capitalism in the postwar era and – on both sides of the Atlantic – created a seemingly unshakeable political consensus behind it. It achieved the overwhelming support of Western peoples during the Cold War and the great domestic political and ideological struggle with socialism. And it made mass Western prosperity a reality, bringing millions and millions into the consumer culture, which previously had been restricted to the very few. The legitimacy of this capitalism in the

West was, of course, based upon its economic performance; its creation, certainly after 1945, of mass middle-class prosperity.

What capitalism is

However, as argued in earlier chapters, this mass prosperity, the basis of the American dream and the world-wide appeal of the West, is now in question. For the first time since its genesis in the 1950s mass prosperity is no longer an expectation: the middle class is fragmenting (up and down), all ships are not rising with the tide and many are sinking, and a new ugly social feature has emerged: a super-rich class existing alongside middle-class insecurities and the poverty of the underclass. So the question that no one would have thought possible now arises: can capitalism deliver?

Alongside this nagging question, and just as important for capitalism's future, for its long-term popular legitimacy as an economic model, is its moral and ideological standing. Social democratic capitalism secured a powerful ideological head of steam, appealing to the moral high ground: its advocates, feeling good about their societies, argued, amongst other things, that post 1945 capitalism was both *democratic* (certainly more so than the command economies in the East) and *meritocratic*, instilling the positive values of work and merit – and the US, the exemplar, stood as a beacon. In contrast those societies (principally in the East but also some in the West) which rejected capitalism were seen not only as inducing poverty, but also as elitist and creating dependency.

Popular capitalism?

During the 1980s Reagan and Thatcher took the political lead in a campaign to give capitalism a moral appeal beyond its obvious material success story. The kernel of their argument was, though, largely negative: an attack upon communism, socialism, even the social democratic state, as representing a serious threat to historical liberties, while capitalism was uniquely able to preserve these liberties. This idea drew upon the body of belief that saw capitalism as the ally (even the begetter) of political liberalism, ushering in modernity by breaking the feudal political and social bonds. Capitalism was democratic because, according to its supporters in the market, there were no commands (unlike in the 'command' economies). Every action in the market – buying and selling – was purely voluntary.

Also, access to capitalism and the market was both free of prejudices and unlimited. Traditional barriers based upon class and background, race and religion (and in the new globalised world, nation) were all irrelevant criteria for membership of capitalist society. It was 'the colour of your money' not 'the colour of your skin' that counted. And although access through money limited the numbers who could properly participate, the great capitalist growth engine would, by 'trickle-down', allow more and more people to participate. Thatcher made 'popular capitalism' a political slogan and promised wider and wider access to capitalism and the market, based upon the idea of wider and wider shareholding.

Yet modern global capitalism, like its nationally based predecessor, is hardly bursting at the seams with participants. Shareholding has certainly burgeoned; yet most of this growth is through pension funds – at one remove from and with no participation by those whose money is used. Just as tax dollars and pounds support programmes of which the taxpayer may not approve, so in today's global overclass capitalist system the people's pension money might easily be supporting companies and industries of which many do not approve. (A recent advertisement by the Calvert Group in an American newspaper highlighted this problem: it asked 'Does your retirement money go places you never dreamed of' as part of a campaign against tobacco.)

Real shareholding – in which the participant knows what he or she owns and can direct his or her money to the desired location – remains a decidedly minority affair both domestically and globally, and shares remain a small proportion of the portfolios of the vast majority of those who own them.

Global capitalism and its markets can hardly be deemed democratic when the vast majority of Western people still come to the market with next to nothing, putting them at a great disadvantage compared with those who bring substantial financial resources to the party. As I will argue later, the idea that modern capitalism – particularly now that it has been shorn of the balance provided by the state – is dynamic and progressive now rings hollow. Indeed it has become a force for stasis and tradition in the way it gives a huge advantage to those with established wealth rather than those whose talent and merit will make wealth.

Some more imaginative market theorists have acknowledged this problem of limited access to the markets. Jeff Gates has argued that modern capitalism needs to be more inclusive but seems unable to make enough capitalists. In order to create such a capitalism he suggests a whole series of reforms, including bank credit without collateral, conditional tax relief on capital gains and a reengineering of estate taxes to advance broad-based ownership.[2]

Others seek to rectify this deficiency in modern capitalism by using state money for vouchers or indeed cash rather than services. 'Give em the money' as a one-off in order to increase access to the markets. As Arthur Seldon has suggested in the context of how to fund education, health and pensions, 'the obvious alternative [to state funding] was to provide purchasing power in cash, general or earmarked, rather than services in kind'.[3] This provision would presumably come from taxes, and be subject to downward pressure every year as the low-tax regime developed. But not even the most radical policy of income redistrubtion would provide those outside the capitalist world with the asset base necessary to join it seriously – to become 'a player'.

Popular capitalism will remain a pipedream as long as the global system has no way of opening itself up to mass involvement. The fact remains that mass asset ownership without a revolutionary programme of *asset redistribution* – from the asset rich to the asset poor – is impossible. Only a political programme to break up the accumulated asset base of families and companies could achieve this objective. No promarket theorist, not even the radical Seldon, is proposing such a shocking departure.

Such a programme of egalitarian capitalism is simply not yet an electoral runner. The idea of a political party taxing wealth in order, say, to fund mortgages for the young is fanciful. The existing Western political consensus behind new capitalism sees no role for government as an agent of widening the distribution of capital. New capitalism has no use for Huey Long's cry of 'every man a King' or Lloyd-George's aim of everyone owning an 'acre and a cow' (and it sees nothing wrong with one man, the Duke of Westminster, personally owning huge tracts of Britain's capital city).

Instead new global capitalism seems to be inducing a two-class world of super-rich investors and their professional advisors on the one hand and the rest on the other (insecure wage earners or welfare recipients). And as long as global capitalism remains geared to rewarding established capital it can have no other social outcome.

Furthermore, the future for these wage and salary earners looks increasingly bleak. Preglobal capitalism had the capacity to include these 'bit players'. The big rewards may have eluded them, but there were rewards (jobs) nonetheless. In the great capitalist game they became participants of a kind. As Eric Hobsbawn has put it from a

Marxist vantage point, capitalism may have exploited the masses, but in the process of exploiting them it included them.

The devastating news is that this 'democratic', inclusive aspect of capitalism may now be gone. The truth is that modern, globalised capital will no longer need a majority of people to procure growth. The majority will become utterly redundant, surplus to requirement. As Hobsbawm puts it, 'now, suppose a majority of the population is no longer needed for production. What do they live on?' Obviously no longer on the surplus they create! 'In one way or another', he suggests, 'they have to live by public transfer payments... social security and welfare' – and all this in an epoch in which footloose capital will be excerting downward pressure taxes and public expenditure.[4]

Rights

Capitalism has also been associated with that other face of democracy: the liberal notion of rights. Indeed both capitalism (and its markets) and the regime of rights of constitutional liberalism are based upon the philosophical idea of the sovereign individual. And it is in the US, the home of modern capitalism, where the most advanced and extensive system of rights exists.

Capitalism does indeed tend to coexist with, even engender, an open and free society, and rights applying to all citizens are a key to such democratic freedom. Even so, this is only part of the story – for in the contemporary, globalised, Anglo-Saxon capitalist countries these rights are severely restricted to political and social issues. Americans are particularly well served when it comes to protecting free speech, freedom of worship and assembly, the right to abortion and privacy, and to outlawing racial and sexual discrimination. Intriguingly, though, economic rights – such as employment, participation in the workplace, social benefits – remain both unarticulated and undefended; whilst, of course, the rights of property (capital) are robustly protected. Indeed in contemporary Britain and America there remains a lively debate about whether these economic rights are in any sense rights at all!

Of course outside the Anglo-Saxon home base of modern global capitalism, in the capitalist economic zones of the developing world, life is raw. In order to become competitive, millions are subject to what even Western opponents of economic rights at home would consider gross abuses. Issues of safety and dignity at work, including basic sanitary conditions, long hours and child labour, all make the issue of economic rights a reality. Yet they may only resonate in the US and Britain if our own need to become competitive brings these Third World conditions to our own shores.

The work ethic

The traditional capitalist order was also portrayed by its supporters as one which induced a work ethic. Certainly the work ethic – the idea that hard work (application, delayed gratification, making sacrifices) is good for economic growth – has consistently been espoused as public doctrine by supporters of Protestant, liberal capitalism. In their famous works both R. H. Tawney and Max Weber argued that Protestantism, and specifically Calvinism – with its belief in the value of work – was a crucial ideological ingredient in the rise of capitalism; and Gutman has shown how a large number of American economic historians have tended to associate the work ethic with the US's economic success.[5]

This Protestant, capitalist 'work ethic' was, though, seen as more than simply an engine for economic and material advance: it was also a moral good, good for the person, good for personal growth. Peter Saunders has argued that Max Weber's idea that some kind of spirituality fuelled the original dynamic of capitalism – particularly in Britain – had some truth in it, but that the puritanism and dynamism may have since drained away. He presents a sad case that 'today, this religious motivation has all but vanished and we have inherited the behavioural husk having lost the spiritual kernel. We therefore continue to work methodically each day in pursuit of the next dollar, even though we may be hard-pressed to provide an adequate explanation for why we do so. . . . This for Weber is the poignant tragedy of the modern age, that we are locked into a system which has lost its substantive meaning for us.'[6]

Whilst she was prime minister, Britain's primary capitalist proselytiser, Margaret Thatcher, made this Weberian moral case for the capitalist work ethic by evoking 'Victorian values'. She argued that hard work, thrift, delayed gratification and the like built self-reliance and independence; and she counterpoised all this to what she described as the 'dependency culture' – the socialist welfare state – in which hard work was replaced by inducements to idleness, if not sloth. (Intriguingly there was no similar rhetoric from market supporters about the problematic values of the 'idle rich'. Such criticism had, interestingly, been a feature of procapitalist Victorian radicalism.)

Some argue that the work ethic may already have been losing its pervasiveness within capitalist culture in the 1980s. The link between hard work and income – the argument that those with high incomes earn their economic rewards because they work harder (by taking more responsibility) than others – may have been broken by the publicity surrounding some of the very large salaries 'earned' by private sector executives. Some of the egregious salaries and packages enjoyed by top executives in the corporate world have raised the issue of the proportionality of work to reward and the question of 'how much is enough?' It has been difficult for supporters of global capitalism to defend such examples as the notorious rise of half a million dollars a year paid to chief executive officer Roger Smith of General Motors following the collapse of the company's market share and the huge reduction of its workforce.

Also the work ethic, particularly the idea of delayed gratification, may have been eroded by the commercialism of modern capitalism, particularly with regard to advertising, and by the search for short-term financial gain, which is now almost endemic in Western capitalism. Indeed Michael Rose has argued that in contemporary capitalism hard work is no longer valued highly, certainly not as much as performance – a very different idea that may no longer be linked to hard work. He suggests that what matters now is effective work, not hard work.[7]

Meritocracy

Linked to the work ethic is the idea of merit. Capitalism, its supporters have argued, may not create the utopian, democratic, classless society (there are too many inequalities for that), but even in its pre-twentieth-century raw form it was nonetheless progressive. It has been a modernising force: for, as both capitalists and Marxists agree, it ushered in the modern world by breaking the 'feudal bonds' between lord and serf, master and servant, and began at least to establish merit instead of inheritance as a social value.

Of course the core institution of capitalism, the market, is not meritocratic, for the market, so globalists argue, exists specifically to cater to the public's tastes and needs, those of the majority not the meritocracy. However, from the supply side, to take advantage of the market some degree of merit or business acumen is needed, a characteristic that requires ability, not position; intelligence, not social standing.

The problem for contemporary capitalism is that the rewards for merit (and work) are no longer as substantial as they used to be; other rewards – most particularly from the inheritance of capital – are often much greater, enough to secure a very, very good standard of living indeed. It is not overly dramatic to believe that without serious rewards for merit and work, the case for capitalism will, for millions and millions, simply begin to dry up.

Individualism

Alongside hard work and enterprise, individualism was at the heart of the value system of old-style capitalism. Calvinism, with its commercial values, believed that 'Grace alone can save, and this grace is the direct gift of God, unmediated by any earthly institution.'[8] English liberal thinkers – from Hobbes through Locke to the American democrat founding fathers in the new world, the new Liberals at the turn of the century and the neoliberal globalisers of today – have all, irrespective of their differing views about the exact role of the state, placed 'the sovereign individual' at the very centre of their world view. In the contemporary era, supporters of capitalism have compared, favourably, this individualist ethic with the values of socialism, and even social democracy, which were seen as weakening the sense of individuality through the conformity that collectivism – through the medium of the state or the trade union – inevitably induced.

Yet in today's capitalism this polemic is difficult to sustain. The free enterprise system no longer has a lock-hold on individualist values: how can it when it was the capitalist ancestors and not the present economic players who, by hard work or enterprise or even sharp practice, amassed the wealth? How can it be when it is the family unit, not the individual, from which all good things, primarily capital, flow?

What's more, modern capitalism can hardly become an engine for individuality while its primary institution, the large corporation, promotes corporate cultures and corporate hierarchies and rules of the kind that, instead of promoting individual flair and creativity, induces all the opposite attributes such as conformity, routine thinking, lack of imagination and risk. With corporations triumphant, global capitalism can be expected to witness a quantum leap in the deadening hand of private bureaucracy.

Risk

Alongside the decline of the individual has gone the decline of risk. Risk was always the great capitalist value; risk taking was the prized hallmark of the entrepreneur; risk was the lifeblood of the daring, the unusual, those who stood out from the crowd and deserved – through talent or luck – their riches.

Yet more and more critics are now asking a question well worth asking: who, in fact, in the modern global capitalist economy are actually taking real risks? Certainly not the capitalist corporations. When companies get into trouble they can all too often switch their investments with minimal losses. On the other hand, in the age of flexible labour markets and downsizing, workers lose their jobs! In the modern capitalist economy it is the employee who increasingly takes the risks. It is a topsy turvy world when those without capital are laid off or casualised when the gamble of investment fails, whereas those who make the investment decisions are all too often protected against loss. This is perverse, what British economist Will Hutton has called an 'unfair distribution of risk'; and it is another reason why modern global capitalism has lost the moral edge that the preceding form of capitalism arguably possessed.[9]

Global investors are also shedding risk. When markets collapse it is the state, not least through the taxpayer-supported IMF, that is often readily available to help out the investors, and the bigger the investors the greater the state bailout. As Martin Wolf has argued, 'unregulated flows of short-term international capital are a license to rack up losses at the expense of taxpayers'.[10]

The 1998 Asian financial crisis provided an illuminating example of how, in the new global economy, risk is no longer borne by those who are supposed to bear it: the great Western capitalist risk takers, the lenders of capital – banks and financial entrepreneurs. Instead the losses were borne by local Asian borrowers and peoples. As Edward Luce has argued, 'Apart from those who lost money on regional stock-markets or bet the wrong way on currencies, most banks which lent money to the three economies [Korea, Thailand and Indonesia] will be repaid in full.'[11] And incredibly, following the IMF-imposed recovery programme, some creditors received a higher rate of interest than that which they had negotiated before the crisis occurred.

The tenacious critic of modern capitalism Larry Elliott, focusing on this loss of risk, reports with some glee Professor K. Raffer's wicked idea that debtor governments should be able to seek protection from creditors in the same manner as US domestic entrepreneurs, who, in a stark example of relatively risk-free capital, are able to use the bankruptcy procedures of 'Chapter Eleven' in the US to avoid serious penalties for failure.[12]

Banks, particularly the big ones, are also in the risk-shedding business. Although they play on both sides of the public–private street, in reality banks are, part of the public sector. They are seen, not least by policy makers, as performing a reserve function, and usually the lenders of last resort will simply not let the bigger ones fail! However these banks still use their special 'protected' status to make money as though they were wholly private sector institutions.

The inheritance culture: a return to feudalism

Marxists and non-Marxists alike continue to argue that, historically, capitalism (and its freemarkets) was a progressive force that – by breaking the feudal bonds and hierarchies between master and servant, lord and serf – opened up the road to modernity and new social values: individualism, hard work, the ethic of responsibility, merit, and rewards for talent and risk.

The problem for today's global capitalism, however, is that it is has become seriously unprogressive: unleashing a dynamic that is, incredibly, taking us back in time, back to the values and society of the feudal world from which the earlier form of capitalism helped to set us free. It is doing so in large part through the practice and culture of inheritance. Inevitably inheritance (which amounts to a gift) erodes the value of work, of earning money as opposed to making it. It has no connection with work – neither hard work nor Michael Rose's 'effective work' – or creativity. It is a reward for bloodline rather than merit. And it is creating a class – or rather a caste – at the top of our Western societies who have inherited, or stand to inherit, enough wealth and income to enable many of them to avoid work for ever.

Historically, work has been the key to productivity, both material and cultural. It may be argued that in advanced societies economic productivity (though not cultural productivity) can increasingly be fostered by improved technology rather than work. However, even should this be true, a society and culture that marginalises the importance of work, relying instead for rewards based upon inheritance, will come up against the issue of the incalculable and intangible loss of human dignity.

Inheritance is very big business, perhaps the biggest business of all in today's global economy. In Britain the free-market Conservative governments of the 1990s talked approvingly of a future economy dominated by inherited wealth as wealth 'cascaded down the generations'. In the US, Robert Avery of Cornell University has predicted that 'we will shortly be seeing the largest transfer of income in the history of the world'.[13] In 1973, 56 per cent of the total wealth held by persons aged 35–39 had been given to them by their parents. By 1986 the figure for 35–39 year-old baby boomers had risen to 86 per cent, leading political scientist Kevin Phillips to argue that inheritance is 'about to become a critical component of the younger generation's future, *something America has never before experienced*'.[14]

In one of the few studies of the inheritance transfers of the super rich – in this case American millionaires – it has been estimated that, on present trends (in 1996) 'the number of estates in the $1 million or more range will increase by 246 percent during the next decade; these estates will be valued (in 1990 constant dollars) at a total of more than $2 trillion ($2 000 000 000 000). But nearly the same amount will be distributed by so-called predecedent affluent parents and grandparents to their children/grandchildren.'[15]

The amounts of individual wealth transfers by inheritance are staggering. Looking to the future, economist Edward Woolf has projected that if inheritance follows the pattern of US wealth concentration in the 1990s then in the early years of the new century the wealth going to each of the top 1 per cent of Americans will average $3 million, and the next richest 5 per cent (the 95–99 percentiles) will average $900 000 each. Also looking to the future, Kevin Phillips suggests that inheritance taxes might slightly alter the future social outcome, but that 'baby boomers would be the most polarized and stratified generation in US history', and that 'the overall pattern would be unmistakable: inherited wealth would create a hereditary caste; class lines would harden'.[16]

However in the late 1990s in both Britain and the US conservative parties were seeking to *increase* the pool of inherited wealth by lowering inheritance taxes even further, or removing them altogether. They could find no theoretical objection to inheritance and seemed to believe that 'an inheritance culture' could exist side by side with an enterprise culture. Even the great man of economic liberty, Frederich Von Hayek, saw no reason to oppose, or even limit, private inheritance. He supported what he called 'the transmission of material property' because 'there is a natural partiality of parents for their children', and because if inheritance was seriously threatened people would 'look for other ways of providing for their children'. In a very, for Hayek, defensive mode of thinking he also argued that 'men being what they are, it [inherited capital] is the least of evils', and inherited capital is a 'lesser evil' to be tolerated.[17]

In a further line of argument Hayek reveals a near-irrational hatred of the state when he asserts that 'those who dislike the inequalities caused by inheritance should recognise that the state will not be capable of splitting up inherited capital leading to its dispersal'. (The reader is tempted to ask: why not? Isn't every redistribution, from inheritance

taxes to lower income taxes, to welfare benefits, to road building programmes, to education, helping to split up inherited capital and disperse
it?)

Irwin Seltzer has recently broken ranks with many of his fellow free-
marketeers by suggesting that their opposition to taxes on inheritance is
wrong, that 'revenues from [inheritance taxes] could be used to lower
income tax rates, especially on low earners. . . . This would reduce the tax
on work by increasing the tax on the less productive activity of being
around when someone dies.' He also argues that inheritance taxes do
not deny children what Gary Becker, the Nobel Laureate economist,
calls 'endowments of family reputation and connection; [and] knowledge, skills and goals provided by their family environment'.[18]

Inheritance remains a decidedly underresearched and underdiscussed
subject in the debate about free markets and modern global capitalism.
Grossly unjust and deeply unfair – rewarding lineage not merit or work,
and undermining the enterprise culture so beloved by neoliberals –
support for inheritance appears contradictory, if not hypocritical. The
inheritance of capital has become the intellectual Achilles' heel of free-
market theory, the 'guilty little secret' of modern global capitalism.

Inheritance: the super rich welfare state

Of course inheritance has always been part of the way of life in both
capitalist and precapitalist societies. Passing on wealth from one generation to the next (via the eldest son) kept relatively large accumulations intact, and was defended on moral grounds by virtue of the right
of the giver to dispose of 'his' property as he saw fit. During the age of
the mixed economy – the mid to late twentieth century – inheritance
taxes started biting into the inheritance culture, but at the same time
inheritance became a feature of middle-class life, primarily through the
inheritance of housing.

Now, though, with inheritance taxes falling throughout the globalised capitalist world – as part of the necessary 'competitive tax environment' – the individual amounts handed down the generations are
becoming larger. Also, it is far easier to make these inherited accumulations grow than it used to be. To create a large amount from a smallish
one used to involve considerable work and talent; now, however, in the
'sleeping money' economy it can often happen automatically.

Worse still, many of today's inheritances are being used to live off. A
huge private dependency culture – dependence upon the family rather
than the state – is being erected. American analysts have described this

derisively as 'economic outpatient care'. And such outpatient welfare care is now massive. It has been estimated that a huge 46 per cent of the affluent in the US give at least $15 000 worth of economic outpatient care a year to their adult children or grandchildren.[19] If this estimate is accurate and an 'affluent' person is defined as a net dollar millionaire, then there is an annual transfer of $15 billion from the super-rich to their descendants in the US alone.

This super-rich welfare state involves the transfer from one generation to another of 'entire coin collections, stamp collections ... payments of medical and dental expenses, plastic surgery' as well as straight cash gifts. It is estimated that 43 per cent of millionaire parents fund all or a large part of their grandchildren's tuition at private primary and/or secondary school, 32 per cent fund their adult children's further education 59 per cent provide financial assistance in purchasing a home, 61 per cent provide 'forgiveness loans' (those not to be repaid) to their adult children, and 17 per cent give gifts of listed stock to their adult children.[20]

All of this is producing a new generation – children of the super-rich who, because they are partly or wholly financially dependent upon their parents – even when they are well into their forties and sometimes their fifties – exhibit, and are likely to transmit, non-productive, idle and dependent values. And they are likely to experience poor social relationships. As in any dependency culture, relationships can be distorted by inheritance. Reliance upon inheritance can induce animosity and squabbling amongst family members:

> The fact is that many 'thirty something Americans' cannot maintain anywhere near the lifestyle they had while living with Mom and Dad. ... In fact, many are unable to purchase even a modest house without financial subsidies from their parents. It is not unusual for these 'rich kids' to receive substantial cash and other financial gifts until they are in their late forties or even early fifties. Often these UAW's [under accumulators of wealth] compete with each other for their parents' wealth. What would you do if your economic subsidy was being threatened by the presence of your equally dependent brothers and sisters.[21]

And these cash gifts often go to the less financially successful and less independent children of the super-rich – daughters who have married and become homemakers, thus losing their earning power, or less successful sons. 'Consequently, an increasing number of families headed by the sons and daughters of the affluent are playing the role of successful members of the high-income-producing upper-middle class. Yet their lifestyle is a facade.'[22] This gift culture – which is seen an acceptable part of the contemporary capitalist system – represents not only a huge misappropriation of resources but also a distortion of values, elevating failure and idleness over personal success, merit, work and enterprise.

Such a massive inheritance economy will inevitably polarise Western societies. It has been estimated that in the US the wealth given to the top 1 per cent averages $3 million and that given to the richest 5 per cent (the 95th to 99th percentiles) averages $900 000, whereas the middle fifth (the 40th to 59th percentiles) on average receive $49 000. For those further down the inheritance is negligible.[23] Thus modern capitalism promotes sharp and mounting inequalities and creates a caste system in which the overclass are inheritors not achievers.

The Western world is already becoming divided between those with skills and those without (as outlined in the early 1990s in Robert Reich's path-breaking analysis). Yet in the age of inheritance even those fortunate or talented enough to acquire skills may be in for a rough time. Skills will continue to be much less well rewarded than capital or its associated professional services, and the gap between skilled employees and the rich and super-rich will probably continue to grow. The sad fact is that an economy that supports and nurtures inherited capital simply cannot create the right environment for skills to flourish. Footloose capital, as it exerts downward pressure on the tax regime and hence the public education system, will inevitably limit investment in skills. (There is also some evidence that inheritance encourages greater consumption, less savings and investment and more dependence upon credit amongst those who receive it.)[24]

Hence the free-market system, which rejects government interference in individual decision making (even at the point of inheritance) cannot act as the radical, democratic and 'classless' force some of its supporters claim it to be. Instead, under the pressure of globalisation it is becoming a conservative force, an economic system for stasis, fit only for the protection of 'sleeping money'. The ancestry of today's American millionaires points up this conservative nature of inheritance. The fact is that the descendants of the early migrants to North America – British and German – still dominate the American super-rich scene.[25]

Indeed markets are not necessarily progressive in their social and cultural consequences. Charles Hampden Turner has argued that markets are not independent of culture. To 'leave it to market forces' in the hallowed tradition of classical economics is not to submit to an impersonal mechanism of allocation, but rather to existing, indeed traditional, classes and cultures. Britain under the supposed radicalising impact of Thatcherite capitalism is a case in point. All that privatisation and deregulation, regardless of the independent case for these measures, may simply have served to give an unexpected lease of life to the 'old money' conservative (inheriting) class and culture.

The reactionary nature of the global market

The image of the free market implanted in Western minds by globalist intellectuals and propagandists was that of a progressive force: open, liberal and democratic, reforming old institutions, making vested inter- ests (primarily an overweaning public sector) conform to consumer needs through the market. Neoliberal economics – as its very name suggests – was also associated with the 'liberal' side of politics. Adam Smith, the Manchester School of free traders and free-marketeers in the nineteenth century were all liberals. This derived from the historical association between capitalism and Whig, then Liberal, politics, primar- ily in England, where the opponents of the market and the rising merchant class were often conservative and Tory.

The political ideas of the leading contemporary free-market neolib- erals are more difficult to identify. The Frankfurt School of economists, clustered around the legendary Freiderich Von Hayek, and the later Chicago School of monetarists, with Milton Friedman at the helm, were fairly disdainful not only of the state but also of politics and politicians. Seeking a minimal state and a small, sometimes tiny, role for politics, their social values were normally 'liberal' in that they tended to place the individual at the centre of things, although they believed that this sovereign individual was best protected and enhanced by the market rather than the state and a programme of rights.

Hayek himself made clear in a famous postcript, 'Why I am Not a Conservative?', to his major work, *The Constitution of Liberty*, that he did not stand in the European conservative tradition. The latter, he argued, lacked principles and represented little more than a 'widespread attitude of opposition to drastic change'.[26] Hayek did not seek change for chan- ge's sake, but at the time of writing – at the height of postwar social democracy – he did seek change, even drastic change.

Hayek saw himself as a liberal but not as a democrat, or at least not a modern democrat. Like his supporter, the monetarist Milton Friedman, he saw democratic politicians as demagogic, and elections as problem- matic because they tended to entrench parties commited to welfare and enlarging the state. In the 1970s and 1980s the politics of Chile became a testing ground for their proposition that limited democracy, or even its temporary abandonment, was sometimes necessary in the construction of a free-market system.

Sometimes the disciples of these free-market gurus would adopt a social and political position that was ultraliberal – indeed libertarian. They possessed a 'moral commitment to the idea of a polity that maximises the scope for individual human beings to give material expression to personal values and perceptions of self-interest' – a view that often took them towards a liberal view of such policy issues as homosexual law reform and the decriminalisation of some drugs.[27]

During the 1970s and the 1980s this liberal and progressive image of capitalism made a lot of headway with intellectuals, journalists and the media. Leading Thatcherite Arthur Seldon was not a supporter of the Conservative Party and called himself 'Whiggish'. Thatcher herself presented some of her political battles as 'progressive' compared with the views of public school traditionalists in her cabinet, the hierarchy of the Church of England, even the royal family. Her rhetoric praised the liberal, 'open' character of the free market, and depicted the left as socially reactionary, as favouring the trade union power of the 1950s, the old British class divisions and a bureaucratic centralisation of the state that kept 'kept people in their place'. Her Conservative government – particularly Cabinet Minister Norman Tebbit – talked of 'upward mobility' as a positive social aim and saw traditionalist upper-class England as attempting to frustrate a new social openness. (Indeed most leading market economists would tend to place themselves in support of the general liberal postulations assembled in Karl Popper's *Open Society and Its Enemies*.)[28]

And the 'freer' market system she introduced certainly liberalised and modernised some aspects of traditional British society, for example its consumer laws and pub and shop opening hours; and the privatisation programme led to a managerial flexibility and consumer consciousness that had not been present under the old state systems. (Of course these liberalising changes in the 1980s were part of the process of modernisation – of the sloughing off of the social stultifications of empire and class hierarchy, which would probably have taken place under social democracy as well.)

In the US, Ronald Reagan succeeded in backing his democratic opponents into a conservative corner: isolating them as supporting 'old-fashioned' spending plans and 'unreformed' welfare programmes. Part of Reagan's 'progressive' appeal was simply to do with vision. He and his free-market supporters seemingly had a vision, while his political opponents, lacking anything new to add to New Deal economics, appeared to be stuck in the past, traditionalist and conservative. Reagan, like Thatcher, was also continually hitting home by counterpoising the democratic 'free market' system with the reactionary, indeed authoritarian, command economies of the Soviet Union and the Eastern bloc (and encompassing social democracy – as a moderate part, but a part nonetheless – in this depiction as at least incipiently undemocratic.)

By the late 1990s the perception that free markets – as opposed to social markets or even social democracy – were in some senses more socially and politically progressive and liberal than alternative Western models, had begun to look somewhat superficial. After almost a decade and a half of triumphant global capitalism, as the full hand of unchecked globalism began to reveal itself, a different picture was emerging: on the fundamental questions – the big issues of prosperity and power in society – the supposedly free market was turning out to be deeply conservative, indeed reactionary in character.

The essentially conservative character of the free market – certainly as it operates at global level – is often revealed by the way in which it inevitably encourages stasis. The image of the free market as a challenging arena where competition erodes tradition and vested interests is a distortion. A clearer way to see the free market is as a strategy for freeing up tradition, freeing up existing power centres and removing the forces that might threaten, challenge or change them.

By removing the ability of politics, of the state, to encourage or institute change, it leaves existing institutions, classes and interests without challenge. The free market does not challenge existing institutions, classes, or interests, except at the very margin; rather it operates in their favour. Existing capital remains undispersed. In crude terms, the position of those with money, with capital, is entrenched *vis-à-vis* those without. Those with money are not overly challenged, and in the absence of cataclysmic financial crashes they have to work very hard to lose their capital.

The return of aristocracy

A progressive, liberal or dynamic economic system would not freeze existing social relations. However a strong case can be made that, socially, the global market, although encouraging upward social mobility at the margins, *has* ultimately served to bolster fundamental inequalities not only globally, but within national communities as well. Indeed, even worse, over time it may so improve the economic power of the existing group of super-rich people that they become entrenched in their positions at the top. The ability to neuter governments by bidding down taxes, particularly inheritance taxes, and bidding up the rewards to capital, means that they will be able to pass on awesome riches to their children.

The new global capitalism is causing nothing less than a return, on a global basis, to an older form of social life – aristocracy. In this new global aristocratic system, the few, those who start life with large amounts of capital, do increasingly well, but the rest are caught in job insecurity and a shrinking welfare state.

If today's super-rich resemble the lords of medieval times, then the vast majority of peoples, billions world-wide, millions in the West, including many who count themselves as middle class, are like mod-ern-day serfs, with either a minimal stake or no stake at all in the economic system. (The political stake created for the masses by demo-cracy – the regime of rights and votes – is, as I shall argue at length in the next chapter, increasingly irrelevant.) Of course, in this new world the middle class (and middle-class values and aspirations) cannot be unin-vented; but it will become fragmented and lacking in confidence.

Just as in aristocratic times past, the few – the super-rich – wield incredible power. These modern-day 'lords of the universe' do not, like medieval lords, exercise detailed, local control over most or every aspect of the lives of others. However their individual, personal command over huge resources and their disposal gives them inordinate power over people's livelihoods, if not their lives. It also gives them the non-economic power to construct politics, society and culture in their own image and according to their own needs, which sits ill alongside the pretensions of democracy.

Of course there are some major distinctions between the old European aristocrats and today's global rulers. The old aristocrats were, at their core, domestic, or 'national'. They identified with the nations they lived in, and rightly so, because they owned them. Their assets were based primarily upon land. Today's aristocrats are global, owing no loyalty or affection to any particular landmass or group of peoples. Their assets are financial and they make money as rentiers. French economist Alain Parguez has called the system they operate – lending to governments and companies – 'the international rentier economy' and the 'rentier welfare state'.[29]

The old aristocrats' social outlook was that of *noblesse oblige* (not necessarily out of sentiment, but for sensible, prudential reasons). The new aristocrats have no such condescension (or, as some critics would put it, 'they could care less'). Politically, the old aristocrats were conservative – believing in organic development and slow, piecemeal change, and even sometimes in moderate reform, like the English Whigs. The new global aristocrats are neoliberal, indeed radical, in the sense of seeking the removal of any obstacle in the way of a universalist creed – of individualism and self-interest.

On the question of heredity, there remains throughout the West a strange contradiction between political values and economic reality. Hereditary rulership – a role for heredity in government – has for some considerable time, except in Britain, become utterly unacceptable. In the world of politics – in constitutions, legislatures, voting – democracy has carried all before it, and the idea of a patrician ruling class is risible. Yet at the same time heredity as a qualification for economic power remains well entrenched, and in the real, hard world of money an aristocracy is flourishing.

Nowhere is this schizophrenia more prevalent than in contemporary Britain. At the turn of the millenium the British are finally getting around to abolishing the hereditary element of their upper house (though not, as yet, their monarchy), but at the same time Britain remains one of the most unequal societies in the West as it plays host to a tightly knit economic and financial elite, most of whom have lineage and gifts (not work or merit) to thank for their position.

This turn-of-the-century British super-rich class – which *includes most of the same super-rich who were at the top before Thatcher's 'free-market revolution'* – is in some senses truly aristocratic, in the old English sense. Many of their number owe their resources, power and position to inheritance, but newcomers, the 'new money', are easily assimilated. And although they exist in a formally democratic country, certainly in a democratic culture, in the world that really counts, the world of finance, all the rules are written just for them.

Through tax breaks, privatisation and lower inheritance taxes on the one hand, and integration into a global economy that encourages low costs and high profits on the other, the capital and wealth of this aristocracy is given priority by public policy. In this environment, removing hereditary peers from the upper house of the legislature amounts to a democratic *gesture*, an essentially meaningless act, further underscoring the reality that power no longer resides in the world of politics (a theme of the next chapter.)

This reactionary social character of new global capitalism is all the more marked by the fact that the formation of this new aristocracy is arising out of the ashes of a fragmenting and insecure middle class. Capitalism was supposed to be the economic vehicle for middle-class objectives such as an open society, social mobility, mass prosperity and mass freedom, not an instrument for the enhancement and protection of an elite.

And the cultural result of the triumph of the 'free' market has been reactionary as well. As with social life, global capitalism simply reinforces the existing culture, marginalising the new and creative and blocking the improvement of cultural standards. In the US it may simply reinforce the worst aspects of existing mass culture to the point where 'dumbing down' – the phrase itself displays a low level of articulacy – throughout the media, exemplified by TV shows based upon the Oprah Winfrey formula, descends further and further into sensationalism.

In Britain the market (in this case the media market catered to by the big-business owners of mass-circulation tabloid newspapers) often reinforces militant cultural proletarianism – sometimes resulting in extraordinary xenophobia (such as the 'Gotcha' headline in the *Sun* newspaper following the British torpedoing of an Argentinian battleship during the Falklands War, killing a large number of Argentinian sailors) and the stirring up of superficial mass sentiment about, and idolatory of, the live and then dead Diana Spencer (Princess Diana).

New capitalism, new values

The new global capitalism, no matter what its aristocratic (indeed reactionary) character, still exudes a spiritual and moral dimension. This idea that capitalism is not only seriously productive but also good, is nothing new. Indeed the idea that private wealth accumulation is a sign of grace goes back all the way to the puritans, arguably the founders of American commerce. Benjamin Franklin's writings, particularly *The Way To Wealth* and *Advice To a Young Tradesman*, were cited by Max Weber in *The Protestant Ethic* as portraying the essence of this ethical aspect of capitalism, a moral case – at least for self-made capitalism – that still resonates in today's America.[30]

Peter Singer argues in his critique of contemporary self-interestedness, *How Are We To Live?*, that this puritanical religious justification for capitalism conjoined with a later, increasingly secular, ethics that also supported capitalism, the free market and the importance of wealth. Capitalism was good for character building, and good for the poor.

The idea that the market builds character was a theme pursued by Herbert Spencer, who saw a positive value in great wealth being accrued through exertion and risk – a viewpoint that, admittedly, would make him cast a suspicious glance at modern capitalism's inheritance culture. And it is also ethical because, as George Gilder argues in his influential book *Wealth and Poverty*, capitalism is good for the poor too. The wealth made by the super-rich will benefit all by 'trickle-down', and capitalism and wealth creates an incentive for the poor, who, he argues, 'need most of all the spur of their poverty'.[31]

Of course old capitalism's puritan values – independence, individuality, enterprise, risk, delayed gratification – may have told only half, or less than half, the story. Traditional capitalism was always Janus-faced, and the obverse face was of course a countenance of greed and selfishness. The late mid-twentieth-century consumer culture – which spawned the label 'consumerism' – certainly emphasised material possessions and encouraged self-centredness. Critics of old capitalism made their antisystem pitches by painting capitalists – indeed even simply the ownership of small amounts of private property – as greedy. This criticism was often somewhat high-handed, for old capitalism had created a consumer society in which masses of people who had previously been shut off from life's material pleasures began to enjoy them. For the first time masses of ordinary people were experiencing some limited, very limited, economic power.

The excesses of consumerism, though, pale into insignificance compared with the greed unleashed by the egregious, stunning amounts of wealth created and flaunted by the new, more global, financial capitalism during the 1980s and 1990s as exemplified by such super-rich money men as T. Boone Pickens, Michael Milken, Donald Trump and John Gutfreund.

Today's global capitalism is increasingly being shorn of its erstwhile puritanism, particularly the puritanical notion of the value of delayed gratification. The huge amounts of super-wealth now being generated need to be justified, and in the process not only do such accumulations of wealth become morally acceptable, but so too does greed itself. Greed becomes good. As Ivan Boesky, the 'king of the Wall Street arbitragers', told students at Berkeley, 'Greed is alright . . . greed is healthy. . . . You can be greedy and still feel good about yourself.'[32]

Greed received a good press in the 1980s when supporters of the free market suggested that greed was healthy because it recognised human nature as it was, not as we wished it to be. Greed was also sold as a spur to activity and productivity. What is more, freemarket apologists propounded, with some truth, that 'greed...is the motive of mankind in all economic systems, socialist as well as capitalist', but that the capitalist system succeeds in releasing it and harnessing it.[33]

These ideas echoed an older rationale for capitalism that is no longer heard – that self-interest was positive and to be encouraged because it was efficient, and out of this efficiency would come a broader interest, some kind of 'general good'. The idea of the ultimate good being the prosperity of the people or some kind of 'general good' – achieved by an invisible hand – has disappeared under a welter of economism (of statistics, returns, performance indicators) and growing scepticism about whether such a thing exists at all. Market capitalists tend to see the general good as but a contrivance for some hidden self-interest. But if greed can no longer be justified by its contribution to the general good, then we are left with nothing beyond saying amen to individual self-gratification.

An insistent question about contemporary greed remains: how much do the super-rich actually need? Is ten times the average wealth enough? Is a thousand times needed? As Bud Fox asks of Wall Street wheeler-dealer Gordon Gekko in Oliver Stone's movie about greed, *Wall Street*: 'Tell me Gordon....How many yachts can you water-ski behind? How much is enough?'

The view of a leading American social critic was that 'it seems safe to conclude that there is *never enough* for the very rich in our society – whether they are the chief executives of America's largest corporations, scions of the country's wealthiest families, or major recipients of the great bulk of stock dividends parcelled out each year'.[34] Another American view, from a surprising, pro-free-market quarter, is that it may now be time to put 'a limit on greed' – 'now that these accumulations have reached what anyone would agree has no conceivable purpose other than to preclude others from the modest accumulations essential to economic self-sufficiency'.[35]

'These huge accumulations' not only raise questions about basic material greed, but also about greed for power: and about how much power is enough. The way things are developing the owners of capital are achieving inordinate amounts of power – power over individuals, power over families, power over society, even power to make history. The satirist Tom Wolfe's depiction of Wall Street financiers as 'masters of the universe' sums up this power aspect of big capital. And arguably such power is even more concentrated than that in the hands of individual politicians – those usually associated in the public mind with the the ownership of power. Politicians, however, have to live within the constraints of having to share power with other politicians and other institutions. Furthermore they are accountable to their electorates. The super-rich 'masters of the universe' are, theoretically at least, accountable too – to markets. Yet this accountability is less formal than that of politicians, whose lines of authority – committees, cabinets, parliaments and ultimately voters – are clear. Also, financial and economic power is also far less transparent and open to the scrutiny of the media than is political power.

It is difficult to discuss the values engendered by late-twentieth-century global capitalism without considering guilt. For greed often, indeed normally, leads to guilt. And intriguingly, guilt may be an even more powerful human trait than greed. Thus the new capitalism may present us with an unfortunate 'double whammy' – for not only does it create egregious accumulations of wealth, but it then compounds the problem by adding to it the distorting effects of the guilt that flows from such inequity.

Along with a social conscience, guilt is the primary fuel for charity. And global capitalism's super-rich are very charitable in monetary terms – the sums given to the charitable or voluntary sector in the US are awesome.[36] Britons too donate very large amounts: in 1993–4 super-rich David Sainsbury was reputed to have donated £11.1 million, Peter Beckwith more than £5 million, Martyn Arbib more than £4 million, Lord Rayne about £2 million, Vivien Duffield and family and Robert Edmiston about £3 million each.[37]

Yet charitable donations can never begin to address the huge social problems thrown up by the new capitalism. Even so, those who give to charitable causes often see it as an alternative to taxation, and charity often also serves as a favoured method for the super-rich to avoid paying taxes. Therefore the world of charity serves as a pressure group for lower taxes. In a superb ironic twist, the burdensome weight of guilt acts – conveniently – as an agent for a low tax or no tax regime.

New capitalism, new man

There is, however, a deeper problem thrown up by contemporary global capitalism than the issue of greed. Greed and guilt are at least human – indeed dimensions of humanity that, *à la* Gordon Gekko, may have positive side effects that we too often repress. There is a narrowness, a certain lack of rounded humanity, at the very centre of modern global capitalism. At the core of its being, capitalism has always, naturally, been about capital, about the rewards to capital, and about creating an environment for capital. It has also been about economics. Harvard economist Amartya Sen, in his erudite, theoretical essay on contemporary economics, argues that the separation of economics from politics – and thus from questions of ethics – had a long gestation period and was a fundamentally wrong development. Yet old-style capitalism, existing in a religious time and bounded by community (essentially the nation-state) was able to limit this separation, and also limit *economism*.

The fact is that in our modern global market, economics is so dominant, so total a preoccupation, that Aristotle's 'life of money-making' now rules. Increasingly modern man and woman are literally not ethical. Ultimately they have no interest in rights and wrongs and are 'completely unaffected by the reach of self-examination induced by the Socratic question, "how should one live?"'[38]

It sounds trite, but other people are not of central concern. In the new global economy they are literally extras – hirable and fireable tools of competitiveness. The culture of the modern corporation – the great victor in the Cold War, the model for modern global capitalism – increasingly displays this idea of people as a commodity. The 'idea of a corporation as the property of the current holders of its shares is an affront to natural justice in that it gives inadequate recognition to the people who work in the corporation', and 'it might even be immoral for people to talk of owning other people'.[39] These are serious considerations. Can some people essentially own others? Are people commodities? Such questions still remain largely unasked, let alone answered, because of their association with Marxism during the Cold War.

5
A World without Politics

A distaste for politics

When, in the mid 1990s, the American social theorist Peter Drucker suggested that 'if this century proves one thing, it is the futility of politics' he was echoing a widely held view that politics had been made increasingly redundant by the growth of markets, the privatisation of assets and the globalisation of finance; and that change was no longer forged by politics, but rather took place in new arenas – primarily economic and financial, but also technological and cultural.[1]

'Futile' was of course something of an exaggeration. Even at the turn of the millenium, with global capitalism rampant, politics is still important, and potentially able to make a comeback. What it has lost, though, is its *special* quality. Politics (like the state) has lost its special role as the arbiter between economic interests and the court of final appeal between business and social interests. It is no longer the ultimate forum, or the overarching way of thinking about the public world.

That arch-priestess of globalism, former Prime Minister Margaret Thatcher, summed up this toppling of politics from its special status with her dictum that 'there is no such thing as society'. She argued – and it was a powerful thrust – that politicians were nothing special, that they were little more than a vested interest, an elite who evoked images such as 'society' and the 'public good' in order to dress up their personal agendas in selfless language.

Above all, and invidiously, the world of politics has come to be seen by influential supporters of the market as a mechanism for elitism. Arthur Seldon called 'the democracy of politics' the 'government of the busy, by the bossy, for the bully'. while the market operated in favour of 'ordinary men and women', 'the political process' was constructed for elites and specialists 'in the arts of persuasion, organisation, inflitration, debate, lobbying, manipulating meetings'.[2] It was a polemical bullet that hit home, particularly in the 1980s in Britain, which had just witnessed the excesses of a minority on the extreme left in local councils and trade unions.

From this market vantage point, the world of politics has become an interest group like any other – no longer concerned with the best for the country, with 'the big picture' essentially no different from farmers, teachers, small businesspeople; politicians always have an axe to grind and a nest to feather; politics is lacking in virtue; public service is a sham, merely a cover for personal aggrandisement; the great political creed of 'rights' is a cover for selfishness (and more stress should be placed upon responsibilities). Even the political art of compromise is derided, and is often compared unfavourably – by the privately owned media – with the risk taking of business.

It is little wonder, then, that the authority has drained out of politics. Political leaders are no longer held in high regard, indeed the very word 'politician' has become a term of derision. The careful, contrived public language of politics – dubbed 'woodenspeak' – increasingly bores the public. The widespread use of public relations advisors – the politicians' response to the massive growth of the political media – tends to reduce politicians to little more than a branch of the entertainment industry. And, in the British and US systems at least, successful politicians are those who – like President Bill Clinton and Prime Minister Tony Blair – are presentationally skilful, highly polished performers in front of the cameras and concerned to court the media elites. In a sign of the times Tony Blair even agreed to a lower billing on a television talk show than that of a popular singer.[3]

By the late 1990s the role of the politician had changed radically, not only from the days of Roosevelt and Churchill, but also from those of Reagan and Thatcher. With the exigencies of the Cold War fast becoming a distant memory, the 'heroic' style of political leadership – the image of distance, gravitas, character, vision – had given way to softer traits: warmth, concern, understanding, sensitivity. For the successful politician at the turn of the century, 'doing the right thing', or thinking long-term and strategically is less important than the day-to-day management of the polity and society. Testing policies before they are advocated (President Clinton and Prime Minister Blair used Phillip Gould's and James Carville's political consultancy, GGC-NOP) has become a leadership skill. An ear to public opinion – via the use of sophisticated polling techniques and focus groups – has become a more important aspect of the job description of a politician than a grasp of the details of policy, let alone a sense of history.

Some believe that, in the era of the global economy, the only function left for national politicians is that of 'role model' – of representing the polity, being the polity's face to the world, and even setting personal standards. However politicians now seem to be being denied even this role. The individualistic, less deferential, media-driven public life in which every body is perceived as having a blemish or two (even if they don't), means that the very idea of 'role models' has lost some hold. Also, in the contemporary culture the people to emulate are increasingly to be found in the private sector – television presenters, sportsmen and women, and above all entrepreneurs such as car maker Lee Iacocca in the US and music and travel mogul Richard Branson in Britain. Increasingly, the most that the public sector politician, increasingly devoid of power and no longer needed as a role model, can aspire to is to become a celebrity.

This collapse in the traditional standards of political leadership is in part a reflection of a lowering of what the public expects of its political leaders. So low had US public expectations become that opinion polls in 1998 showed that a majority of Americans believed that their president had lied under oath – and to them! Yet they still approved of the way he was doing his job and did not want him removed from office, even though he had probably committed a crime. This public reaction to the Clinton scandal probably reveals a general view that politics matters less and less, certainly much less than during the Cold War. It increasingly seems that Western publics are simply not listening to their politicians; instead they are turning to 'experts', journalists and a range of non-traditional authority figures, even celebrities, royalty and talk show hosts, for social and political views and guidance.

Political institutions are also in trouble. In the global market democracies of the US and Britain, governmental institutions – from the US Congress and presidency to the British Parliament and monarchy – are losing their appeal with the public. No longer viewed as remote, authoritative and above all neutral, political institutions are no longer separated from the political class who inhabit them, and thus even the institutions themselves have come to be viewed as players in a kind of market system. The US public's low regard for the US Congress has become a settled feature of political life, and intriguingly the elected members of the Congress regularly fall well below the respect and trust ranking of the unelected members of the Supreme Court; while British opinion polls regularly report that large numbers of Britons, particularly amongst the younger age groups, no longer believe that the monarchy and royal family have much relevance to their lives.[4]

The most democratic political institution of all – elections – is faring no better. No longer viewed as 'democracy's great day', elections are increasingly seen as exercises in manipulation, their outcomes governed by public relations advisors and, in the US, by hugely expensive television advertising campaigns. On the right, mass democracy, and the politicians who operate within it, are seen as pandering to left-wing sectional interests and as a direct cause of the overblown, unfundable welfare state.[5] For many on the left, elections are dismissed as a middle-class preserve that have no meaning for large numbers of the excluded, particularly the growing underclass.

Turnout rates in elections are falling. In the US, only about 50 per cent of electors normally vote in presidential elections. In the 1988 contest 91 million people voted, but *the same number* – largely composed of inner-city blacks, Hispanics and the rural and urban poor – stayed away from the polls. In elections for Congress the turnout figures are even lower. Even after several well-publicised registration drives the turnout amongst American blacks is still alarmingly low. In Britain the turnout for general elections fell from a high of over 80 per cent in the early 1950s to as low as 70 per cent in the 1980s. The European Union elections usually attract significantly fewer British voters, and the turnout for local elections is often in the region of 20–40 per cent.[6]

Causes

Many American analysts believe that the contemporary crisis of confidence in the US government is essentially a feature of a breakdown in the legitimacy of political leadership and institutions – the inevitable result of specific, avoidable events, particularly the 'political sins of deception' surrounding the Vietnam War, Watergate and in 1998 the scandals, lying and law-breaking surrounding the proposed impeachment of President Clinton, all made highly public by mass media attention.[7] Others place the crisis at the feet of what, in the fashionable arguments of the 1970s, came to be known as the 'overloading' of government, or the inability of political institutions to deal with the extent and complexity of the changing demands upon them.

Yet these causes of the crisis in politics are by no means the whole story. The now worrying, seemingly endemic distaste for politics has not arisen without considerable help along the way – to the point of fanning the flames – from the burgeoning corporate media. It is often forgotten that for Western publics the world of the public sector – the world of politics – is filtered through privately owned media by a business world that can hardly help but bring its own values and opinions to bear. In the US television journalists, pundits and newspaper editors are employees of big-business enterprises, many of them global companies.

Although the media class – well-off, highly educated, urban and relatively sophisticated – tend to be progressive on social issues, they are apt to reflect their employers' views on economic issues, particularly taxation – of course this may reflect their high earnings rather than conformism. The private sector, particularly in the US, tends to take a jaundiced view of the efficiency and honesty of the public sector, and it is unsurprising that, from the US media's vantage point, the life of politics and public service should be derided, that 'politics' itself has become a demeaning term, evoking images of deceit and corruption, and that the skills of the politician have been devalued (becoming the 'black arts' of unprincipled compromise) compared with the more acceptable skills needed to make a profit in the business world.

The media's destruction of the reputation of politics has not, though, simply been a function of its ownership by private sector moguls. The mix of mass democracy and the new technology of mass communications (the inherent questioning of authority, the probing of leaders and public figures, the need to feed the cadres of opinion formers and critics) would, even if the Western media had been less wholly located in the private sector, inevitably have led to a popular disillusionment with government and politics.

When the Cold War and the contest with Soviet Union came to an end, the Western corporate media began to lower their political content in favour of new concerns: lifestyle issues such as sexual morality, abortion, fashion and sport. These kinds of issue – aired regularly to huge television audiences – tended to marginalise politics, turning the world of public life into a boring arena occupied by men in suits. And in the process the focus of public attention was turned away from traditional concerns of economic and social justice.

However this growing disdain for politics was more than simply the product of a change in a cultural mood induced and directed by the corporate media. There were more profound social and political changes at work. As I discuss later, in the age of global economics, national politicians (and at the turn of the millenium *all* politicians are still national politicians) have become increasingly marginal figures. Also, the 1980s witnessed a huge increase in small businesses (many of them sole proprietorships), which was partly the design of market policies and partly the result of the failure of the market – many workers who were laid off started up their own small commercial operations.

In such an environment the roles and images of the 1950s were reversed, with the businessperson becoming the hero and the politician the hack even the crook. The private sector and entrepreneurship came to be highly valued, whereas the public sector – populated by bureaucrats – was seen as endemically inefficient and of little productive value. And in this process even the very best examples of the public sector – the meritocrats, the highly educated achievers who ran the civil service, even those in France and in the European Commission in Brussels – were branded as technocrats and seen as much less worthy than the risk takers in the private sector. Somehow the craft of administration and management in the public sector came to be labelled as bureaucratic, whereas the same bureaucratic functions in the private corporate sector went largely unnoticed. (And in the real world, the bosses of the public sector – the politicians, the bureaucrats – often directed far fewer resources than the chief executive officers of the private sector or the major financial families.)

Of course this distaste for politics was really a distaste for *government*, for its reach, its heavyhandedness, its interference in what was seen as private domains, and, above all, for the tax-raising power of the state. One of the most underpublicised social changes of the postwar period has been the rapid growth in the number of people who pay tax. In the 1950s tax paying used to be a concern of a 'rich' minority only; but as broader swathes of the population became subject to 'Pay As You Earn' (in Britain) and 'Withholding' (in the US), let alone started paying inheritance taxes, a rich vein of populist resentment against 'government' became available for tapping. President Ronald Reagan's famous electioneering soundbite – 'Get the Government off the Backs of the people' – successfully exploited this sentiment.

The coming world without politics

As the new millenium approached, so battered was the reputation of government, politicians and politics that the free-market dream of the minimal state, of minimalising politics and marginalising politicians, was well on the way to fruition. Some could even glimpse a coming world in which global capitalism and global markets would replace politics completely.

In this future free-market world the *forms* of politics would continue. The great buildings of politics – the Parliaments and Congresses – would continue to stand and the institutions (political parties, elections, governments and above all the nation-states) would continue to operate. And, crucially, the media would continue to report their activities as though they were of urgent concern. Yet in reality little of *substance* would be decided in the political arena; politicians and their institutions would be be hollow things, mere shadows of their former selves, going through the motions because no one wanted to admit they had become redundant.

In this brave new world markets alone would rule. Markets would become the mechanism for democracy and participation, the forum for choices, for determining social values. And crucially, markets alone would provide the mechanism for allocating economic resources. They would decide the very way we live. In other words a world without politics would be complete.

The persistence of politics

The idea of a world without politics is of course somewhat farfetched. Certainly at the end of the 1990s the trends were still working in its favour. As long as global integration continues (and governments lose more and more control) it is hard to envisage any forces that could turn back the tide of the market.

Yet such a world without politics would amount to a revolution. We would have seen nothing like it before. From the dawn of time, certainly from ancient times – from the time when humankind began to organise itself (and arguably even before that, in the relations established between two people) – politics has existed in some form or other. In the days of the Greek polis Aristotle depicted politics as 'the master art', concerned with the allocation of resources and much more besides. The ancients seemed to possess a clear understanding of the limits of economics ('the dismal science').

In the middle ages, too, economics was subordinated to a host of social goals, such as the idea of a socially 'just price' or protectionist and producer interests (often called guilds). In medieval local communities the church often held sway over economics, and in Catholic Europe, in an approach reaching down to today's Christian democracy, very definite ideas about the economy – almost amounting to a Christian code of economic policy – were propagated.

This subordination of economics to politics was inevitable in a world of traditional communities where non-economic loyalties took precedence, where community goals were seen as transcending individual economic advancement. People were loyal to their communities in a way that is difficult to understand today. These communities were not instrumental or contractual, establishing obligations in return for services. Rather they were seen as living organisms which, existing long before the individual was born and surviving long after he or she had gone, could demand not only loyalty but also obedience.

Also, the sheer religiosity of these traditional medieval communities ensured the supremacy of politics over economics. Spirituality took precedence over the material world; and the debate over religion (what today we might call ideology), much of it with a highly political content, compared favourably with the dim, or dimmish, understanding of economics.

Politics and the nation-state

In Europe during the seventeenth and eighteenth centuries, as local markets expanded into national ones, the emerging nation-states slowly took over the political functions of the localities and the church, and began to impose their own regulations and taxes. This new world of nation-states brought, if anything, a strengthening of politics.

A transcendent sense of community remained, but was given form and life by the emergence of a new and larger political unit, the nation-state. These nations, and their states, became the primary focus for loyalty – often even competing with and winning out over the family unit.

Mulhall and Swift have suggested that a sense of identity 'is inseparable from an awareness of ourselves as members of a particular family or class or community or people or nation, as bearers of a specific history, as citizens of a particular republic; and *we look to the political realm* as a way in which we can develop and refine our sense of ourselves'.[8]

In fact nowadays we tend to forget the strength of this identification with the political realm, the political community, represented as it has been over the last three hundred years or so by the nation-state. Alan Milward suggests that the ultimate basis for the survival of the nation-state is 'the same as it always was, allegiance'.[9] During the twentieth century millions of people have displayed their allegiance to the political idea of nation by making very serious sacrifices, including a willingness to make the ultimate one.

Of course the *genuine* level or intensity of political allegiance, or loyalty, is very difficult to measure. The nation-state also had ultimate legal authority over the lives of its people. It could (still can) fine, tax, imprison, even take life. There was no higher legal appeal, and most people were powerless to leave its boundaries. In such circumstances a degree of political loyalty or allegiance was hardly surprising, perhaps more as much a measure of *force majeur* than of genuine feeling. Linda Colley has attempted to measure this political loyalty by the yardstick of willingness to serve in the armed forces. She reports that by early eighteenth-century standards 'they [the statistics organised by the government in 1798 and 1803 to find out who would serve in the armed forces] confront those who argue on the one hand for widespread loyalty and deference throughout Great Britain ... and those who claim on the other hand that the mass of Britons were alienated from their rulers'.[10]

Business and the Victorian nation

So powerful was the nation-state that even during the high point of the unfettered market relations of the nineteenth century, politics remained in charge, managing to constrain the raw economic power of Victorian capitalism. Trade and commerce may have blossomed, and increasingly broken free of borders, but in these Victorian times – in the leading capitalist nations, Britain, the United States and Germany – political sovereignty went unquestioned. The Victorian nation-state was not to be trifled with, or at least not in the way in which globalism treats the contemporary nation-state.

Of course this was the age of imperialism in which the nation-states (and their ruling groups) directly and politically controlled vast territories and peoples. The fundamental dynamic here, therefore, was political – involving ideas of contests between peoples and civilisations, conquest, predemocratic values such as racial superiority and paternalist political views such as elite governance. These empires were geopolitical systems, in which trade might not always exactly 'follow the flag' but was always securely wrapped in it. Commerce played a crucial but ultimately secondary role to the political dynamic of empire, being run from London, Paris, Amsterdam, Madrid and Lisbon.[11] And it was politics – through imperial expansion of the European nation-states – that fuelled the globalisation of this Victorian era (whereas today's globalisation is the product of economics, of companies and capital, not nation-states).

At home, the Victorian era saw politics – in the form of an expanding political community based on the emerging middle-class male democracy – establishing ascendancy even over the confident, burgeoning capitalism of the era. Victorian capital may indeed have been confident, and profitable; but in an era of strong political loyalties, and being unable to move as freely as it can today, Victorian capital was ultimately subservient to politics, to the Victorian state, in a sense in which it is not in today's global economy. The political community, through the state, could improve labour conditions, take the first tentative steps towards a welfare state, and increase public expenditure and taxes without provoking capital flight.

The great Victorian debate was not about whether society or politics existed, or should exist, but rather about how big the state should become – about how much regulation economics should endure. Even the great free-market thinkers of the Victorian era saw politics as sovereign. They may have seen the means towards achieving the free society as largely economic, but their ends were usually political.

It is an interesting twist, but many of these same free-market Victorians were political radicals whose overriding concern was not economics, but political and social change. For them the state was wrongly ordered and should be reformed, although not abolished. Also, unlike today's supporters of the market, these Victorian free-marketeers were keen on securing rights for the broad mass of people, and saw the state – in the form of the law – as a crucial mechanism. For them the central problem was social: the power of the aristocracy and landed interests (reflected in the monarchy, the House of Lords and the limited franchise for the House of Commons). And it was the political ideology of freedom – of freeborn Englishmen – which fired the minds of these radicals. Certainly Tom Paine, Herbert Spencer and Auberon Herbert were supporters of minimal government. They saw the state controlled by a corrupt aristocracy, and sought a greater space for business and the market which would promote a less paternalist, less objectionable, more middle class, society, with better, more democratic values. The aim was social and political, not economic.[12]

Even during the gilded age of American capitalism in the late nineteenth century, capital was political and social – that is, bounded by the idea of limits placed upon its reach and power by the needs of a wider community. Max Weber in *The Protestant Ethic and the Spirt of Capitalism* (1920) and the Christian Socialist R. H. Tawney in *Religion and the Rise of Capitalism* saw a direct link between religiously inspired ethics and capital, 'a code of Protestant conviction which said that gaining wealth was connected to virtue but was also a trust'.[13] There was wide acceptance of the idea that making money (profits) was morally acceptable as long as there was an ultimate social goal. In the US this notion of capital's ultimate social responsibility was given practical form in the great philanthropic trusts and foundations of the Rockefellers, the Mellons, the Carnegies and the like. These moguls were certainly not keen on state interference in the making of capital, which was often a grubby and ruthless business, but once the pile was made the idea of wider social responsibility (often in the form of charity) took over.

As an historian of the robber baron period has argued:

> in short order the railroad presidents, the copper barons, the big dry-goods merchants and the steel masters became Senators, ruling in the highest councils of the national government, and sometimes scattered twenty dollar gold pieces to newsboys of Washington. But they also became in greater number lay leaders of churches, trustees of universities, partners or owners of newspapers ... and figures of fashionable, cultured society.[14]

Indeed, as Thorstein Veblen suggested, these robber barons with a conscience, and with a 'becoming gravity', offered themselves as guides 'to literature and art, church and state, science and education, law and morals – the standard container of the civic virtue'.[15]

Business and the twentieth-century nation

The supremacy of politics over economics in the twentieth century was exemplified by the ideology of the rapidly expanding corporate world. These new corporations, which over the century had replaced the traditional family firm, were large, multi-unit operations. They represented a new managerial capitalism where month by month, year by year, decisions were increasingly taken by a race of professionally and technically competent managers. As Pulitzer Prize winning management theorist Alfred Chandler has argued, these modern big businesses were rather like independent political units, and 'took the place of market mechanisms in coordinating the activities of the economy and allocating its resources'.[16]

By controlling the market rather than competing within it, these big new corporations increasingly acted politically. As Werner Stombart argued during the 1930s, they began to take on a life of their own, the emerging managerial class having as much political and social interest in the land as any trade unionist or civil servant.[17] They sought, and often obtained, influence over legislation by financing congressmen and senators.

And crucially, the new breed of career managers and corporate bureaucrats 'preferred policies that favoured long-term stability and growth of their enterprises to those that maximised current profits'.[18] Although often driven in part by profitability, and certainly living by the rules of the world of economics, the new culture of the big, multi-unit, largely American corporation saw the company as part of the wider political community, with political and social obligations.

One such political obligation was obeying the law. Of course preglobal corporations used their muscle to attempt to bend legislatures to their will and sway laws in their interests, but once political decisions had been made, the corporations, ultimately bound by the political requirements of their nations, continued their operations within the national boundaries. (Although today's global corporations all make a point of declaring that they also obey the laws of the lands in which they operate, their ability to relocate in territories where laws are more amenable means that their protestations are something of an empty boast.)

Some of the these big, preglobal companies operating in the Victorian and Edwardian eras saw themselves as political and social communities rather than organisations of property seeking only to make profits. The workforce – often in order to forestall trade union activity – was given the view that the company was a community, almost a family (Henry Ford even became a kind of agony uncle); and a 'community of feeling' was promoted by providing employees with long-term jobs, pensions and health benefits. This approach amounted to a form of micro welfare capitalism. Elton Mayo, the founding father of the human relations school of management, publicised the corporate welfare practices of AT&T's Hawthorne Works in the late 1920s and early 1930s. Management theorist John Sheldrake has argued that 'the package of benefits at the Hawthorne Works was, by contemporary international standards, impressive and included a pension scheme, sickness and disability benefits, a share purchase plan, a system of worker representation, a medical department and hospital'.[19]

In Britain the same kind of community attitude could be seen in the mid-Victorian mill towns where, according to F. M. L. Thompson in *The Rise of Respectable Society*, 'life centred on the mill, not simply because it was the source of work and wages but because it formed a distinct community and attracted specific loyalties'.[20] Indeed the cotton textile industry became the focus of paternalistic activity – what would later be termed 'welfare capitalism'. From the middle of the century it became increasingly common for big employers to provide reading and newspaper rooms at the mills. By the 1890s works sports grounds were common, as were brass bands.

The growth of interest within these new corporations in the idea of scientific management demanded a mental revolution and a mutuality between managers and workers. F. W. Taylor's work on management, which advocated such a mutuality, attracted a considerable following in the US, Japan and Germany, as did the ideas of his disciple, Henry Gantt.[21]

The notion of businesses as communities – of a social or political leavening of the raw economic commercialism of the corporation – did not normally go as far as seeking to involve the 'community of workers' in commercial decisions. After all, this kind of capitalism was paternalistic, not democratic. The corporation was for the workers, but not of them. Even so, after the Second World War codetermination, in which employees were allowed some kind of general input into commercial strategy through reserved positions on the governing boards, became a feature of West German corporations following the country's enforced reorganisation by the victorious allies (who would not have given house room to the idea in their own countries.) What stopped worker participation in its tracks in the Anglo-American world was not just the, often visceral, opposition of some business leaders; it was also the strength of the trade union movement. Trade union leaderships remained unconcerned about the question of participation in the firm, seeing their function as primarily adversarial, as negotiating over wages and conditions.

This kind of pre-global capitalist business was, though, in no way sentimental. It was ruthless, and often hugely profitable. Its precursors around the turn of the century had been dubbed the 'robber barons' or (by Teddy Roosevelt) those 'malefactors of great wealth'. Yet these tough-minded capitalists not only tended to see business as a form of community, but also displayed a wider social concern beyond the factory gates: business was seen as part of a wider community, with community responsibilities. The tone was set by one such robber baron, John D. Rockefeller, a serious critic of whom conceded that his 'prodigious investments in public charities which, begun in 1890, were conducted upon a scale befitting the man's princely power, and most certainly fitted to scale Heaven's walls'.[22] And long after the age of these robber barons, the American companies of the twentieth century continued to invest in local communities – in the townships and villages in which they operated, and expected to continue to operate. All manner of local cultural services and amenities, including symphony orchestras and opera companies, were aided by large corporations.

Of course this political and social dimension of business – the idea of business as a community, albeit a paternalistic one, and as an integral part of a wider political community – often made good business sense. A contented workforce could be expected to work more efficiently and thus produce more profits, and, crucially, would be less likely to demand trade union representation. And the local community activity would be good for the image of businesses by improving their public relations over the long term.

Yet for all their self-interest, businesses in the preglobal capitalist era saw profitability and politics as somehow linked; and believed that the interest of the shareholder could not be completely extricated from a social context. The aim of the corporate game was certainly to make profits, but power, prestige, acceptability and recognition were, along with money, powerful business motives, and the path to business success did not always involve lower and lower social costs.

Of course the view of business as bound up with the interests of a wider political community was enhanced as the twentieth century progressed by the deepening relationship between the state and the corporations. The rapid growth in government before, during and after the Second World War opened up for the private sector, for companies big and small, particularly in the defence industry, a veritable cornucopia of government contracts.

And later, during the growth of the state after 1945, politically driven procurement policy often became even more important to the corporations than operating in the market. In such an environment, big business increasingly saw itself, or said it did, as contributing to national (political) goals, not just profit maximisation. As business and state (and sometimes relatively well-behaved trade unions, 'business unions') worked together and helped each other in an 'every one a winner' kind of symbiotic relationship, a new ideology of cooperation, or corporatism came into fashion.

The idea of cooperation between business, unions and state had been floated officially in Britain during the Mond–Turner talks in 1928–9, and big business organisations (such as the Business Round Table in the US and the CBI in Britain), sensing it would make life easier and more profitable, warmed to the idea. In the political world, many big-business supporters of the moderate wing of the Republican Party and 'One Nation' Tories in Britain propounded these corporatist views way into the 1970s, when the Thatcher and Reagan revolutions marginalised

them. But in continental Europe proponents of the social market continued to stress the advantages of cooperation (between the social partners of capital and labour) and the state and big business continued
to work together on long-term, strategic plans for investments and
markets.

Business, democracy and war

With hindsight this cooperative approach between business and the
state was bound to be a temporary affair. After all, the big corporations
were the coming players, and national governments were slowly losing
their authority and autonomy. The dynamic of restless, borderless, burgeoning capitalism could ultimately be expected to destroy the nation-
state, even the well-established nation-states of Europe. Indeed some
theorists argue that even the Victorian economy saw a more pronounced form of globalism than that operating today.[23] Also, the
growth of consumer individualism could be expected seriously to
weaken the broader hold of community identity and loyalty.

In the final decades of the nineteenth century it would have been a
rash man who predicted that what lay ahead was a new age of nationalism. Yet such a new age was indeed about to dawn, and with it,
surprisingly, continuing ability of the nation-state (and therefore of
politics) to constrain the power of economics, business and the market,
and to keep capitalism civilised.

This comeback for the nation-state was the product of two extraordinary twentieth-century phenomena – mass democracy and mass war.
It is an intriguing thought, but without either the mid century might
have seen the demise of the nation-state and the full emergence of a
global economy and culture. As it was, both democracy and war rode to
the defence of the nation and, in their different ways, reinforced particularism (at the expense of the universal) and communal loyalty and
identity.

By the second decade of the twentieth century mass democracy was
well under way in the advanced industrialised countries. The franchise
was becoming a majority affair and the middle classes were seeking to
participate. The idea of popular sovereignty – that the people owned
their government – was growing: strongly in the US, moderately in some
continental European countries and somewhat less in Britain.

And, crucially, the nation-state became the forum – the only possible
forum – for the expression of these democratic instincts and aspirations.
Parliaments, congresses, assemblies – all of them *national* institutions –

were the accepted and unquestioned institutional expression of the people. Thus any weakening of the nation-state was a weakening of democracy itself. (Indeed even today, on the very eve of the third millenium, the British left-wing politician Tony Benn continues to argue that the nation-state, as represented in his case by the parliament in Westminster, is the only real mechanism for democratic expression, and that European integration, even should it involve a strengthened European Parliament, ineluctably reduces democratic control.)

Mass democracy led to mass society. The growing consumer culture of the twentieth century linked up with technological changes (radio, movies and then, probably more important than any other, television) to produce in most Western nations a mass culture. But because it emerged during the age of nations, this mass culture was primarily national in its content, creating a popular national literature, a populist national imagery and even a popular national history (and national heroes) for the masses, all of which strongly reinforced the legitimacy of the nation and its state, and therefore politicians and politics more generally.

Nationalism – and thus politicians and the state – received a mid-century shot in the arm from the new mass communication industry. The most significant of all the new consumer technologies, television, began to project into millions and millions of homes the images of a wider nation. The image and authority of the US presidency was hugely enhanced by television. And the coronation of Queen Elizabeth II in 1952 was the first mass television event in Britain, hugely strengthening the symbolism of the monarchy and the sense of national unity. (The BBC, under the pressure of its funding by taxpayers, adopted a 'national' ethos, believing it needed to broadcast national events that would 'bring the nation together' and act as a kind of recorder of national affairs.)

The movie industry and the popular literature of the twentieth century, which reached millions, also reinforced national particularism by the heavy use of national stereotypes. The 'national traits' of Americans, French and Germans (particularly Germans) were both established and exaggerated by early popular and populist culture. 'Englishness' was a particular victim – one writer suggested that a group of dinner guests would describe Englishness as 'a bowl of scented roses on a sunlit table and the muted thwack of leather against willow. Umbrellas clashing on city streets and felt trilbies brim to brim at the races. A cup of tea, or a pre-prandial glass of sherry. The first cuckoo of spring and the first Pimms of summer. Kipling and Just William.'[24] In the movies, central casting produced, amongst other national stereotypes, an exaggerated view of the 'English gentleman'. In Britain, Ealing Comedies presented Ian Carmichael as the perfect representation of the type, while Hollywood had David Niven and Rex Harrison playing the part to a tee.[25]

Although some sections of the late-twentieth-century mass communications industry – perhaps CNN and other global broadcast systems who brought global shows and global perspectives to a mass audience – may have lessened provincial, nationalist particularism, they were the exception. By and large the age of mass communications reinforced national identities and loyalties, and gave nationalism a new lease of life. And in the process national politicians, claiming to speak on behalf of both the national state and its people, gained a secure measure of legitimacy over business and businesspeople.

Politics, business and war

War, more than democracy, rescued the twentieth-century nation-state. The sheer nationalistic fervour of 1914–18, when millions volunteered to fight (and die), remains inexplicable for many. But it existed. It produced a huge emotional commitment to the nation-state, not only during the war, but afterwards too, resting on the legions of heroes who it was claimed gave their lives for the nation, for king and country. And war benefited the craft and calling of politics too – for the Second World War leaders (Churchill, Roosevelt, De Gaulle) were politicians, and their mythic status gave authority and credibility not only to the political class but, more broadly, to the state. Business and businessmen were marginalised by war, were thought to play little part in the great military clashes and political crusades, except perhaps as shadowy and sinister armaments manufacturers. The state, not the market, won wars.

The Second World War, unlike its predecessor, was a 'good war' and produced little subsequent pacifist and internationalist sentiment. As argued earlier, a major media industry – primarily Hollywood, but television and the literary world as well – hugely reinforced national sentiment in many of the victorious countries. Patriotic themes and negative images of defeated foreigners ('Huns', 'Japs') conspired to enhance postwar nationalism. The war against Hitler was conducted by an alliance, but each nation separately was able to claim an heroic role.

The nation – with its centralised state and its politicians – not only 'won the war', but in its aftermath was also appearing to produce the economic goods. The state, like the nation, came out of the Second World War rather well. It had mobilised resources in a righteous cause, and it had been victorious. In the postwar decades it constructed a popular welfare state which brought education and health care to those who had been unable to afford it. The state still had negative aspects – it was seen as inefficient and ridden with bureaucracy – but the majority of the population still did not pay a large amount of their income in taxes so the unpalatable 'tax and spend' public sector was a thing of the future.

As a social-democrat theorist Anthony Crosland wrote at the height of the postwar boom in the 1950s: 'Whatever the modes of economic production, economic power will, in fact, belong to the owners of political power' – in effect the owners of the nation-state. He believed that this political world would last, that 'political authority has emerged as the final arbiter of economic life', and that 'the brief, and historically exceptional, era of unfettered market relations is over'.[26]

Yet this enhanced credibility of government and the state went hand in hand with the renewal of the private sector and its enormous productive capacity. The reviving capitalism of the 1950s and 1960s, the high point of social democracy, took place in the context of an extraordinarily productive balance between economics (and the market) and politics (the state and government) that lasted until well into the 1980s.

During these decades business still deferred to national leaderships, to government and politics. Part of the reason for this was the inherited 'authority' still inherent in the idea of the nation, and in politics and the political world. The emerging big businesses, however, also found the nationally based, social-democratic, 'mixed economy' conducive to its needs. The nation-state was providing a healthy infrastructure for the private sector and was subsidising business in numerous ways. This was the age in which a Republican president (Richard Nixon) and a Conservative prime minister (Edward Heath) introduced wage and price controls; in which big business supported the election of a big-spending, 'Great Society' president (and turned its back on Reaganite Barry Goldwater); in which industrial policy or national planning was not anathema in Britain. It was an age in which business believed that trade unions had to be taken seriously, indeed often appeased. And as I shall argue later, the welfare state – existing in an age when, in Europe certainly, socialism and communism were on the political agenda – was seen by many business leaders as a force for social stability.

The Cold War, politics and business

There was to be yet another major international 'war' during the twentieth century: the Cold War – the four-decade intense hostility between

West and East. The Cold War began in the late 1940s, the same period in which huge amounts of American public and private capital were invested around the world and later pump-primed the era of global capital. Paradoxically, it was also the Cold War that staunched the process of globalisation. The intensity of the East–West conflict locked what today would be called the 'emerging markets' (of Eastern Europe, the Soviet Union and above all China) out of the world economy. Also, the Cold War breathed life into the nation-state, and gave it a centrality that for fifty years would keep it from being overwhelmed by global capital, global business and the global market. J. G. Ikenberry goes further. He sees the Cold War as a 'long era of global struggle' that not only strengthened nations, nation-states and national governments but also 'centralised' them.[27]

Thus did the Cold War keep politics in the ascendant over economics and business. For the duration of this conflict the 'big business' of the US was no longer business itself, but rather the very *political* objectives of protecting the country and fighting for democracy! With political objectives taking centre stage, the world of politics was given a shot in the arm. That most political of institutions, the US presidency, came of age during the Cold War. The president became the leader of 'the free world' and the focus of the West's resolve to face down the challenges of the Soviet bloc. The presidency (and the president) was potent, more powerful than any institution (or person) in the history of humankind, as he could, theoretically, destroy the world by ordering a nuclear holocaust. (And, of course, the same applied to his opposite number in the Politburo in Moscow.)

In this political contest, anticommunism – the great cause of the West – became a focus of loyalty. The business world, with its anticommunist instincts, naturally fell in behind the cause, and corporations, even the largest and most powerful of them, remained subordinate to the broader political, ideological and indeed cultural struggle.

Of course during the Cold War decades, particularly in the 1970s during the period of detente, business began doing what it inevitably does: breaking the political and ideological bonds. Some theorists argue that globalisation was proceeding quite handily during the Cold War, and 'the immediate reaction [to the end of the Cold War] was to exaggerate the discontinuity, neglecting underlying forces for change that were having a transforming impact in any event'.[28]

There was indeed during these Cold War years a decided increase in economic relations between Western corporate capitalism and the communist bloc. Western companies were pioneering the economics of globalisation: in particular they were increasingly taking advantage of the Eastern bloc's low-paid, strike-free labour. An intricate process of buy-back agreements – dubbed 'Vodka–Cola' in which 'you bottle our Coke and we'll buy your Vodka' – were developed in order to bypass the non-convertibility of communist bloc currencies.[29] The delights of Western capitalist access to the low-cost, union-free command economies of the Eastern bloc were recognised early on by such prominent business figures as Armand Hammer of Occidental Petroleum and Cleveland billionaire Cyrus Eaton. Many European business leaders also saw great advantages in dealing with the Eastern bloc and supported and encouraged the West German policy of Ostpolitik between the Federal Republic of Germany and the Communist bloc.

However, during the rule of the communist parties (in the period up to 1989) trade and capital flows were minimal, certainly compared with the opening of the floodgates following the collapse of the Berlin Wall and the dissolution of the Warsaw Pact. The requirements of politics – international geopolitics – took precedence over business. In the US, Congress politicians – as part of a major act of political interference with free trade – were able to pass into legislation 'national security' measures whereby whole sectors of Western industry and commerce, particularly those connected to the defence industry, were denied trading rights with communist countries by law. These national security laws of the West, primarily aimed at denying technology transfers from West to East, were of course never fully complied with, but during the Cold War most businesses continued to place loyalty to the Western political community ahead of profits.[30]

Of course this restraint of the Western business class was also to do with self-interest, as corporations that skirted the legal rules and traded with the Eastern bloc might find it difficult to secure highly lucrative defence contracts from the Pentagon. Also, because of strict western legal restrictions, the Soviet Union was unable to use its large reserves of gold as a means of financing the purchase of western technology. And capital injections into the Eastern bloc were risky because of the inconvertibility of the communist currencies and the limits to simple barter deals in return for massive transfers of capital and services.

However, for most businesses, trading with the communist world remained off the agenda for no better reason than that it was 'off limits' for political reasons. There was immense political and social pressure on companies not to trade with the East, pressure made all the more powerful by the anti East–West trade alliance in the US of Republicans and

Cold War liberals. Business leaders did not want to fall foul of Reaganite Republican sentiment or be attacked by neoconservatives. *Vodka–Cola*, the title of an influential book published during the period of detente, became a term of abuse amongst those in the resurgent conservative and neoconservative movement in the late 1970s and early 1980s. Armand Hammer became an American hate figure amongst Republican and Democrat Cold Warriors for a time. In the great cause of 'making the world safe for democracy' business was expected, even by the most probusiness elements in the political class, to toe the line.

Many Western business elites, and their political allies, not only saw themselves as part of a broader political cause opposed to the Soviet Union and communism, but they also believed, certainly in the early years of the Cold War, that the West needed to be defended at home, within the domestic societies, against the spread of communist ideas. The Soviet Union, its Communist Party and its ideological and propaganda apparatus around the world, was taken extremely seriously as a threat. Its ability to attract Western converts by proferring an 'alternative model' of society was not underrated.

A wide range of business people – including the 'super-rich' of the time – saw social democracy as the best antidote to world communism. A sizeable state sector, a welfare system and above all full employment (guaranteed if need be by deficit financing, some subsidisation, higher taxes and even a little inflation) would ensure sufficient social stability for alternative models of society (particularly socialism and communism) to have little allure for Western peoples. For the same reasons, some of the richest people in the Western world promoted the politics and culture of social democracy amongst Western intellectual elites in the universities, the media and politics. And of course a sizeable state – the public sector no less – was needed to organise the military opposition to the Soviet Union and communism.

The Cold War not only served to promote a political loyalty that was larger than the needs of business, it also gave a further kiss of life to the nation-state. Of course in one sense the Cold War was prosecuted by an international alliance – the North Atlantic Treaty Organisation (NATO). But NATO, although it possessed (and still possesses) a single command structure with a single (normally American) commander-in-chief and a single secretary-general, was, as its name suggests, an alliance, multilateral not integrationist, and based upon the cooperation of sovereign nation-states. (Other Western organisations, for example the International Monetary Fund and the Group of Seven, were similarly organised.)

The nation-state, and in particular the US government, remained the organising principle around which the military force of NATO was built. And it was the political leaders of nation-states (the US president, the British prime minister and the French president), not the NATO political or military chiefs, who were responsible for the most important of all decisions: the global life and death decision about the use of nuclear weapons. In this sense the nuclear age, although fought out between two large blocs, was ultimately an age of separate nations.

The end of national sovereignty

Of course, although the nation-state endured during the twentieth century it was fighting a rearguard action. Even during the Cold War, with strict limits placed on mobile capital, creeping globalism meant that the nation-state was slowly losing power and credibility. After the fall of the Berlin Wall (with the spectacular collapse of communism and the emergence of truly global markets) the last pretensions to national sovereignty were stripped away.

Pioneering analysts, such as Kenichi Ohmae, David Held, D. D. Marshall and many others take the view that the dynamics of globalisation will ultimately render the nation-state redundant.[31] Robert Reich has argued that 'the very idea of a national economy is becoming meaningless, as are the notions of national corporation, national capital, national products and national technology'. Ideas such a a 'national economy' are to Reich 'vestigial thought'. 'So who is "us"?' he asks.[32] Indeed the sovereign state may have become little more than a facilitator, 'reduced to the role of adjusting national economies to the dynamics of an unregulated global economy'.[33]

Even the school of thought that dismisses these projections as exaggerated or 'hyperbolic', still see the nation-state as somewhat weakened, needing to come to what Ian Clark suggests will be a 'new accommodation between state power and the forces of globalisation'.[34]

The early warning signs of collapse were there for all to see. One such was the Americanisation of the Western world, which proceeded apace after 1945. The earlier structure of a 'concert of nations' first gave way to alliances, and then, after the Second World War and the start of the Cold War, to a superpower structure. So-called 'sovereign' European states were defended against the Soviet threat by US military power and foreign military bases and personnel were accepted on sovereign territory. American popular culture, spread through the growing mass media industry, became the popular culture of other nations, and nowhere, ironically, was this Americanisation more pronounced than in Britain, where national sovereignty was still highly prized in the late 1990s.

Yet the hold of national sovereignty remained very difficult to prise open; and even today it retains its power over the human imagination. We still, all of us, even the most ardent globalists, often think in national terms, still instinctively look to national governments to solve problems, and believe the highest appeal is to 'country' and the political authority that represents 'country' – the nation-state. The concept of national sovereignty may be vestigial thinking, but it is powerful nonetheless.

None of this is very surprising. The idea of national sovereignty has had a long run. It was first revived in modern form (that is, after the long period in the Middle Ages when the classical notion of sovereignty had collapsed) by Jean Bodin in *De La Republique* (1576 in French, 1606 in English). Bodin 'worked to find some basis of ideas on which the harmony of the political community could be restored'. Thomas Hobbes also played a crucial part in the popular development of the idea of sovereignty 'by substituting for the Prince the abstract notion of the state'.[35]

Over time the idea of sovereignty became a veritable holy shrine, particularly in England, where it was meat and drink to monarchists and those who supported hierarchy and centralisation; and it came to represent Sir William Blackstone's 'quintessentially Anglican version of the traditional English unitary and absolutist doctrine' of governmental authority.[36]

Later Hegel also got in on the 'sovereignty' act. During the latter part of the nineteenth century the influence of Hegel's ideas, particularly his conception of the state 'as the realisation of the moral ideal and as an absolute end', made headway even in supposedly liberal societies such as Britain; and this renewed interest in the sovereignty of the state went hand in hand with the rise of nationalism, and thus the 'sovereign state quite easily became interchangeable with the "sovereign nation"': they were in fact one and the same thing.[37]

Of course ideas of nation-state sovereignty rarely went uncontested, for they ran up against contradictory liberal beliefs. During the nineteenth century the powerful free-trade ideology and instinct rejected national sovereignty – mainly implicitly but sometimes openly. So too did that aspect of liberalism which elevated individual conscience and pacifism over the demands of the nation-state. Indeed, Lord (Harold) Acton was very influential, though ultimately unsuccessful, in trying to persuade his contemporaries of the unfashionable idea that nationalism was not a liberal idea at all. And of course the business class was always wanting to limit the role of the state, and thus, at one remove, the nation too. Scepticism came from the democratic left too. The potential for absolutism at the heart of the idea of sovereignty led the political theorist Harold Laski to argue that 'it would be of lasting benefit to political science if the whole concept of sovereignty were surrendered ... it is at least probable that it has dangerous moral consequences'.[38]

Yet (as has been argued earlier) both the collectivism and the wars of the twentieth century boosted the nation-state and the idea of national sovereignty. And strangely, so too did the rules of international law and practice drawn up by both the League of Nations and its successor, the United Nations. The UN based the fundaments of post-Second World War diplomacy on the 'sovereignty' of nation-states, only admitting to its ranks countries that were deemed to be nation-states and recognising only them as the principal actors. As late as the early 1990s a great military conflict in the Middle East (the Gulf War) was justified by US President George Bush on the ground that the 'sovereign' national borders of Kuwait had been crossed by Iraq.

But (as was also argued earlier) the process of economic globalisation was slowly making the territorially bound nation-state increasingly irrelevant. This author – as is obvious – shares the view that it is the new, virtually unrestricted mobility of capital that is the key here – a dagger at the heart of nation-states. But there are other forces at work as well. One such is the revolution in technology. Intriguingly, it may have been in the military field – traditionally the bastion of nationalism – where changing technology made a decisive breakthrough against the nation-state.

During the 1930s in Britain the policy of appeasement was suddenly given a serious boost when it became clear that one of nationalism's great imperatives – the defence of the territory of the nation-state – was no longer possible. The frightening slogan of the time – 'the bomber can always get through' – displayed in vivid terms the limits of the nation-state. And the nuclear age, with its technology of intercontinental missiles and space weapons, opened traditionally secure national territories to instant destruction – and from thousands of miles away. There was little sovereignty, either inherent in Britain or in its 'mother of parliaments', when the Soviet Politburo, sitting at the other end of a continent, could destroy the country in a matter of minutes.

Changing technology, both with a military application and without, was of course at the very heart of the growing power and reach of the transnational corporations. For instance the transportation, communications and computer revolution allowed transnational corporations – the single most organised and dynamic force to weaken national sovereignty – to develop and expand on a truly global basis. As Mathew Horsman and Andrew Marshall have put it, 'its [trans-national corporation's] access to knowledge is central to its success: to its production techniques, to its distribution and marketing, to its financial operations. ...In sectors ranging from financial services to management consultancy to commodity trading, there is no longer production as it is traditionally understood. There is only information, communicated efficiently within, between and among companies.'[39]

'Sovereign' national decision making can hardly exist in a global economy in which transnational companies, many of them with financial resources the size of small nation-states, can move those resources around the world at will. Anthony Sampson suggests that 'the huge flow of foreign funds, whether from Arabs, mafias, or multi-national corporations, tests the integrity of every institution to the limit', and rightly concludes that 'in the global context, national politicians or administrators begin to look more like local councillors confronting big-time developers'.[40]

When meetings about interest rates in Washington or Frankfurt or about investment or mergers and acquisitions in Paris, Brussels, Riyadh or Tokyo can have a greater purchase on a peoples' future than any decision taken in its own capital city, then national decision makers have indeed become 'local councillors'.

And sovereignty is also eroded by the very institutions set up to attempt to manage the global economy, to give some order to the world market-place. The International Monetary Fund, the World Trade Organisation and more particularly the international meetings, both formal and informal, of national politicians, all serve to limit sovereignty even further. Indeed it could be argued that the single most important institution affecting the economic lives of the peoples of the world in the late twentieth century are the G5 or G7 meetings of finance and other ministers, for it is often within this framework (or ones very much like it), and not in the national capitals separately, that global economic policies – interest-rate policy, exchange-rate policy and, ultimately, taxation and unemployment levels – are set.

And increasingly, as the European Union begins to take hold, then – certainly in Euroland (those countries in the euro currency zone) – interest rates, exchange rates, perhaps even taxation and unemployment levels will be decided in a non-national forum: the supranational European forum of the EU Council of Ministers or the Central Bank. In the interplay between European political, financial and corporate actors – the real environment in which decisions will be made – the role of the national politicians will be limited, perhaps even marginal. Just as the national central banks of Europe will become hollow institutions – rather like the Federal Reserve Banks in the states of the US – so too will sovereign national parliaments.

Culture, as well as economics and finance, is also eroding the nation-state. In the age of national sovereignty, culture too was largely national. Public information was controlled by domestic national media outlets, and popular culture was national too, pumped out to a national audience by a national media. In Britain the public broadcasting authority (the BBC), because it used taxpayers' money, was obliged by law to broadcast great national events. Of course during the 1950s, 1960s and 1970s the US mass entertainment industry – fuelled in part by the power of the English language, but also by its skilful appeal to popular taste – was making huge inroads into world-wide national markets outside the communist-blocs. Since then changing technology – satellites, telecommunications, computer networks – has enabled a massive penetration of the domestic market by foreign culture (principally American at the start). National, sovereign control of culture has become a thing of the past.

Also, the global economic market will allow increasing foreign control of media outlets. An Australian (by birth) owns large tracts of US and British media; a German publishing company is one of the biggest publishers in the English language; the very American world of Disney has arrived in France; and there is fierce competition amongst big corporate Western media to service the Chinese media market. There can be little doubt that this increasingly cosmopolitan nature of media ownership, together with changes in technology, will inevitably take its toll on indigenous national culture. Of course global culture, together with the tourist industry, will continue to demand national particularism. But the 'Englishness' or 'Frenchness' or 'Italianness' constructed for the tourists will be largely fake and superficial, and will not in reality amount to anything particularly distinct from the global culture. Whether the replacement global culture – the culture that will replace national cultures – will be what amounts to an 'Americanisation' of the globe, or to a new and exciting cosmopolitanism, is yet to be seen.

The two 'classic' modern nation-states, France and Britain, are now going through a serious adjustment to this world without national sovereignty. As France becomes locked into the single European currency, and into a symbiotic relationship with Germany in a more and more integrated Europe, the famed and jealously guarded sovereignty of France can hardly hope to survive. The same, though less forceful, pressures are operating on British national sovereignty. Europe is forcing change on the sovereign United Kingdom: from the weakening of ties between the mainland and Northern Ireland (a pivot of the old UK) and England and Scotland, where the push for an independent Scotland in Europe is also fracturing the old UK nation-state. As for France and Britain, so too for the smaller European nation-states, and in a sense more so because they are amongst the leaders of the movement for greater and greater European integration.

On the other hand the US remains an intriguing exception, but perhaps one that proves the rule. The federal government in Washington DC is the one nation-state apparatus that is powerful enough to disprove the 'end of national sovereignty' thesis. Yet the US is not really a nation-state in the sense it is being used here; it is more a continental government, a regional grouping. But also, and crucially, the US government has chosen not to confront globalisation – or at least not yet. The US nation-state has stood on the sidelines and positively cheered as US-based corporations, US media and American culture have become the forcing grounds for globalisation, for the erosion of nation-states and their national borders and sovereignty. Of course in the process US national sovereignty has also been eroded. It becomes increasingly difficult to assert national sovereignty when foreigners own huge chunks of US-based assets, and when Japanese penetration of the US bond market can create a fear of another Pearl Harbour should they pull out. Even so, the US nation-state (in essence the federal government) is unlike any other national government: it is still in the game, in reserve so to speak, able to make a comeback against global forces should it so decide.

In place of the old idea of national sovereignty there is already arising a more fluid, tangential and pluralistic theory to fit the new reality. The writer Neal Ascherson has already been reaching towards a new conceptual framework. He argues that

> sovereignty [in Europe] will cease to be a one way flow, going either downwards (as in Britain) or upwards (as in Germany). Instead it will become a sort of all-permeating medium, like water in a swamp, in which clumps and floating islands of self government will relate to one another in many different ways. The 21st century will be a period not only of fuzzy logic but of fuzzy democracy.[41]

Put another way, 'the theory of sovereignty will seem strangely out of place in a world characterised by shifting allegiances, new forms of identity and overlapping tiers of jurisdiction'.[42]

The end of national identity?

What, though, of national identity in the global age? A consensus seems to have emerged that although the nation-state may be in trouble, perhaps terminal trouble, nationalism – the feeling for nation (particularly for smaller subnation-state nationalisms such as Scottish or Basque nationalism) – is not. Indeed such sensibility may be on the rise. The argument is that old nation-state nationalism (the kind of British, French, German, Indian, Pakistani, Japanese, Chinese and American-nation-state nationalism we have seen in the last few decades) will still resonate, will continue to form the basis of loyalty and affection.

However, if the nation-state was a major transmission agent for the idea of nation, then, with the state seriously weakened, rather like a croaking and spluttering radio becoming fainter and obscured by other stations, its nationalist message will be weakened too. Indeed, perhaps a much more radical, indeed revolutionary development may be under way – *national identity itself may also be eroding.*

Of course people will presumably continue to need to identify with something bigger than themselves; and a sense of self can be secured, honed and developed by a relationship with others. Indeed it has been suggested that the sense of identity

> is inseparable from an awareness of ourselves as members of a particular family or class or community or people or nation, as bearers of a specific history, as citizens of a particular republic; and we look to the political realm as a way in which we can develop and refine our sense of ourselves by developing and refining forms of community with which we can be proud to identify.[43]

Yet how important in the global capitalist age is the nation as a category of identity? How central as a community with which to identify is the old-fashioned European nation-state, such as Britain or France? How does 'belonging to Britain' or 'belonging to France' compare with, say, belonging to or identifying with the family, the immediate locale, the city or village, the local sports team, the office, the network of friends? And, crucially, how intense is nation-state identification compared with identification with subnational entities such as Scotland, Wales,

Yorkshire, Cornwall, Brittany or the Basque country, or indeed with cities such as London, Paris or Rome, or with multi-or supranational entities such as the European Union, the United Nations or even the OECD?

Certainly, as a point of identity, nation-state nationalism *used* to compare extremely favourably with both subnation-state nationalism and multinationalism. Alan Milward suggests that the ultimate basis for the survival of the modern nation-state 'is the same as it always was, allegiance'.[44] The nation-state certainly appeared to generate unique and remarkable levels of loyalty in its peoples. During the twentieth century alone millions of people, the element of compulsion notwithstanding, have apparently displayed this kind of allegiance by making serious sacrifices for their countries, including a willingness to make the ultimate one.

It is, though, possible to measure a real shift amongst the post-Second World War generations away from military service – perhaps the ultimate test of allegiance to nation. Fighting and dying for one's country – for the political community – is no longer a test of young manhood in most Western nations, and joining the military has become a job like any other. In the US the middle-class young's resistance to conscription during the Vietnam War was in marked contrast to the kind of self-sacrifice that prevailed during that earlier, ill-defined, bloody conflict of the First World War. And in Britain, too, the willingness of young men to risk their lives for their country, or any other abstraction, also declined. The abolition of conscription – the draft – was a popular act. And the supposed war fever and xenophobia unleashed by the Falklands War and the Gulf War was, for most of those who exhibited it, more a case of vicarious valour – the real fighting was safely distant, in colour, on television.

The late-twentieth-century's tests of national loyalty and allegiance are much less rigorous. Norman Tebbit, a British conservative politician, declared that one test of national loyalty might be to ask whether a person supported his or her country when its national team was playing its national sport against a foreign team (the sport in question was cricket). National sentiment and national loyalty has indeed become an aspect of the leisure and consumer society, primarily expressed (often vociferously) through support for national sporting personalities and teams. Identification with nation – in soccer in the world cup, in the Olympics, or during the Cold War when the US met the USSR at ice hockey – may heighten patriotic sentiment but is ultimately little more than taking sides in an entertainment. It is not ultimately serious.

Nor are the plethora of empty nationalistic rituals that the entertainment and tourist industries often offer up as authentic 'national' experiences.

Individualism and nation

This loosening of both allegiance to nation and identification with it, was of course an inevitable result of the new liberal world that, ironically, nationalism had helped to usher in during the seventeenth and eighteenth centuries. And later, the great liberal idea of 'the individual' – indeed of the primacy, the sovereignty of the individual, and his or her autonomy and consciousness – was to shake the very fundamentals of allegiance to nation and nation-state, arguably paving the way for another battering with the later arrival on the scene of economic globalisation.

The 'sovereign individual' has always been at the centre of Western liberal thought, but a powerful argument can be made that the decisive breakthrough for the idea of 'the individual' took place in the post-Second World War era with the arrival of the mass consumer society. The industrial and commercial age may well have fostered a technology (mass communications) that temporarily enhanced national sensibility, but it also set in train, and decisively so, the rise of individual consciousness.

The growing political culture of individual rights met up with the economic development of mass markets catering to individual needs and desires to produce a powerful assertive individualism. In the modern global capitalist system, more so than under traditional capitalism, 'the individual's relationship to the economic system is a highly atomized one. Individualism, not collectivism, typifies consumerist society, even for those who do not possess the wealth required to fulfil their desires: I consume therefore I am.'[45] Increasingly, as individuals began to count, and as consumerism inevitably induced a greater self-consciousness and self-awareness, then the old virtue of selflessness lost its erstwhile allure. Increasingly selflessness came to be seen as self-sacrifice or self-abnegation, whether of the mild kind such as public service or of the egregious kind such as the sacrifices made by millions for their country in the First World War. In this environment, collectivities – including the nation, one of the most important of collectivities – were bound to weaken.

Nationalists saw the threat posed by the modern individual consumer very clearly indeed. At the turn of the century George Eliot suggested that 'our dignity and rectitude are proportioned to our sense of relationship with something great, admirable, pregnant with high possibilities, worthy of sacrifice, a continual inspiration to self-repression and discipline by the presentation of aims larger and more attractive to our generous part than the securing of personal ease or prosperity'.[46] And the English reactionary Tory, Lord Hinchingbrooke, bemoaned the damage done by '*individualistic* businessmen, financiers and speculators', 'who were 'creeping unnoticed' to 'injure the character of our people'.[47]

In this individualist environment, identity itself – what the Oxford English Dictionary calls 'the condition of being a specified person' – was bound to begin to weaken its hold. The assertive and self-conscious individual seeks to become his own man or her own woman, less constrained by reference to groups – particularly large and relatively anonymous groups such as nations. Schiller's advice to his fellow Germans – 'Do not seek to form a nation, content yourself with being men' – nicely captures this dichotomy between nation and individual.[48] Or as Eric Hobsbawn has put it, 'the cultural revolution of the late twentieth-century can thus best be understood as the triumph of the individual over society, or rather, as the breaking of the threads which in the past had woven human beings into social textures'.[49] The 'wondrous machine' of global capitalism has done more than break the threads, it has torn them into pieces.

In this increasingly global and atomistic environment, whatever group consciousness – and identity – continues to linger may no longer be national or even local, but more personal, based upon individual characteristics such as being male, female, young, old, middle-aged, 'thirtysomething', tall, short, disabled, homosexual, heterosexual and so on. Thus being English, let alone British or American or French, becomes much less important than being young or a student or a woman. And, geographically, being a New Yorker or Londoner or Texan or Yorkshireman or Parisian or Berliner or Bavarian certainly becomes more important than being American, English, French or German.

One of the features of individualism was a slowly growing scepticism of authority, an inclination that may, by the last decade of the twentieth century, have turned into something near contempt. Institutions, including the nation-state itself, were increasingly becoming subject to market consumerism – judged on their performance, not their historical import. This 'individualistic', market approach to nation-state was intriguingly exhibited some two centuries ago when a London coachman, way ahead of his time, provided a superb description of the instrumental citizen of today. Asked whether he would fight for his country during the heightened anxiety over a French revolutionary invasion in 1803, he replied, 'No law or power under the canopy of heaven shall force me to take up arms.... I pray to God, that I may never live to see my country become a province of France, but if this war is suffered to go on I know it will be conquered, for I am positively sure that the King, Lords and Commons... have long since lost the hearts, goodwill and affection of a very great majority of the people of this nation.'[50]

National feeling, severely weakened by the rise of individualism, is also threatened by the growth of more local and regional loyalties and identities, principally the emergence of ethnic nationalisms. Since the collapse of the Soviet Union the intensity of ethnic identification that existed within the former Soviet empire has been fully revealed, and in the case of Yugoslavia these resurgent identities have been so powerful that thousands have been willing to fight and die to defend them. And subnational ethnicity may also be unleashed by the European Union as it weakens the hold of those other mini empires – the larger European nation-states. As Neal Ascherson has argued, 'we can formulate a law of politics here. When European Union advances, so does regional autonomy.'[51]

Although the Scots, the Bretons, the Basques, the Welsh, the Northern Italians, the Bavarians – unlike the Serbs or the Bosnians or the Croats – may not be prepared to die for the cause of their 'ethnic' or substate nation, they are likely to identify ever more strongly with it and ever less strongly with London, Rome, Paris or Berlin.

The temporary nation

The decline in national allegiance – indeed in national identity – which overcame the nation-states in the West during the latter quarter of the twentieth century, still surprises many observers. The 'resilience' of the nation-state is still the currency of much comment and analysis – and certainly at the turn of the millenium a life without nation-states is still widely considered unthinkable. The idea and image of 'country' (still largely associated with the nation-state) is still for many the final appeal, the final justification, the final good.

There is, however, nothing particularly inevitable or immutable about the nation, or about 'country'. National sensibility has only held sway over the imagination of the peoples of the planet for a small proportion of the time since the emergence of recognisably human life. Both the

nation-state and a sense of nationalism were absent during both classical times and the Middle Ages. Indeed, during medieval times 'nation'
connoted 'race' (in the Cursor Mundi of the fourteenth century 'English'
meant the English race). Then, traditional organisations such as blood-
based tribes, kingdoms and empires were the primary political units,
and in some respects sources of loyalty and identity. Most of the serious
analysts of nationalism agree that there was little or no nationalism in
the world until the end of the eighteenth century, and that only since
the French revolution has it dominated 'the political thought and
action of most peoples'.[52]

Kenneth Minogue has sought to find 'a general condition of things
from which nationalism seems primordially to spring', and suggests a
general answer: 'Our clue may be that nationalism in both France and
Germany became the spearhead of an attack on feudalism.'[53] The late
Ernest Gellner also portrayed it as the inseparable ideological counter-
part of modernisation, of the transition from agricultural to industrial
society. He argues that the ideology of nationalism provides 'an integra-
tive structure both assisting and easing the shocks of modernisation in
all its facets – the breaking down of tribal, social and intellectual barriers, the reorientation of politics, the spread of education and literacy,
the expansion of equal opportunity, the introduction of agricultural and
industrial techniques'.[54] And other analysts of nationalism do not dispute its modernising character, its crucial role in the transition from a
feudal order, but argue that the nation, and the nation-state, was not the
sole transporter of modernity. Gerald Newman suggests that the modern
era was formed during 'the nationless universalism of the early enlightenment, the age of Locke and Pope and Voltaire'.[55]

Also, some experts believe that far from being a popularly rooted
aspect of political life, the nationalism of modern times was all got up
by the intellectuals, and was sustained by propaganda. 'Nationalism is, at
the outset, a creation of writers', argues Gerald Newman.[56] And Minogue
has described the initial phase of nationalism in eighteenth-century
England as being created by native intellectual 'stirrings' against French
domination of literary life.[57] There is little doubt that in the forging of
English, and later British, national sensibility the role of writers, thinkers, polemicists and others with a reflective temperament and time on
their hands was utterly crucial. As was the wider dissemination of the
nationalist ideas of intellectuals that was secured by the burgeoning
internal market and the advances in printing and publishing.

The idea of 'the temporary nation', with its arguable lack of rooted-
ness, and the perspective of nationalism as being but a 'blink of an eye'

in historical time, are both instructive. If, indeed, nation and national-ism are not as resilient as many think, no nationalist comeback against the forces of globalisation is in prospect; and that is bad news for the political community, for the state.

The death of the state

If the all-pervasive reality of nation was an obstacle in the path of revolutionary global capitalism, then so too was the state, or govern-ment, the collective political organisation that operated general rules for common welfare. Yet of course the state – essentially a function of nation, and the only form in which the nation could realistically be organised – would have been lost without the nation. Nation and state seemingly rose and fell together.

As the twentieth century came to its close, no matter what the endur-ing hope, an 'international state' was still a pipedream, as the ineffective history of the League of Nations and the United Nations fully under-scored. The signs were that the state might reappear within a 'regional' guise (as I argue in the final chapter); but in the period between the decline of the nation-state and the state's reformulation in the arrival of the region-state, capital and markets saw a window of opportunity – and they were not slow to exploit it.

As we have already seen, by the late 1990s the reputation and validity of the state was already in deep trouble – irrespective of the state of the nation. Belief in government (the nice word for the state) in the thirty years or so following the Second World War was built around the suc-cesses throughout the Western world, including the US, of the social-democratic welfare consensus. This consensus started to fall apart as early as the late 1960s as the Vietnam War, and later the oil price rises, fuelled an inflation that caused a crisis of social and political stability throughout the West.

Quite simply, postwar social democracy – the 'Great Society' in the US, welfare capitalism in Europe – came apart at the seams. The politicians of social democracy could no longer maintain high employment rates and an adequate welfare state paid for out of growth or, if there was no longer growth, the taxes of the growing, and voting, middle class. In W. B. Yates' famed words, 'the centre could not hold'; it was dividing up, with social democrats leaving the centre field for pastures left and right. The intellectual world of social democracy collapsed. In the US a group of highly influential neoconservatives – writing in magazines such as the New York Jewish Committee's *Commentary* – joined more traditional conservatives around President Reagan to argue that the fight against Soviet Russia and communism was more important than traditional social-democratic – or liberal – ideas (and that, anyway, many of the centrist nostrums of the 1960s were mistaken). In Britain the political and intellectual elite that had sustained social democracy also broke up under the powerful onslaught of the new right in such think-tanks as the Institute of Economic Affairs and the Centre for Policy Studies.

The collapse of this social democratic consensus also coincided with the obvious failures of the command economy in the Soviet Union and Eastern Europe, which – even in the eyes of the most sympathetic Western observers – could no longer pose a serious alternative model to Western capitalism. Thus the way was opened for an unstoppable scepticism about, and even hostility to, government and the state. To many of the new, ascendant supporters of global capitalism and global markets, the state would continue to be necessary to carry out some residual and helpful functions, but little more.

This death of the nation, and of its state, the reality of which began to dawn after the end of the Cold War in the early 1990s, marks the real beginning of globalisation, of raw, rampant, global capital, of the modern capitalist revolution. The scene was set for what is now, at the turn of millenium, the raging triumph of a new economic order, ringing changes not only in the economic life of the planet, but also in the culture of the world, including the very foundations, built up over centuries, of the democracy of the Western world.

6
A World without Democracy?

Supporters of the brave new world of global capitalism argue that there is no need to fear a world without politics and government. They suggest that the idea that politics, political ideas, government and constitutions – based upon the state, until now the nation-state – created democracy is mistaken. Instead, they argue, it was the growth of capitalism, and its idea of the market, that gave birth to the democratic society and way of life.

Indeed market enthusiasts like to associate capitalism with democracy. During the Cold War 'capitalism' and 'democracy' became synonomous, and both were claimed by people in the West to represent their system against the communist or socialist (or totalitarian) systems of the Eastern-bloc. Indeed a strong case can be made that the history of capitalism is interlinked with the history of democratic development – in the sense that, by casting aside the feudal world, capitalism helped usher in modern democratic ideas of equality and freedom. And after three centuries of capitalism it is undeniably true that democracy has become the governing ideology, indeed the very spirit of the times, almost the religion of the West.

Just as capitalism helped forward a more democratic world, so for many it remains the best bet to preserve it. Market theorists see markets as providing more democratic safeguards than government ever can. They also see 'market democracy' as more real than 'political democracy', because they see political democracy, or government or the state, unlike markets, as inherently abusive of power. When the classical liberal economist and founder of public choice theory, Professor J. M. Buchanan, presented his pioneering promarket ideas to a British audience at the Institute for Economic Affairs in 1978 he set them in a democratic context, quoting John Stuart Mill against government. Mill had argued that 'the very principle of constitutional government requires it to be assumed that political power will be abused to promote the purposes of the holder...such is the natural tendency'.[1]

Freedom and liberty

At the very heart of the more serious marketeers' world view is, intriguingly, a political proposition: that the most important value of all is that of individual freedom – preserving, and enhancing, the freedom of the 'sovereign individual'. Market supporters suggest that only the pluralism of the market allows this sovereign individual to develop freely. This, they argue, is because the market, unlike the state, avoids compulsion. Marketeers proceed from the proposition that the state compels us to obey its laws by force and gathers its resources forcibly. They argue that the state, unlike the market, is backed by the law, which in turn employs the sanction of punishment, indeed jail; and that, ultimately, what lies behind the power of the state – of the world of politics – is the military.

The central promarket contention here is that the resources held by the individual (money, property, other assets) are inalienably his or hers – and that, whereas in the market the individual releases these resources voluntarily and by invitation, the state and government compels their release.

On a propagandistic and polemical level this *compulsion* argument of the global free-marketeers is very appealing – particularly when the issue is tax. People naturally tend to believe that the resources they hold are indeed 'theirs', and the idea that 'my' money is being taken forcibly by the state's tax collector taps a populist vein. Also, public bodies, unlike private bodies (even those in a monopolistic or oligopolistic position), tend to become very defensive about their use of taxpayers' money. For instance public bodies (such as the taxpayer-funded British Broadcasting Corporation) worry about accountability, whereas privately funded organisations (such as the commercially funded television companies) are much more free-wheeling, believing they are automatically accountable – to market forces! (When in fact they are accountable to the whims and opinions of advertisers.)

Yet the intriguing questions remains: does not the private sector also engage in compulsion? To continue the television analogy: the idea that there is no 'compulsion' involved in the financing of commercial television, simply because it takes no money from the state, may be fanciful. The fact is that if the market determines television output, then in the real world is means that the advertisers – interpreting public taste – determine this output. Rarely are consumers or shareholders consulted by the advertisers on their month-by-month decisions, and these short-term decisions can be very important indeed. The advertiser then places the costs of the advertisement onto the price, which is passed on to the unwitting consumer in the supermarket. Thus in the real world of the real market, as opposed to the imagined 'free market', a host of little 'compulsions' are forced on the individual – acts that are not, in truth, voluntary because of shortages of time, imperfect knowledge, rigging of market entry and all the other real world constraints. Compulsion is certainly present in the market and the private sector. It is simply more subtle and circuitous than that imposed on the individual by the state.

George Soros and the idea of 'compulsion'

Intriguingly the global financier George Soros (who became famous for his speculation against the British pound during the Exchange Rate Mechanism crisis of 1992) has argued that the new global market system is not only undemocratic, but also represents threat to what he calls – taking his definition from Karl Popper – 'the Open Society'.

The kernel of Soros' argument is that the global free market is not based, as some neoliberals would argue, upon the democratic interplay of supply and demand. 'The assumption of perfect knowledge proved unsustainable', he argues, 'so it was replaced by an ingenious device. Supply and demand were taken as independently given ... [but] the condition that supply and demand are independently given cannot be reconciled with reality, at least as far as the financial markets are concerned. Buyers and sellers in financial markets seek to discount a future *that depends on their own decisions.*' (Nor can supply and demand be taken as independently given in areas other than finance; in fact there is hardly any economic activity at all in which supply and demand are 'independently given'.)

Thus according to Soros, markets, and market players, 'have the capacity to alter the subject matter to which they relate'.[2] He suggests that market players are inevitably imposing their will – in the form of their expectations, but inevitably also in the form of their values and interests – upon the rest of us. Such an imposition – arguably as much an imposition, or compulsion, as any imposed in the democratic world by politicians – affords a new view of the moral balance sheet between state and market. It opens us to the little heard proposition that the market can limit freedom as much as can government, that the market can create a class system – now on a global canvas – as insidious as any created by old-time feudalism or the modern political class.

The state and the law

In the real world the 'sovereign individual', although sometimes, undeniably, reduced or even threatened by the state, can also be protected by it. Indeed the state may be the sovereign individual's only ultimate protector. After all the state, the polity, is the only body that can guarantee the rights of citizens and their space, not only against private interests, including big corporations, but even against itself and its own subdivisions of government. (In fact this notion of the state protecting the individual against the state is at the very heart of the American constitutional idea drawn up by the men of Philadelphia. The state would be split up – separation of powers – in order to protect the individual from any one part of it; and the state, through its bill of rights, would protect minorities from majorities using the state to oppress them.)

This work of liberty is done by the law – by the state's law. That erudite political thinker, the late Maurice Cranston, has argued that the rule of law is utterly central to ensuring the liberty of the individual.[3] It is a stark fact that the more zealous marketeers sometimes overlook the fact that the state remains the only possible mechanism not only for creating law, but also for enforcing the rule of law. Thus without the state – even with a severely weakened state, as in post-Cold-War Russia, a society of mafias and gangs – society would be lawless. And lawlessness poses a much more serious threat to the individual – to his or her property, even life – than do the oft cited 'excesses' of government, such as bureaucracy or tax-gathering. The rule of law is arguably the state's most profound gift to civilisation.

There is now little doubt that what William Greider called the 'manic logic' of new global capitalism seriously threatens the reign and rule of law, or at least as we have known it. Supporters of business continue to proclaim the importance of law, about the responsibility of businesses to exist 'within the law'. Yet this obeisance to the law by businesses can often be disingenuous. The fact is that many big corporations see the law as their primary threat, as they make a point of escaping, or threatening to escape, from those laws they do not like, and relocating, or threatening to relocate, to more conducive legal environments. It is a stark reality, but in this sense, for corporations, the rule of law no longer exits. In the ideal world of global capitalism the long arm of the law will not always reach. There will be no extradition treaties for mobile capital or for corporations in pursuit of lower social costs.

As well as securing the law, there is another powerful argument for the state as protector of the individual and of individual freedom. Historically, a strong case can be made that the freedom and space of the individual has best been protected, even enhanced, where there has been a balance between public and private, state and market, where the public sector can cooperate with and compete with an equally strong private sector. The pluralism inherent in such a balance can at least secure some autonomy for the domestic citizen.

Obviously for supporters of individual freedom it is the character of the state, rather than its existence, that matters. Yet in the new global order the democratic state – the state that enforces the law properly and fairly, even the state that remains in balance with the private sector – has also become the enemy, to be circumvented if possible, defeated if necessary.

Conflict resolution and an age of peace

The freedom of the individual can only exist if conflicts can be resolved sensibly and peaceably. The political world, rather than the economic world, was always considered the primary mechanism for such accepable conflict resolution. After all, at the heart of the idea of the modern study of politics is both the recognition of conflict and difference and disagreement, and also the processes whereby people resolve, or do not resolve, conflicts.

Thus according to some schools of thought there is no politics in agreement, nor in forced agreement. The political philosopher Kenneth Minogue has argued that 'despots don't belong' in the definition of politics.[4] As Maurice Duverger puts it, the 'two-faced god Janus is the true image which...expresses the most profound political truth' of group conflict and its resolution based upon discussion and compromise.[5] Politics only comes into operation once a single power centre – crown, dictator, party (as in the communist system) – is removed or fades away.[6] In contrast, of course, a market can exist under a dictatorship, or even, as we are still seeing in communist China, a one-party state.

The skills of the politician are democratic skills, so much so that today the much maligned skills of 'politics' – the ability to read public mood, the sense of what is possible and what is not, the ability to compromise between interests, the ability to articulate goals and values – are essential in mastering the arts of democracy. In contrast, and it is a crucial distinction, the skills of the businessperson – organisation, management, risk taking – are leadership skills, aimed at helping forward an individual unit or company. They are certainly creative, but they are not particularly democratic. They are aimed at producing a product or a profit, not at securing certain values or resolving conflict.

However, regardless of this huge history behind politics and law as conflict resolvers, global marketeers still see the market as a much better way of resolving conflict. They correctly point to the history of politics as being the history of the nation-state (as much as the history of law), and to how this self-same nation-state was the source of the great and deadly conflicts of war.

In contrast with this sorry history of conflict and war, they suggest that the new world market now being brought into being will usher in, on a global scale, an epoch of peace (and that the global market will ensure peace not simply because it is a market, but because it is global). This argument, a powerful one, rests on the proposition that it was the market, not politics, that created one global system, and one global system is inherently more stable and peaceable than one with subdivisions – nations – that cause emnities and conflict.

However one world economically does not mean one world politically. And intriguingly, globalisers may be pushing for a world market but they do not want world government. The dynamic of global capitalism seeks no balance between public and private on a global basis, and resists – largely for tax reasons – world government. So in the real global economy that is now under construction, economic inequalities and resentments can be expected to grow; and these inequalities could spawn serious rebellions and violence. As Soros argues: 'I can already discern the makings of the final crisis [of global capitalism]. It will be political in character. Indigenous political movements are likely to arise that will seek to expropriate multi-national companies and re-capture the "national" wealth. Some of them will succeed in the manner of the Boxer rebellion or the Zapata revolution.'[7] There is no reason to believe that whole nations will not opt out of the global economic system, causing conflict with their neighbours, and ultimately violence. Could Malaysia, which in 1998–9 was resisting the imperatives of global capitalism from a very, very small base, be a prototype?

And all this in an environment where there is no democratic world government to resolve these conflicts through the exercise of law. The 'one world' of global capitalism may become a very unsafe place indeed.

And crucially, without world government, without a global political dimension, those economic conflicts that are resolved will not be settled as they broadly are under political regimes, in favour of majorities or on the basis of rights upheld by the law. Rather they will be resolved in true market fashion, in favour of those with economic power, with that rawest of measurements: most money, most resources. Again, unavoidably, those who control the market, the super-rich with their super-capital, will inevitably win.

People rule

As well as securing the rights and freedom of the individual, governments – proper, democratic governments – were supposed to ensure that 'the people', rather than elites, ruled. Supporters of global capitalism, however, dispute this idea that politics can ensure popular sovereignty. They suggest that only through the market mechanism can true popular sovereignty – the idea that people, rather than elites, rule – become a reality. This is the notion of 'people's capitalism', made popular in the 1980s by Margaret Thatcher and Ronald Reagan. In its essentials it argued that politics and government limit access.

This question of access is at the heart of this criticism of politics. The capitalist theorist Arthur Seldon has taken the lead in arguing, with force, that the sizeable government and state created during the post-1945 era produced a class of 'political people' who manipulated this state system in order to achieve an advantage for themselves. This idea of 'political people' could also be extended more widely to many in the middle classes, and was most evident in health and education, where the 'political people', the well-connected people, through their social status (which in the postwar period was still very, very important in European countries such as France and Britain) or contacts in the system gained what amounted to preferential treatment within the state system.

This populist appeal – that in the state and public sector, special 'elitist' people gained at the expense of 'ordinary people', or 'the common people' – subtly or not so subtly undercut the political left as the protector of the weak and underprivileged, portraying socialists not as caring democrats but rather as 'top people', uncaring mandarins. This was a more effective rerun of a theme from the early 1970s whereby the political and intellectual left were depicted as phonies: in the US as 'limousine liberals' and in Britain as 'Hampstead do-gooders'.

This populist marketeerism was effective because it possessed some truth. There remains a strong case that the middle classes gained disproportionately from the welfare state, and that the welfare system was open to manipulation by the articulate and well-connected. Also, the social democratic state, as it developed in the 1950s, 1960s and 1970s, did indeed become both bureaucratised – producing, as anyone on the receiving end could readily testify, insensitive and bossy elites – and politicised, creating political classes who saw both the state and the world of politics as exclusive preserves for their own benefit. And in the process government did indeed cease to operate as a neutral referee between private interests or as a well-organised welfare system, but instead became 'an interest', rather like a 'special interest' or a 'corporate interest'. And many of those who worked for government, who served the state, no longer saw their occupation as a special vocation – a proud vocation uniquely allowing the office holder 'to do the people's work'.

The only problem was that all these charges about state bureaucracy, about special interests and about unfair advantages gained through influence and connections in the governmental system could just as easily have been made of the market-based system. Corporations produced their own bureaucracy and organisational rigidities, inefficiencies often successfully hidden from shareholders by managers. 'Who you know', rather than 'what you know' – a corporate term called 'networking' – worked just as powerfully in the private sector. Large businesses thrived on 'connections'. Unsavoury (even outright corrupt) connections between large private corporations and the state (such as the US Congress and executive departments such as the Pentagon) were the routine meat and drink of the lobbying system. Job appointments were less regulated than in the public sector, with fewer rules about interviewing and discrimination. And amongst small businesses, nepotism – almost by definition – was an acceptable form of business recruitment.

Participation

As well as securing popular sovereignty, marketeers claimed that market capitalism achieved another crucial democratic outcome: a high and wide rate of participation, higher and wider than that offered by *political* democracy. Arthur Seldon suggests that modern capitalism, by minimising the writ of politics and maximising the writ of the market, 'creates a more effective form of democracy' by enabling 'all the people, the common people as well as the political people, to decide their lives'.[8] Seldon then goes on to posit what he calls 'the central question': 'is it . . . easier for the political process to include all the heads or for the market process to endow all the people with money?' The obvious answer to this rhetorical question was that the political process would include fewer.

There was a misreading of 'political democracy' here. Modern democratic politics, political democracy, was never just about 'counting heads' or participation. It was certainly about allowing those who wanted to participate to do so, *and to do so as of right*. (You had the right to vote because you were a human being, whereas you participated in market democracy because you were endowed with money.) But it was more than that. Under the democracy of the state, access and participation were to be secured through rights, not just votes. And rights (as I argue later in this chapter) can allow 'the common people' access to the governmental system and the decision-making forums of society just as effectively, in fact more effectively, than voting every few years.

Some probusiness intellectuals believe that the private capitalist sector can help participation through means other than the 'democracy of the market' – for instance by encouraging participation through companies themselves. Company workforces already take part in company decision making in many small ways, but Charles Handy, amongst others, has suggested that a restructuring of the corporation could allow for a real advance in corporate democracy. He suggests that the modern corporation is 'inadequate for modern times', that 'a public corporation has now to be regarded as a community, not a piece of property', and that we need a 'citizen corporation' in which 'the core members of that community are more properly regarded as citizens rather than employees or "human resources", citizens with responsibilities as well as rights'.[9]

The idea here is that in these new 'citizen corporations' the private ownership of property will remain, as will the market, but that within the privately owned unit a new sharing of power and decision making should take place. A variant of this is, of course, the existing cooperatives. In the cooperative movement:

> the key idea is that the market mechanism is retained as a means of providing most goods and services, while the ownership of capital is socialised . . . all productive enterprises are constituted as workers' cooperatives, leasing their operating capital from an outside investment agency. Each enterprise makes its own decisions about products . . . prices, etc. . . . net profits form a pool out of which incomes are

paid.... Each enterprise is democratically controlled by those who work for it.[10]

One problem with this private sector model of participation is that, even if it was expanded to include public sector enterprises, the new-style market democracy it advocates takes no account of the millions and millions who have no connection with companies whatsoever – students, the elderly, the unemployed. *Political* democracy, on the other hand, can include everyone. Also, market democracy – particularly in the global market – limits decision making to economic and economic-related issues, whereas political democracy encourages participation in a range of non-economic issues, from international policy to cultural and even social and sexual issues.

Another problem with market democracy is the huge inequalities in participation. Certainly everyone who has access to the market can participate in it, but unlike political democracy, where participation is at least theoretically equal (one person has one vote, everyone has the same rights), the extent of market participation depends on the amount of resources you can bring to the market. Put crudely – for it *is* somewhat crude – big bucks mean greater participation. And under global capitalism, where capital is even more important *vis-à-vis* labour (and the state), then this inequality of participation is even more marked.

The marketeers' criticism of low participation rates in political democracy are powerfully made. However politics is open to reform. In one sense the history of government is the history of adjustment and adaptation to wider and wider participation and access, in other words to democracy. The Greek idea of the polis may have existed alongside slavery, but Greek politics gave us the word and the idea – the gripping, powerful idea of 'democracy'. Democracy remains a political word with a political meaning. The political institutions of the medieval world – kingship and the like – certainly exluded the majority of people and entrenched serfdom, yet the English Parliament was formed in this period. Although the great political/constitutional document of American independence was written in Philadelphia by English landowners, who excluded women and happily ignored slavery, it was malleable enough to become the most celebrated and mature example of democractic constitutionalism (and arguably it still is the greatest single written institutional expression of the democratic idea).

Not only is it possible to reform government and the state, to continue to adapt it to the growing modern need for ever-increasing participation and access, but reforming government in order to achieve this task is now relatively easy because of modern techniques and changing technology. The widespread use of information technology – television, computers, internet and the like – makes a surfeit of political participation now practically possible. We can now participate – discuss, vote – from home. The citizen is now able to vote – monthly, weekly, daily, even hourly – both on single issues and for representatives. It is now technically possible to arrange a fairly competent referendum every day of the week. (So rather than political democracy limiting access or participation, the modern-day problem may be democratic fatigue.)

Anthony Giddens, in his theoretical book on social democracy, *The Third Way*, sees the possibilities of renewing rather than shrinking the state. 'What is necessary', he suggests, 'is to reconstruct [the state] – to go beyond those on the right who say "government is the enemy" and those on the left who say "government is the answer".' And he outlines specific strategies that the modern state should employ in order to renew itself: devolution, the further democratisation of democratic institutions, renewal of the public sphere through transparency, administrative efficiency, mechanisms for direct democracy, and government as risk manager (by which he means, in part, regulating scientific and technological change).[11]

Minorities

Market theorists and propagandists sometimes argue that 'political democracy' is potentially authoritarian, and therefore careless of the rights of minorities. In this mindset 'the state' is – if not exactly the door to communism or fascism – incipiently authoritarian, certainly compared with 'the market', which is viewed as inherently libertarian. Even the relatively mature democratic states – say the US or Britain – although not in themselves necessarily oppressive, have a very definite potential to be so. Their problem is majorities! Their 'working method of making decisions by majorities, or counting heads, and ignoring many heads merely because they are less numerous, is a childish and uncivilised way of deciding the use of resources'. In contrast market democracy, by 'counting pennies not heads', provides some power for 'all heads, including those of minorities and . . . independent and idiosyncratic individuals'.[12]

This idea that minorities and 'idiosyncratic individuals' are protected by money, even lots and lots of it, is fanciful. Stable mass prosperity, whereby majorities feel secure and unthreatened, is probably the most effective protection for minorities. But in times of economic trouble the market, by its propensity for increasing inequalities, may make life *worse* for minorities because of the creation of increasing social tensions in which minority groups become vulnerable. And it is in these difficult times for minorities that politics – in the form of an entrenched democratic political culture – and the state – in the form of a written constitution and, crucially, the rule of law – is the best guarantor of minority rights. Whatever the causes of the two great holocausts – the slaughter of the Armenians in Turkey and the Jews in Germany – it was the lack of a political safety net – of strong democratic institutions, of a democratic political culture – not the lack of markets, that led economic failure and social tensions to break out into slaughter.

In a global economy in which no state is strong enough to create this political safety net, minorities may find themselves with less and less protection.

Rights

The battle for individual rights has been the very stuff of the history of Western civilisation. It has exercised the minds of the great liberal thinkers from John Locke to John Stuart Mill, and great polemicists such as Tom Paine and Thomas Jefferson; and it has enlivened the pages of great political documents from the Magna Carta through to *The Rights of Man* and the American Declaration of Independence, right up to the present day and the UN and EU Declarations. These traditional 'rights' – such as freedom of speech, assembly and petition, and the right to worship – are now joined by social rights such as the right to privacy, abortion and non-discrimination based upon equal rights. Even economic rights, to jobs and economic security, are now, more controversially, on the agenda. Rights are so much a part of the fabric of Western life, even a measure of civilised living, that some commentators believe the culture of rights has progressed so far that the concomitant responsibilities are being ignored.

Yet rights are essentially a political idea. They are articulated by politicians and political writers. They are written down in political documents. And political, constitutional and legal systems enforce and encourage them.

It is universally accepted that the state – that is, political authority – is the only mechanism that can entrench rights. This is so because it is the only acceptable mechanism for law making and governing the physical forces of coercion that lie behind the law – the police, the military in 'aid of the civil power'. No one, except extreme libertarians and anarchists, suggests that the much-vaunted market – or market players – should actually make laws (although in the real world large agglomerations of private capital can control legislatures or ignore laws) or take over the role of the courts and the police (although private security services sometimes blur the distinction between state law and private rules).

The fact is that the market – and certainly the global market – cannot create and cannot protect rights. Nor can, or should, the principal inhabitors of the market place – the large corporations! Ultimately we need to face the fact that businesspeople are not in business to protect rights (or, more generally, to make the world a better place!) Regardless of the protestations of the business ethics industry, most honest businesspersons will admit the truth of this. And in a world in which corporations have their way, having outmanoeuvred the state, then the future for any realistic regime of rights looks increasingly bleak.

As the claims for rights come to be extended beyond political rights to economic rights, then the very idea of rights clearly comes into direct conflict with modern market democracy and global capitalism. When, for instance, the 'right to employment' is claimed, this right is obviously denied by supporters of the global markets, and even by market democrats who see it as threatening the smooth working of market capitalism, particularly the ability of employers to hire and fire at will.

Pluralism

For many political theorists, pluralism is the lifeblood of democracy and the democratic way of life. Plural power centres are seen as offering protection against the dangers of centralisation inherent in a single authority, and as giving the individual freedom of space and manoeuvrability.

And pluralism is modern capitalism's strongest suit. Whatever can be said against the global market it does not tend to centralise power – at least not during the early stage it is still in. The global marketplace is simply too big and too diffuse to allow such centralisation. So far, whatever its other democratic shortcomings, modern global capitalism remains a veritable cornucopia of pluralism: almost a bustling anarchy, with many, many decision-making centres. The sheer number of companies and units of capital competing around the world ensures such pluralism. And the new mobile capital of the global economic order also ensures political pluralism because it acts to break up political units so that it can divide and rule.

Of course modern global capitalism is witnessing an increasing number of mergers between corporations. Giant and highly centralised super-corporations are beginning to dominate the various sectors of the global economy. The huge mergers of the 1990s – many of which, such as those between British Petroleum and Amoco, and Deutsche Bank and Bankers Trust, were truly transnational – all point to a worrying future of great agglomerations of economic power. Even so, there is still little prospect of that creature of the imagination, 'one great corporation', dominating the world.

On the other hand the political system, the interstate or international relations system that globalism has largely replaced, tended to concentrate power in far fewer locations. And in the Cold War's nuclear age some of these political power centres – individuals such as the president of the United States and the general-secretary of the Soviet Union, and their respective inner-sanctum colleagues – accumulated so much power that, unlike even the biggest corporation, they held the awesome power of life or death over millions. That the state can possess such an illiberal, centralising potential that may not, in quite the same sense, be present in the market is now widely recognised. Even socialists are now able to accept that in state-dominated economies there is a pluralist deficit. As Christopher Pierson has written:

> what has seemed to many commentators to be fatally damaging to this socialist argument is the continuing failure to generate a satisfactory model for the democratic control of economic life. This objection seems even more compelling now in the light of the recent experience of the two most prominent and quite divergent forms which 'real socialism' took in the twentieth century – the Soviet model and western social democracy.[13]

Of course one of the reasons why democrats and liberals support the idea of pluralism is that, by preventing the growth of any power centre from reaching the point where it can threaten the individual, such pluralism enhances individual rights. Capitalist economic pluralism, however, does not serve this function. It certainly provides many economic decision centres, and this type of pluralism certainly helps consumer choice. But extending consumer choice, important though it is, is not the same thing as protecting political rights such as freedom of speech, assembly and worship – or indeed economic rights such as a job! Political rights are protected by law and the state, and no matter how diffuse economic power may be under global capitalism, if the state is weakened so is the ability to protect rights. And also, we should not forget that no matter the number of economic decision makers in the market, not one of them – not one – has, in their economic role, any fundamental interest or motivation in protecting human rights.

Through the mists and subtleties of the great debate about globalisation and democracy there remains one very worrying political truth. Whatever the politics and values of the new world we are heading into, they will not be democratic – at least as we have known and understood the word. The kind of liberal-democratic political systems that grew from and developed out of the political upheavals of the late eighteenth century in France and North America – what we now call liberal-democracy – were coexistent with nation-states, and are likely to die alongside them.

The new global market system, for all its plusses, is nonetheless creating, remorselessly, a new class system. The broad lines of this class structure are now clear: those who start life with capital do increasingly well, and the rest are caught in job insecurity and a shrinking welfare state. This congenital dynamic towards quite extreme inequality is hardly consistent with a democratic society or liberal-democratic values, rather it is creating nothing less than the return, on a global basis, to an older form of social life altogether – aristocracy. In this new global aristocracy the few – the super-rich – will rule over the many, and construct politics, society and much of culture in their own image. Although the forms of democracy (voting, paper rights) may remain – even be enhanced – they will be images only, restricted to the faltering, increasingly irrelevant nation-states, whilst the real power moves upwards to these transnational elites.

7
The Next Phase: The Brave New World of the Minimal State

The elites of media, business, academia and politics . . . have already made up their mind on . . . the global economic system – and [about] defending it from occasional attacks from angry, injured citizens (William Greider, *Who will Tell the People?*, p. 393).

If there was a bronze age and an iron age, this is surely the age of capital (*Newsweek*, 23 June 1997).

Still triumphant

The brave new world of global super-capital and the super-rich is, even after the Asian shocks of 1998, still looking unstoppable, possessed of a sense of ultimate triumph. Robert Samuelson has described the basis for this optimism:

> After the Cold War, global capitalism offered a powerful vision of world prosperity and, ultimately, democracy. Multinational companies and investors would pour technology and capital into poorer regions, creating a transnational mass market of middle class consumers who would drive Toyotas, watch CNN, eat Big Macs – and, incidentally, demand more freedom.[1]

Francis Fukuyama saw the same vision from a more political and philosophical vantage point. His arresting idea of the 'End of History' had a mixed press when it appeared in the early 1990s, primarily because, in Europe at any rate, it was seen as triumphalist (and too pro-American), but its central forecast looks more and more realistic. Fukuyama posed the theory largely in political terms. His specific point, more hedged around with qualifications than was generally reported at the time, was that liberal democracy was probably, in fact, 'the end-state of the historical process'. But for 'liberal-democracy' Fukuyama's readers could easily read 'capitalist globalisation'. Thus the thesis argues that globalised capital (with its political arm, 'liberal democracy') becomes the 'end of history', and global capital becomes entrenched, victorious for all time, with no more fundamental upheavals or rebellions likely.[2]

Of course global capitalism can have its set-backs. It can begin to look somewhat frayed at the edges. The dramatic lowering of the financial value of stock markets and currencies in Asia (and Russia) during 1998 were signs, even to its supporters, that the new global economic order will not establish itself without problems, even traumas.

However, even after the Asian shocks of 1997 and 1998 it was not clear that these gyrations in world finance heralded any reversal of global capitalism's ultimate grip. As the new millenium approaches mobile capital is still in the ascendant. The Asian financial collapse will allow capital to invest in a range of new cut-price assets, and will also provide international investors with a huge pool of even cheaper labour and lower social costs. In this new post-Asian environment mobile capital will still be able to dictate to national governments, unless they act in concert (to the point of submerging their erstwhile sovereignties); trade unions, particularly in the Anglo-Saxon economies with high rates of part-time, short-contract work with large numbers of women in the workforce, will remain weak; left-wing parties will still fall foul of the majority of voters who remain hostile to high-tax regimes.

The one serious threat to triumphant globalism posed by the Asian crisis of the late 1990s was the response of Malaysia. By shutting itself off from global capital markets it bought itself some temporary relief from extreme social and political dislocations. And as George Soros has argued, 'If Malaysia looks good in comparison with its neighbours, the policy may easily find imitators.'[3] But as I have argued throughout this book, such a comprehensive challenge to global capitalism cannot be sustained by countries the size of Britain and France, let alone Malaysia. Without 'regional' support from an Asian regional superpower of the European Union kind, the Malaysian challenge may attract some support, but will ultimately falter.

A secular religion

Like all triumphant movements and ideas modern global capitalism has developed a 'spiritual', even moral dimension. William Greider argues that 'the utopian vision of the marketplace offers ... an enthalling religion'. 'Many intelligent people have come to worship these market principles, like a spiritual code that will resolve all the larger questions for us, social and moral and otherwise'. And Edward Luttwak describes the orthodox monetarism at the heart of the new capitalism as having 'like all religions a supreme god – hard money – and a devil, inflation'.[4]

And a flavour of the religious fervour – indeed vehemence – behind much of this contemporary antistatist impulse is provided by this intriguing passage from a new right propagandist:

> the New Right must propagandise mercilessly against the state. It must stress unremittingly the enduring moral bankruptcy of government. It must constantly compare the burden borne by the taxpayer, to fill the government trough from which the interest groups are feeding with the benefits received by the swine at the trough ... we must underscore relentlessly to our unorganised fellow taxpayers their direct interest in the unremitting attenuation of the state.[5]

Such sentiments are the food and drink of libertarian economists in think-tanks from the Cato Institute in Washington to the IEA in London.

This religion of the market – of the global market – is of course of the secular variety. This secular religion has its own doctrine: the almost sacred idea of the 'sovereign individual'. This individualism is, though, of the libertarian kind, and is so central to the faith that it allows little limitation or constraint upon its sovereignty. Modern libertarians see most of the serious limitations on individual freedom (such as taxes) as a threat, and even marginal incursions (such as traffic laws) as worrisome. State and public sector constraints upon the individual are feared much more than those imposed by the private sector. (To this day there is no promarket publication – neither book nor pamphlet – that systematically critiques the myriad of private corporate constraints placed upon individuals in their employment. Such constraints – involving intrusions into corporate managers' private behaviour, including family life – are a feature of life in the corporate sector, and can be much harsher and more invasive than anything a Western social-democratic state would impose. Nor do libertarians tend to recognise the way in which families can constrict individual liberty, and, for some, the value of the welfare state as a means of releasing the individual from such dependence. It is also interesting that non-economic – communal, cultural, social or religious – constraints upon individualism rarely meet with such determined opposition from globalists and marketeers as do the economic.

This ethical idea of the sovereign individual fighting a great battle for liberty translates easily into a more prosaic and materialistic economic individualism. The key globalist free market proposition here is that all resources – land, capital, money – belong to individuals (few questions are asked about the origins of an individual's resources) and *not* to communities; and that incursions into this rightful private ownership are infringements of liberty. The state is seen here as the principal agent of community, and therefore as the principal enemy.

Rewriting the history of the state

A religion – even a secular one – needs a favourable history. And the winners, of course, write the history books. So global capitalism's victory over socialism became the occasion for such a new history. In this new history the state took a veritable drubbing. The state came to be associated with limiting freedom, with oppression, even with persecution. Socially it induced sclerosis and politically it automatically centralised and bureaucratised. And most cutting of all, the state was an expropriator – of property and, worse still, of taxes. In such an environment the contrary idea of the state as helping to forward pleasing images such as enabling, helping, opening, democracy and rights could not get house room.

The gravamen of the new globalist history is the view that raw capitalism – the Anglo-American model of free market, minimal government capitalism – is the world's great success story. This well-entrenched thesis is built around the extraordinary material and economic success of the Western world, and in particular, in the twentieth century, of the United States. The received wisdom has it that the US (and to a lesser extent Britain), the two great examples of high, free-market Victorian capitalism, uniquely ushered in the industrialism (and later the commercialism) that made the West the predominant civilisation of the world; and that through the spread of global capitalism this huge success story will be repeated world-wide.

This history of private and market triumph completely undervalues the role of the state – the public sector – in the success story. Britain in Victorian times was by no means the raw capitalist society of myth. Its great free-trade, free-enterprise, free-market system, it should never be forgotten, was built upon the back of a world-wide empire – an empire sustained by government and its agencies in the military and civil services.

Likewise, the history of the economic development of the US is hardly a story of undiluted capitalism. That great engine of American capitalism, the continent-wide internal market, was the result of government – the geopolitical expansion of the US 'feds' through military conquest! The British Royal Navy, the military arm of a foreign state – but a state nonetheless – ensured the protection of the US capitalist economy during the formative decades of the nineteenth century. And American *state* craft helped defeat US capitalism's great enemy – the imperial protectionist system of the old European colonialists. And of course it was the state – the US state (with its *public sector* military, diplomatic and political arms) – that, by prevailing over the Soviet Union and its command economy, preserved Western capitalism and gave global capitalism its lift-off. In the face of such overwhelming evidence it is impossible not to see the history of the US as the history of capital and state working together.

Of course, one of the primary reasons for US capitalism's great leap forward in the twentieth century had nothing at all to do with its economic system, and everything to do with politics and the international game of states. Unlike its competitors in Europe, the US was relatively unscathed by the two world wars – the great conflicts that destroyed the European empires and set back the European nations for over half a century. It was the wisdom of politicians, the leaders of the US state – primarily General George C. Marshall and President Harry Truman – who, by pouring public sector money into the regeneration of the European economies, provided an expanded market and represented the single greatest boon to US corporations in their history, and made them the global players they are today.

The clash of political ideologies and state interests that was the Cold War also helped US capital and capitalism to make their mark. The post-1945 bipolar global political framework, with the US as the leader of the West, helped US capital to penetrate global markets; and the military confrontation with Russia helped create a huge market for American business – the big business of defence procurement and the small businesses it generated.

State and capital worked together in another way too. The American success story in the twentieth century – 'the American century' – is too often attributed to the economic dynamism unleashed by bustling entrepreneurs, tough-minded robber barons and, later, the efficient management of global American corporations. Yet this is only half the story. For there was a political dimension too – a governmental genius was at work as well. To create, and then to bind together this geographically and socially diverse, continent-wide federation was no small achievement. It was a political document, the US constitution (liberal, flexible, adaptable) that helped keep a fractured nation – and thus a single economy – together. It was the political genius, too, of President Abe Lincoln and his supporters, who, by keeping the union together after the defeat of slavery and the south, preserved a single internal market – perhaps the most important of all the reasons for the later blooming of the US free-market system.

Rewriting – that is, talking down – the history of the state, and of government itself, often involves depicting the state as simply a phase of history. In an echo of historical Marxist determinism, supporters of the market see 'stateless' global capitalism as the end-point of history. 'Prehistory' was the history of nation-states; these nation-states may have been progressive in their way (they did, after all, serve to organise democracy and introduce concepts such as rights and accountability), but they were riddled with contradictions, and were unstable. This instability has given way to a new, stable system of globalisation. Globalisation is historically inevitable and represents 'the end of history'.

The minimal state

Global capitalism is a godsend to such antistatists. By disposing of the 'interfering' and 'expropriating' nation-states the only realistic mechanism for state power is marginalised. This in turn allows the libertarian attack on the state – or the public sector – fuller rein than ever before in human history.

In an unusual alliance with libertarians, big corporate capital sees all too clearly the advantages of a weakened state – the unhindered mobility of capital (so those who invest can punish those states and societies that do not encourage sufficent returns), low or zero inflation (in order to ensure low interest rates and thus boost the prices of shares and bonds), low taxation (so that the returns from capital remain high), and 'flexible labour markets' (in order to keep costs, particularly social costs, low and therefore raise profits and the return on shares).

Most serious marketeers, however, are not arguing for the complete abolition of the state – the campaign objective is more limited: to shrink the state, to reduce it further and further until it becomes 'the minimum state'. Adam Smith's aphorism that governments should do only what cannot be done in the market – or what cannot be done by individuals – was the central idea of capitalism, old and new. It allowed for considerable debate about the exact role and reach of government. Today, however, with globalism as their ally, marketeers want a 'minimalist' approach.

The minimal state idea seeks to limit government to a small number of 'absolutely necessary' functions, leaving the rest to the market. In practical terms, minimalists want the state to withdraw not only from economic life through lower and lower levels of taxation, through privatisation and deregulation, but also from the four main welfare services: education, housing, medical care and insurance for income in retirement. As Seldon declared, 'the vision of capitalism is the prospect of minimal government. It excludes the state, or its agencies, from the production of goods and services. . . . The vision thus requires the eventual withdrawal by government from most of its accumulated activities.'[6]

In Britain, advocates of such a comprehensive minimal state began to put policy flesh on these bones – with very practical proposals – during the late 1960s and early 1970s. Clustered around the Institute for Economic Affairs in London, and led by Arthur Seldon, they pioneered many of the ideas that, in the 1980s, conservative politicians began to introduce to a wider public. E. G. West wrote *Education: A Framework for Choice* in 1967, F. G. Pennance wrote *Choice in Housing* in 1968 and Charles Hanson wrote *Welfare before the Welfare State* in 1972. Later, in 1981 Arthur Seldon wrote *Wither the Welfare State*, and in 1985 David Green wrote *Working Class Patients and the Medical Establishment*.[7]

Some extremist minimalisers, still discounted by mainstream minimalisers, even want the government to withdraw from law and order, even from controlling the currency. Another school of thought amongst the minimalisers is that which believes that although government should be largely withdrawn from economic life, it should nonetheless be used to liberate the poor by enabling them to use public resources to acquire the means to exercise choice and take responsibility for their health, education and old age provision.

This amounts to using the state in a sort of enabling function, which, though limited, could in practice amount to a considerably more extensive state sector than the true-believing minimalists would ever want. John Gray's 1989 IEA pamphlet advocated this more expansive form of minimal government, although his most recent thinking would probably now see the need for an even larger state sector.[8] What is interesting here, though, is acceptance of the state as a domestic actor, as an enabler, but not as a balance against mobile capital. Yet without the state as a bulwark against mobile capital the domestic pot would get smaller and smaller, a fundamentally tragic outcome in terms of employment, income and social divisions that no amount of domestic 'enabling' would be able to redress.

The minimal state project

The vision of minimal government – that governments should do only what cannot be done in the market – was, until the 1990s, just that – a vision, a distant goal. Certainly the late 1970s and the 1980s saw a major tilt in the US political world (and consequently in Britain) away from social democracy and towards the market. Ronald Reagan and Margaret Thatcher gave political leadership to a conservative movement, that used simple and populist terminology to get its case across. Politically powerful soundbites – such as 'get government off the backs of the people' and 'government is the problem, not the solution' – skilfully associated the state with bureaucracy, officialdom, 'red tape', inflexibility and, most witheringly of all (as I have argued earlier), compulsion.

Reagan and Thatcher also led an intellectual revival. Unlike many of the more centrist presidents and prime ministers who preceded them – most of whom who took a managerialist view of leadership – they saw the long-term value of ideas. They used their offices to introduce to a wider public a host of classical liberal theorists who, marginalised during the postwar social democratic consensus, finally came into their own. Ludwig Von Mises, Frederick Von Hayek, Milton Friedman and Karl Popper, if not exactly becoming household names, did become the new gurus of the age (taking over from John Maynard Keynes and John Kenneth Galbraith).

In the US a new generation of free-market 'conservative' intellectual leaders emerged in the think-tanks and universities – economists such as George Stigler and George Gilder, sociologists such as Charles Murray, public choice theorists such as Mancur Olsen and J. M. Buchanan, and philosophers such as the former socialist Robert Nozick. In Britain, in an intriguing parallel eruption, theorists such as Arthur Seldon, Madsen Pirie, Anthony Flew and William Letwin, economists such as Samuel Brittan, Peter Bauer, W. H. Hutt, Patrick Minford, Gordon Tullock and Alan Walters gave Thatcherism an intellectual underpinning.

These Reaganite and Thatcherite intellectuals wrote with verve and confidence, with a sense that they were part of a new tide of ideas. In comparison the socialist response seemed intellectually inadequate and the social-democratic response somewhat tired and bereft.

One intriguing aspect of this renaissance was the number of former socialists and social democrats who began to break cover and support market solutions and a reduced role for the state. The primary issue for many of them was non-economic – the Cold War, and they rejected what they considered to be their fellow socialists' anti-Western attitudes – but many of them also began to make a link between the failures of the command economies of the Eastern bloc and the problems of the growth of the state in the West. Robert Nozick, Peter Berger, Robert Skidelsky, Evan Luard, Irving Kristol and – less so – Sidney Hook, Daniel Bell and Daniel Patrick Moynihan associated themselves with this broad conservative revival.

Two magazines became the home for this trans-Atlantic generation of 'neo-cons' ('neo-conservatives', as they came to be dubbed by the American media). In the US the American Jewish Committee's *Commentary* magazine – edited by the redoubtable Norman Podhoretz – not only focused on winning the Cold War but also, month after month, systematically attacked the social and economic agenda of the American 'liberals', including what they considered to be the overblown US welfare state. In Britain, *Encounter* magazine, led by the equally redoubtable Melvyn Lasky, did not set itself against social democracy quite so strongly (in the early 1980s it supported the social democrats' political exit from the increasingly leftist Labour Party), but it did provide a platform for serious arguments from Thatcherite economists and social scientists.

As well as these social-democratic allies, the promarket, antistatist right secured support from another, somewhat surprising quarter: from some traditionalist conservatives. Such conservatives – numerous in Europe, less numerous in the the US – were suspicious of individualism and consumerism, neutral about the power and reach of the state, and saw the market as destructive of traditional values and ways of life. Yet conservative thinkers such as Michael Novak, Roger Scruton and John Casey rode shotgun with free-market capitalism, seeing few contradictions between capitalism – even the rawer kind – and tradition.

Taxes

The intellectual case, with its touch of religiosity, was very powerful, and in the era of the collapse of the authority of socialism it had a real allure for those in search of truths. But the ideology of market capitalism, attractive though it may have been, was not the cause of the break-through of antistate, market, ideas and their public support. The war for the market was really won on the more prosaic terrain of taxes.

Market politicians noticed something that socialists ignored. One of the most pronounced social changes since the 1950s was the hugely increased number of people paying taxes. Low, even average wage earn-ers were not really in the income tax brackets in any number until well into the 1960s. As they, including the growing army of women in the workforce, flooded onto the labour market the anti-tax appeals of mar-ket supporters achieved a previously unknown resonance.

But it was the world of business that had the real resentment against the high-tax regimes of governments, and ultimately, through globalis-ing, broke them. Tax competition by governments assumed 'grotesque forms' to keep companies sweet. The tax rates for companies fell throughout the world. It has been estimated that between 1991 and 1995 Siemens (including its subsidiaries) was able to reduce its world-wide taxes from 50 per cent of its profits to 20 per cent. This new power relationship between corporation and nation-state was summed up neatly in 1996 by the reported comments of Daimler Benz chief Jurgen Schremp, who announced that he did not expect his company to pay any taxes on profits in Germany, and told parliamentarians that 'you won't be getting any more from us'. Schremp summed up the clear, new, market capitalist idea that companies, not the state or society, have the ultimate right to ownership of money and resources – it is 'our' money, not 'yours'.[9]

Globalism and the minimalist breakthrough

Yet even during the 1980s, minimalists, although possessed of a con-siderable *esprit de corps* and a sense of being on the winning side, were ascendant rather than triumphant. They were not able fully to dislodge social democracy – the state, the welfare society, or the mixed economy. President Ronald Reagan presided over a huge deficit budget and did not succeed in lowering the public sector take in the US economy, and Prime Minister Thatcher, for electoral reasons, was reduced to proclaiming that 'the National Health Service is safe in my hands'. Reagan and Thatcher gave way to Bush, Major, Clinton and Blair, all of whom proclaimed various kinds of quasi-social-democratic messages and a role for the state that was much more than minimal. Western leftist intellectuals and propagandists may not have been putting up much of a fight, and were certainly not saying much that was new, but the interests opposed to raw free- market capitalism were still well entrenched. What is more, as the 1980s progressed it became clear that the European social model was still intact – as was the Japanese model – representing a beacon for those who wanted a more cooperative public – private, managerial – labour system and a more involved state.

Even the marked growth of privatisation – which was particularly dramatic in 1980s Britain – did not marginalise the state. Of course it weakened the public sector by depriving it of the assets of ownership. Yet at the same time the newly privatised companies paid taxes to the state, and when they reduced their workforces the state was still there to pick up the social security bill. By the end of the free-market 1980s most Western states were, intriguingly, taking as much in taxes as they had at the beginning of the decade; and of course the state was still a power in the land by virtue of the huge military budgets – and payrolls – it still deployed.

It was globalism that made the breakthrough. Only with the emergence of truly global markets could the minimal-state project begin to assume real proportions. During the 1990s – almost overnight, as it were – capital, freed from nation, began to establish a marked ascendancy over the state. It was this increasing mobility of capital that was the key element in weakening the state: for capital mobility – or the threat of mobility – allowed the market, for the first time, to punish and reward nation-states according to its requirements. The mobility of capital weakened the state more effectively than any proselytising or privatising by Reagan or Thatcher and their market intellectuals.

This brave new world of the minimum state is now under construction. As we enter the twenty-first century we are only at the beginning of the project. Its contours are now clear. Unless new political realities intervene to prevent it, the minimum state of the mid-twenty-first century will shrink welfare, reduce or abolish regulation (particularly of the labour market) and – globally, under the banner of 'free trade' – remove the state from any control of trade and resist the construction of any serious international economic order (ensuring a 'minimum international state').

Minimum welfare

Of all the projects of the minimum state, reducing welfare may be the most difficult. Most of the leading continental European nations have serious welfare states that, though reformable at the margins, are so entrenched that any dismantling would lead to political revolt. And in the US the welfare system is so bound up with inner-city, underclass politics that any major surgery would, even though unintended, produce real racial divisions.

In the push for a minimum welfare state marketeers will argue on two levels. On the moral and ideological level they will continue to assert that there is simply more dignity in providing for yourself than relying on 'handouts' from the state. Those relying on welfare will become supplicants. This argument was spelt out clearly by a leading free-market theorist, who argued that the welfare state turned 'paying customers in the market' into 'importunate supplicants in the political process'. This contrasts clearly with the traditional social-democratic view, set out crisply by Will Hutton, who argued that 'the vitality of the welfare state is a badge of the healthy society; it is a symbol of our capacity to act together morally, to share and to recognise the mutuality of rights and obligations that underpins all human association'.[10]

Yet at the heart of the minimalist view of welfare is the question of efficiency and cost. Minimalists would have it that the four main services of the welfare state – education, medical care, housing and pension income in retirement – can be provided much better by private organisations – through insurance and charging – than by the state through taxation.[11] Indeed taxes are the real point here. Capitalism used to be able to sustain a welfare state through taxes on businesses – the 'social costs'. Yet with the growth of demand in some welfare areas – such as health and pensions – the same level of service can only be provided by increasing taxes, by raising these social costs on businesses. Minimalist reformers of the welfare state believe that such social costs are no longer sustainable – certainly not at the level operating in continental Europe, in the so-called 'European social model'. They offend against a principal globalist requirement: by eating into profits they – unless prices or employment take the strain – threaten share performance.

British and American supporters of the new capitalism regularly focus on late-century France as the prime example of the unsustainability of this 'high social cost' model. the *International Herald Tribune* investigated a French decorating company, BDM, in the Normandy town of Bray-et-Lu and found that 'employing a worker at a gross monthly salary of 10,111 francs ($1,702) ends up costing a total of 15,306 francs, or an additional 51%'. The paper revealed that these social costs go towards family allowances, low-cost housing loans, unemployment insurance, work accident compensation, pensions and professional training, and even towards reducing the social security budget; and the clear implication emerged that in the Anglo-American market model much of this kind of provision cannot be expected to be funded by businesses.[12]

In the future minimalist state there will be a trade-off between welfare and unemployment. If social costs remain high then companies will simply lay off workers in order to keep profit margins high. A leading French banker argued in 1997 that 'If costs in America were the same as in France...perhaps 25% of Americans would be unemployed.'[13] Of course in such a regime the minimal state would not be able to afford much in the way of unemployment benefits. So low-paid – very low-paid – part-time work for millions of people might be the answer.

Minimal regulation

This minimal state would also be a minimal regulator. The American Nobel laureate and minimal statist George Stigler argues that regulation too often ends up favouring the regulated through cosy deals and the inadequacies and corruptions of the political process.[14] Stigler, and the minimalists, would obviously consider Will Hutton's ideal 're-publican' regulator – 'flexible, negotiating, focusing on competence, imbued with a sense of wider interests, conscious that citizens have a right to participate in decisions' – as not just, according to Hutton, 'conspicuous by its absence', but also as highly fanciful.[15]

Yet the real regulatory battle will take place over the labour market. The brave new minimalist world will want to deregulate this market in order to create a 'flexible' workforce. The key 'flexibility' demanded by the minimalists is the legal ability of corporations to hire and fire at will, and to use part-time, largely unprotected labour to respond quickly to changing profit margins caused by changes in demand.

Minimal international political order

Of course triumphant globalism has probably already ensured the victory of the minimum state within the domestic economies of the various nations. (As I have argued earlier, mobile capital will penalise any individual nation whose state is not minimal.) The key for minimalists, now, is to ensure that, beyond the water's edge, a minimum regime is also established. The ideal political structure for minimalists is a fragmented global political order with a host of medium-sized states, all competing with each other, none able to command a purchase over capital.

The new global capitalism will continue to subvert any form of serious international political order, anything that even smacks of global economic government. It can be argued that such a global order existed, at least in embryonic form, during the Bretton Woods regime, when the world financial system – with its fixed exchange rates, regulated financial markets and currency risks borne by the public sector – provided some form of political and thus democratic authority as a balance against markets. Of course individual nation-states brought Bretton Woods into being, and in essence it remained the creature of the government of the most powerful of them – the United States.

This era ended when, in response to the pressures of the early 1970s, the US government decided to dump Bretton Woods; and during the following two decades exchange controls were abolished, domestic limitations on cross-market access to finance were removed and controls on credit were scrapped. During the 1980s, amidst a quantum leap in speculative financial flows, financial risk was privatised and a global market in monetary instruments emerged; and in the 1990s this flow became a tide.

Today's globalists seek a world order that is not only far more minimalist than Bretton Woods, but also far slimmer than the *ad hoc* internationalism of the post-Bretton Woods era. And they are getting it. With the state weakened at the national level, the aim is to ensure that the state does not regroup at the global level – that the world order remains fragmented into a host of states, none of them too big to establish political authority over global finance, and all of them competing with each other for capital's favour.

In the twenty-first century international relations (where the essential characteristic is relations between nation-states) will, in all but a rudimentary, residual sense, cease to exist. In its place we will inhabit what John Burton, as early as 1972, described as a 'world society'. An intriguing vision of this 'world society' has been outlined by John Vogler: 'the units of the system will not be billiard ball states but can be corporations, overlapping ethnic groups, classes or even individuals'.[16]

The American business economist Joel Kotkin also caught the flavour of this modern global society when he introduced the idea of global tribes – for instance the British, the Japanese, the Jews, the Chinese and the Indians – establishing global networks 'beyond the confines of national or regional borders'. And as for global tribes, so too for global corporate units and global individuals – our super-rich.[17]

In this new global society there is no government. The state is not minimal, it is non-existent. For instance the G7 or G8 group of countries, or global organisations such as the World Trade Organisation, do not begin to rise to the level of a state, even an international state. At best they represent an attempted coordination of policy by weak national states, at worst they protect the myth of an international order.

In this anarchic global environment each nation-state competes with each other in order to keep and attract the huge amount of mobile money now washing round the system. Governments are measured by how 'market friendly' they are – whether they offer the full range of the new capitalism's needs (low inflation, prudent monetary policies, public spending under control, low taxes) – and are rewarded and punished accordingly.

Some analysts believe that this lack of political authority – and the need to be 'market credible' – have imposed deflationary strategies on the leading Western economies. John Eatwell has argued that the 1960s model – of a managed international financial system creating full employment – has been replaced by a 'contagious' dynamic that has elevated financial stability above employment and 'ratcheted up real interest rates, which have in turn reduced domestic investment and slowed the growth of world trade'. The late Susan Strange went further, arguing that the present unordered financial system, what she witheringly described as 'casino capitalism', threatens world living standards.[18]

There is little likelihood, though, that in the short or medium term any global political or democratic authority – a world government – could limit this market-driven globalism. World institutions such as the United Nations and GATT (General Agreement on Tariffs and Trade) remain fora rather than authorities – essentially the creatures of agreements amongst the larger, fragmented nation-states. If the Western world – through international groupings such as the G7 or G8 – cannot rise to the occasion and create a political authority, then there is no hope for the broader international community. (The European Union is a different matter, particularly if it can establish with the US federal government some enforcible regulations.)

The victory of free trade

Preventing government – any government, national or global – from interfering with the world of trade is a major aim of the new capitalism. Ever since the Bretton Woods agreement free trade – including, crucially, the free movement of capital – has been a veritable sacred cow; and any political involvement in trade (protectionism) has been considered economically injurious, indeed one step away from war.

A formidable coalition supports free trade in the West. At the heart of this coalition – its engine room – are the great US-based corporations, which in turn ensure a political consensus of Republicans and Democrats in the US. Every single president since 1945 has needed to support free trade. Opposition to free trade comes from the weakened labour movement and from marginalised political figures such as independent presidential candidate Ross Perot and conservative columnist and presidential candidate Pat Buchanan. A more substantial, though still embryonic, challenge to the free trade consensus was made in the late 1990s by the Democratic leader in the House of Representatives, Richard Gephardt.

In postwar Europe free trade was also the orthodoxy, but had less of a firm hold. It was the policy and rhetoric of most of the European political establishment – including that of West and then united Germany – although French policy often flirted with a measured European protectionism. Yet at no time could free trade be seriously, frontally challenged. As Ravi Batra has argued, 'the idea [of free trade] is now embraced as economic theology around the world'.[19]

The powerful grip of the ideology of free trade on Western intellectuals and public imagination (indeed its virtual divinity) is reinforced by a particular view of history – principally the belief that interwar protectionism was a cause of the 1929 financial crash, the interwar depression and then the war itself. The fact that the Smoot–Hawley Tariff Act – now almost raised to the point of demonisation – followed, not preceded, the great Wall Street crash, and unemployment rose from 3.2 per cent to 8.7 per cent long before the effects of the tariffs were felt, has little effect upon this powerfully embedded received opinion.[20]

Another part of the governing mental construct about trade is that protected markets – protectionism – hinders economic growth. Much of this comes from the British experience in the nineteenth century, when the flourishing protected imperial market system was mistaken for free trade. So well propagated is the benign character of free trade and the malign nature of protectionism, that the fact that the United States protected its home market for most of its spectacular growth period during the nineteenth century is often overlooked – as is the role of protectionism in the postwar Japanese economic miracle, the rise in the 1980s and 1990s of the newly industrialised 'tiger' economies of Asia, particularly Taiwan and South Korea, and the selected protectionism in the US during the Reagan era, particularly in the car industry.

Free trade ideology

In theory the old verities of free trade – pioneered by David Ricardo – retain a residual charm. The theory holds that 'comparative advantage' dictates that two countries forming a partnership – that is, a single market without trade restrictions – and specialising in the goods and services in which they have an advantage, whilst importing the other product, will be more productive together than separately.

Edward Luttwak has taken the lead in attempting a contemporary critique of this well-entrenched theory. In his new book *Turbo Capitalism*, Luttwak concedes that free trade theory may be more efficient globally – producing the same goods by replacing expensive workers with cheap workers – but adds that 'in affluent countries ... now increasingly afflicted with the return to poverty in the most vulnerable fraction of their population, it is not necessarily a good idea to enrich the kingdom by turning some of its subjects into paupers'. (And he criticises free trade economists for 'leaving the scene' whenever compensation schemes for the unemployed and low-waged – which are 'never implemented' – are mentioned.)[21]

In 1995 the late James Goldsmith introduced a refinement to this argument by drawing the attention of anyone who would listen to the fact that with the end of the Cold War four billion people had suddenly entered the world economy, and that these newcomers would 'offer their labour for a tiny fraction of the pay earned by workers in the developed world'. Consequently, 'it must surely be a mistake to adopt an economic policy which makes you rich if you eliminate your national workforce and transfer production abroad, and which bankrupts you if you continue to employ your own people'.[22]

Another critic of free trade, Ravi Batra, has gone further, arguing that the theory of comparative advantage, or partnership between nations, may make the partnership as a whole more prosperous but it says absolutely nothing about the individual prosperity of the two participants – one of the partners could be much worse off even with higher all-round productivity.[23]

These criticisms of free-trade theory predate globalisation, but their hand has been immensely strengthened by the new global realities. However contemporary theorists increasingly argue that free trade has been made redundant by mobile capital, because, with companies no longer rooted in nations, the profits from free trade no longer revert – in one way or another, as they used to – to companies rooted in nations or to domestic populations.

Here to stay?

Many still believe, though, that free trade is here to stay, immovable, unyielding Indeed its grip will be very difficult to loosen, let alone remove. For the foreseeable future any medium-sized nation-state that attempts to interfere with free trade – either in capital or goods and services – will be punished by capital flight, under investment and political unpopularity following lower living standards caused by public sector cuts or rampant inflation or both. At the turn of 1999 the economic fate of Malaysia – which turned its back on mobile global capital and thus offended against one of the central tenets of the ideology of free trade – was very much in the balance, and might yet set a fearful contemporary example for those who stray from the faith.

Only very large political units such as the United States or the European Union could, should the political will be present, withstand the consequences of intervening in the mobile trade flows. Yet in both North America and Europe critics of free trade will need to contend not only with vested corporate interests but with a broader consensus fuelled by an almost religious conviction, what Edward Luttwak kindly calls the 'emotional intensity' of free traders. The fact is that 'the elites of media, business, academia and politics...have already made up their mind on these questions. They are committed to promoting the global economic system – and to defending it from occasional attacks from angry, injured citizens.'[24]

Protectionism – the idea that the state has a role in regulating trade flows – is not only dismissed intellectually, but is still considered a baleful doctrine of the forces of darkness.

The handmaiden state

Big global capital – its players and supporters – may need a minimal state for taxes, welfare, regulation and trade, but it does not seek a stateless world (only libertarians and some free-market intellectuals want to go that far). Rather, corporate business capital – always more at home in dealing with the state than are the bookish free-market enthusiasts – seeks only to ensure that the state, or the public sector, remains within bounds. It wants a government that is powerful enough to serve capital but not so powerful that it threatens it.

The old role of the state as umpire – between the needs of capital and labour, between public and private, between domestic and international – is, for global corporate capital in the 1990s, certainly passé; but a handmaiden state (that is, a handmaiden or servant to mobile capital) is very much in order. And this handmaiden state – like handmaidens themselves, invisible, not heard, but crucial behind the scenes – will need to be authoritative in order to help big capital realise its full potential.

For instance the state is needed to help guide public resources to the service of capital. The existing transfer of resources from taxpayers – via the state through hidden subsidies, through the costs of the infrastructure that capital readily uses and through bailouts of lenders in emerging markets – to private interests is huge and probably incalculable. An authoritative state is also needed 'to police markets, including labour markets; to sustain law and order; to sustain some of the economic and social conditions for [capital] accumulation'.[25]

It is also needed to secure the crucial reserve functions for capital. One such function will continue to be its crucial, irreplaceable role in limiting inflation. Inflation is a deadly enemy of the super-rich, the global rentier class of wealth holders. As the columnist Bob Herbert has put it, 'Alan Greenspan's purpose is to protect the assets of the very wealthy. The value of those assets erodes with every uptick in the rate of inflation.'[26] Those who earn their income can normally increase their wages and salaries to meet inflation, and the state can index pensions, but those dependent upon income from capital will find that it depreciates in an inflationary environment. Therefore 'the rentiers' core goal was stable money... everything else – sales, employment, social relations, government obligations – was considered secondary.... Wealth holders, of course, benefited immediately from this regime, since it both defended the value of their stored savings and produced the higher interest rates paid to them as creditors.'[27]

Roger Bootle in *The Death of Inflation*, a pioneering book on the consequences of what he believes may be the coming age of zero inflation (or even disinflation), has argued that a zero inflation economy – as long as it doesn't tip over into serious disinflation – can be generally beneficial, but is specifically good news for shares, the engine room propelling the growing wealth of the rentier super-rich. He argues that zero inflation 'would imply a higher level of real equity prices at each stage even if the level of bond yields and the rating of equity risk were the same'.[28]

In a zero inflationary environment real interest rates would be lower and this 'argues for higher real equity prices' and higher profits. What's more, a world without inflation – with low interest rates – would see another building bloc for super-rich wealth creation: a higher price

– earnings ratio (that is, higher share prices at a given level of company earnings). The death of inflation and the resultant fall in interest rates would also lead to huge capital gains for the holders of bonds, as occurred in 1993 when short-term interest rates fell (during the inflationary 1970s bond values fell).

Also, an era of zero inflation would mean less need to hold the traditional hedges against inflation – property, antiques, collectibles and gold – and would free up resources, some of them fixed in location, for even more investment in shares and financial instruments. Zero inflationists, though, also worry that inflation – or rather price instability – would disrupt markets by causing uncertainty and unpredictability amongst market players in the areas of investment and wages, and there are those who argue that even a small level of inflation causes great harm – leading investors into a host of incorrect decisions, primarily in the labour market, about how many people to employ.[29]

In sum, a low or zero inflationary environment is one of the crucial foundations of the new global capitalism; and without the authority of the state (working through politicians and the cental bankers) to impose such a non-inflationary regime the whole international financial edifice might begin to crack. Quite simply, the state cannot help in this function if it no longer possesses the ultimate reserve authority.

Concern with inflation is normally the preserve of bankers and monetarist academics. During the decades of the social-democratic (post-Second World War) era the West lived with inflation. Anyone born after the 1920s has known a world in which prices rise every year. Yet suddenly counterinflation became a political if not a populist issue, gathering a degree of public support. Post-Second World War German opinion was always hostile to inflation, indeed obsessed by it, because of the Nazi experience in the 1930s. But a broader anti-inflation constituency throughout the West emerged following the oil price crisis of the 1970s when unusually high price rises led to serious social unrest and political instability (this was particularly marked in Europe, where radical political change, including the possibility of 'Eurocommunist' governments, was only just averted).

As a reaction to this inflationary dislocation the anti-inflation campaign – led in the early 1980s by Federal Reserve chairman Paul Volker and politicians Reagan and Thatcher – took hold. And since then the goal of low or zero inflation has become orthodoxy, and any policy that can be attacked as 'inflationary' hardly stands a chance of a serious hearing. The arguments against an inflationary society remain strong, even for social democrats, but so too do the arguments against deflation.

Yet the global capitalist orthodoxy appears prepared to take risks for one course, but not the other.

So fixated on low or zero inflation have the Western economies become that those who question the orthodoxy of low inflation are few and they tend to argue their corner rather tentatively. Yet they are beginning to emerge. The late 1990s centre-left political regimes in Germany and France will probably tolerate somewhat higher levels of inflation than their predecessors. Even amongst economists some heads are beginning to appear above the parapet. James Tobin of Yale University has argued that a small amount of inflation helps 'grease the wheels' of the economy.[30] Also, the highly experienced former British Treasury minister Joel Barnett recently suggested that 'it seems untenable to put inflation on a unique pedestal', and that it should be considered alongside other objectives such as 'growth and exchange-rate management'.[31]

Yet the Western consensus is still a long way from replacing inflation as dogma with inflation as technique – as merely a mechanism to help secure economic prosperity and social and political goals. And we are a very long way indeed from understanding that the large internal Western markets (in the US and the European Union) can, partly because of their low exposure to trade, easily tolerate rather higher inflation levels than those which prevailed in the 1990s.

'Bankocracy'

New global capitalism needs some form of political authority to deal with its fear of inflation. However the exact type of political authority desired by anti-inflationists is interesting. It seems that 'politics without the politicians', or a state without elected officials, is the desired model. In other words, modern monetarists seek a political authority that rests in the secure hands of bankers, or more precisely, central bankers. These central bankers are by background normally accountants and economists, but become, in essence, 'political'. They are established by law (in Europe the European Central Bank is established by treaty), they are appointed by elected politicians for a fixed term, and from time to time they justify their actions in public fora – in the US very publicly to the US Congress. (The European Central Bank established for the euro currency area under the Maastricht Treaty is rather less democratically accountable and may present a real 'democratic deficit' problem for the peoples of Europe.)

In theory most central bankers are in some manner accountable. However in practice they are not. Although paid by the taxpayer, this exotic race of money men have little connection with the political world of democracy and even less in common with the masses. They have about them the aura of transcendence, even religiosity. Edward Luttwak sees central bankers assuming a priestly status in the deflationary, market-driven global economy. They see themselves as having no duty, he suggests, to political or democratic authority, but rather to the higher authority, 'the sacrosancity' of 'hard money'. Their own power derives largely from their supreme command of their crusade against the devil of inflation.'[32]

Central bankers are not, though, like politicians – either like the best who determine policy according to history and values, or like the worst who follow almost any policy direction dictated by popular mood and demand. Rather they resemble high priests, guardians of a holy but technocratic gospel based upon the doctrines of the market and 'sound money'. The management of plural social and economic interests and international relations, and the pursuit of values and principles – none of these matter in comparison with the technocratic 'jihad' against inflation. Yet, hugely ironically, the minimalist anti-inflation lobby will need to protect the political authority of the state – or collection of states – in order to enforce their monetarist vision.

Skilling

In the global capitalist mantra and in the doctrine of 'third way' centrists such as Clinton and Blair, states have a crucial role in preparing their populations for the global economy, for 'skilling up' their people. Both new global capitalism and its 'third way' friends have given up on the old-fashioned, Victorian-utopian idea of creating an 'educated population'. Thus although the rhetoric about education remains, the reality of the global economy is that capital does not need educated people; rather it needs a local population that is trained and skilled.

This task of maintaining and enhancing the skills of local populations is conveniently not assigned to global capital itself, but rather to the public sector. British Prime Minister Tony Blair once went so far as to argue that such skilling and reskilling was nothing less than the 'greatest single priority' of government in the global economy.[33] Global capital will of course play its part in this process – as a kind of umpire, picking and choosing between nation-states as to which ones have performed best, and rewarding the winners by investing, for a short period, in their local populations.

Some analysts argue that Western economies will always have an edge in the global economy because they will always possess an advantage in skills. Robert Lawrence argues that whereas 'some processes and technologies can be moved internationally...the most significant sources of higher productivity in the developed countries – the superior levels of skills and the tacit knowledge of the workforce – cannot move abroad'.[34]

I seriously doubt this prognosis. Skilling up the Western populations will put real pressure on budgets, and no matter what the ability of the Western countries to sustain such public expenditure, governments in emerging markets – particularly Asia and the Indian subcontinent – will be able to skill up their populations to the same level at a much lower cost. To dismiss this competitive possibility – probability – is part of a widespread complacency that almost amounts to a huge cultural and psychological block, or indeed a prejudice, in underestimating the technological and organisational ability of non-Western populations.

Can we really envisage a global economy in which, say in two or three decades' time, the skill levels for the bottom half in the West will be higher than those of the top half in China and India? As Australian diplomat Gregory Clark has said, 'today, in Asia at least, some [countries] are equal or superior to the West in work ethic and ability to absorb technological skills'.[35]

Because of the pressures on public expenditure – and the need to maintain a low tax regime – some new capitalist supporters are arguing that the state may not be needed in the Western quest for skilling and reskilling the population. They suggest that 'market forces will do this automatically – 'for instance, if workers with low levels of education in OECD countries saw their wages fall to levels equal to those of workers in developing countries, they would have a tremendous incentive to invest [personally] in education'.[36] Of course an 'incentive to invest' might not translate itself into actual investment because the individual unemployed worker might not have sufficient personal resources, and the state will also be wise to limit its resources. A terrifying dynamic could take hold, in which both public and private investment in skills would be inadequate to attract capital, and the resulting unemployment and underemployment would lead to fewer and fewer resources being available for reskilling.

Bailouts

The minimal or handmaiden state desired by global capital is at its most useful when it comes to the rescue of new capitalist 'risk takers'. Some kind of minimal international political authority is essential for bailing out super-rich and big-capital investors whenever crises in the global financial system – as during the 1990s in Mexico and Asia – lead to the possibility of defaults. The present rules of the game conveniently minimise these risks. Indeed for many so-called financial entrepreneurs the risk of exposure involved in such lending is about as great as those faced by a feckless and spoilt son who, having lost at the gambling tables, turns to an endlessly compassionate patriarch to bail him out. This kind of lending, knowing you will be bailed out by the state, is called by economists 'moral hazard' – rightly so, because for many risk-taking investors there is certainly no *financial* hazard.[37]

Perhaps, though, the metaphor of the insurance company is more apt than that of the patriarch – for our risk-taking financier needs to pay a premium for such protection. These premiums are the taxes that go towards the public sector bail-out of these private sector failures. Yet these premiums are hardly onerous; indeed they are highly reasonable (as they are also funded by the general Western publics) and can often be avoided. Professor Willem Buiter of Cambridge University is right to wax indignant about this cycle being little more than a racket – 'a gift from the taxpayers to the rich'.[38]

These 'gifts' are often arranged very secretively and very swiftly. In the first major crisis of the post-Cold War world of global markets, the IMF–BIS bail-out of the super-rich during the Mexican crisis of January 1995 took place in under 24 hours: no more than a handful of people, all operating outside any real parliamentary control, used Western tax-payers' money to organise the largest credit and aid programme since 1951. In the IMF bail-out during the Asian crisis of 1997–8, billions of taxpayers' dollars were spent on shoring up collapsing financial structures, and at the same time bailing out risk-taking speculative investors.

Typically in these bailouts, equity investors and long-term lenders suffer losses, but short-term international lenders – the 'risk-taking speculators' – are largely saved. Interestingly, though, the US Congress, when asked during the height of the 1998 Russian financial crisis to approve a bail-out of $18 billion, finally balked. Yet for the foreseeable future Western capital and global super-rich investors will have Western taxpayers at their mercy, because the alternative to bail-outs is often thought to be the collapse, certainly the threat of collapse, of the entire global financial system.

New global capitalism may demand a handmaiden state as its helper, but it is by no means picky about which particular nation-state should do the job. In fact any state that picks up the tab – either by a low-tax regime or by bringing to the global table the necessary skilled and competent workforce – will do. Being mobile, capital can always move from a 'non-performing' nation-state to an hospitable one.

Buying the state

From the perspective of business, however, politics still remains highly unpredictable, and governments and states can always turn nasty. The long boom of the 1990s kept the Western publics well within a probusiness consensus. Left-of-centre parties (such as New Labour and the American Democrats) now vie with conservative parties to be business-friendly. But, should recession hit, public opinion could always start to flirt with social democratic or even socialist parties.

Now, though, it is much more difficult for public opinion, even should it begin to change, to assert itself. The old model of the state – in which government was like a referee, neutral between capital and labour, limiting the ability of any sectional interest to manipulate and dominate, thus leaving the way open for public opinion (through geographically rooted constituencies) to make its mark – is now a thing of the past. The old image of independent legislators, disdainful of sectional interests, deliberating on what was best, was always fanciful, and was supplanted during the twentieth century by organised political parties. These parties used to represent separate, often antagonistic interests – primarily capital and labour.

Now, though, in many Western countries, particularly in the US and Britain, the business interest is the only game in town, influencing, even controlling parties of both right and left. The reality is that the business interest has a disproportionate influence, working its will through parties, candidates, the political media, indeed the total political process. In this sense, even before the votes are counted, business has already bought the state.

Of course private interests have a long history of influence-peddling in and around government. There have always been a number of ways in which companies and private interests can place senators, congressmen, members of parliament, even cabinet and government ministers in their debt, if not exactly on the payroll. The 'revolving door' – whereby jobs in the private sector, often in areas directly related to their governmental portfolio, are arranged for politicians when they leave office – is one way. In countries where there is no public funding of political parties, politicians, even party leaders, often find it hard to resist offers from the private sector to help them with their office expenses.

Historically, of course, this private sector influence has been tolerated because it has been balanced, often more than balanced, by the lobbying and financial power of organised labour. The trade union federation, the AFL–CIO, was still, even in the late 1990s, one of the most powerful of all lobbying organisations in the US, even though its declining membership meant it had less clout than during its heyday in the 1960s. In Britain during the era of 'the social contract' in the 1970s, the trade unions were treated more seriously by government than was business, and were even invited to 10 Downing Street to help determine a range of economic and social policies. Throughout continental Europe organised labour is still a serious force in the land – either because it is institutionalised as a 'social partner', or because, as in France, it can still exert pressure on government by its militancy.

The quantum leap in business influence over the state, though, is not just a product of the late-twentieth-century victory of capital over labour. It is also a result of the changing nature of democracy and technology. The fact is that in the media age, serious and sophisticated political campaigning amongst the huge populations of many Western nations takes huge resources. Parties and politicians can no longer raise the necessary money through subscriptions from the faithful, and in countries where there is no public funding for parties, private business is all too willing to help out.

Campaign contributions from big businesses are a standard feature of political life in the US. One frightening assessment has it that 95 per cent of the successful candidates for Congress are those who have spent the most money to win the race (comment by Dale Bumpers, former US senator, in *New York Times*, 8 Jan., 1998). These campaign contributions are usually funnelled through political action committees (PACs). Big business PACS tend to be more influential than unions, not only because they are more acceptable to most middle-class electors (the vast majority in the US's low turnout polity), but also because they can guarantee longer-term financial support, even jobs or consultancy work after political careers are over.[39]

Business influence on government is also guaranteed by the political and electoral influence of the media, particularly media that reach into millions and millions of homes – such as television and tabloid newspapers. Much of this media is owned by big corporations or super-rich individuals, and thus, over time, private interests help both to set a political agenda and to hype a party or candidate (as well as to destroy opponents).

This political power of the private sector sometimes allows an egregious amount of power to reside in the hands of individual media barons – a problem highlighted by the well-publicised 'virtual veto' over British European policy that the British prime minister allowed foreign media owners Rupert Murdoch and Conrad Black to exercise in the early days of the euro. Even though evidence remains that television – which maintains a reasonable balance between parties – is the main informational channel for politics, some British politicians remain in awe of the opinion-moulding power of populist tabloids such as the *Sun* and the *Mirror*. (In the premedia age a more dignified posture was adopted by British Prime Minister Stanley Baldwin, who attacked a political campaign by press barons – in a manner unthinkable today – by describing them, in a famous phrase, as 'having power without responsibility, the prerogative of the harlot throughout the ages'.)

The victory of business has also helped to change – in a probusiness, promarket direction – the all-important cultural and intellectual environment (the 'tenor of the times'), which, although its impact is not as directly felt as are elections and lobbying, ultimately, over time, works its will on government. Universities, particularly those funded mainly by the public sector, have tended to remain a bastion of liberal-left thinking, but they are increasingly marginalised in the public debate as it operates through the mass media: on television, in newspapers and in influential magazines. A new race of accessible think-tank analysts and very accessible political, social and cultural journalists has emerged to fulfil the role of public intellectual. These 'infotainment' journalists are able to voice opinions on a wide range of topical issues and are more able to communicate to a wide audience than are traditionalist academics. Also, typically, they are employed by large corporations or super-rich individuals, and thus are more likely to have business-friendly opinions.

8
The Hope of Europe

A continuous revolution

Globalisation is a continuous process; indeed it can never be finished. Like Leon Trotsky's 'permanent revolution', the 'reforms' of the new capitalism can only be the beginning. With little or no serious opposition left, the global super-rich and their aspirants and supporters will continue to demand performance and profits from their capital. This will cause pressure for lower and lower costs – both labour costs and social costs – and as China and India come on stream, these lower costs for business will become a reality, in turn creating a further dynamic for lower and lower costs in the Western world. In the global market eternal vigilance over costs is the price of success.

To ensure these lower costs, and without any one or anything to stop them, transnationals and global capital will continue to insist upon 'hire-and-fire' flexible labour markets – one mechanism for keeping labour costs low through the emasculation of trade unions, and by more and more part-time, temporary, largely benefitless work. And decade after decade, indeed year after year, these lower social costs, together with low tax regimes throughout the west, will mean that Western welfare state provision, particularly health provision and pensions, will need to be cut (although education, meaning training, may be spared somewhat because of the perceived need for skills).

In this environment the long-term social effect is clear: standards of living in the West, expressed through wage and salary levels and working conditions, will need to fall. Some will not of course, and inequalities, even pauperisation, will grow sharply (as I argued in Chapter 1, this happened in both the US and Britain during the 1980s and 1990s).

This stark, indeed frightening process will certainly be uneven – all change is. The additions to the global labour market from South and East Asia may be less fulsome and more spasmodic than envisaged; the potential skill levels in Asia may indeed be less impressive than they now appear; Western service and high-tech industries may see major short-term benefits from growing demand and open markets in Asia; and as a result the economies of the West – and the Western peoples who are dependent upon them – may enjoy more prosperity and stability than the logic of this fateful dynamic would suggest.

Yet at the turn of the millenium this 'continuous revolution' was well underway. In the US and Britain some of the necessary reforms needed to live successfully in the global economy were already operating. Headway was made with flexible labour markets, allowing downsizing and cost cutting, and in Britain the all-important battle to weaken the trade unions (without which no adjustment to the global economy would have been possible) was won. And, in a neon sign that these reforms can only be the beginning, by the late 1990s 'Third Way', left of centre politicians in the US and Britain were already introducing proposals designed to erode some of the erstwhile untouchable programmes of the traditional welfare states.

A comeback for the state?

Any aim or campaign to overthrow or even reverse this new capitalism would be utterly unrealistic. For social democrats a much more profitable route would be to use the existing framework of political (or public) power to negotiate with capital and corporations. Of course, with the demise of the nation-state the state's hand is weak. However it could be immeasurably strengthened by the pooling of power and authority in new region-states or super-states. In other words, the only way globalisation can be tamed, and its consequences limited, is by the emergence of continent-wide government – by the ability of super-states (such as the European Union or a more integrated ASEAN, or indeed the United States itself) to make deals on a more or less equal basis with the global economic players.

Even so, some still argue for a national – even a local – solution. 'If we really want to throw sand in the wheels of global capital', argues Larry Elliot of the London newspaper the *Guardian*, 'then the answer is to think national and think local. Heading down the Euro-route is the blindest of blind alleys.'[1] Former US Labour Secretary Robert Reich also seeks a national response, a 'positive economic nationalism, in which each nation's citizens take responsibility for enhancing the capacities of their countrymen for full and productive lives', that is, providing skills for the global economy rather than confronting it.[2]

Global governance

Others seek a global solution to what is after all a global problem. In what is becoming a typical line of argument, a leading member of the European Parliament has suggested that 'as they play one government off against another, companies often evade national laws on everything from workers' rights to environmental protection ... [and] to stop the downward spiral in labour and environmental standards, there needs to be new national and international regulations ... regulating multinationals'.[3] Nawal el Saadawi ended his BBC radio essay on the perils of globalisation with a heartfelt plea not just for an international solution (that is, an agreement between states) but for a *global* political solution:

> This cannot go on. We have to shift this agenda to develop a global people's movement which will force the hands of the multinationals, liberalise, democratise and free the creative forces of hundreds of millions of men and women everywhere. The seeds of this movement are being born before our eyes everyday.[4]

Labour unions and developing countries are at the forefront of the movement for some form of global regulation of corporations and capital. They want mandatory regulation of the globals, including such issues as disclosure of information, taxation questions such as tax evasion and transfer pricing, employment protection, industrial relations and antitrust policies. Yet, unsurprisingly, none of these ideas have been implemented, not least because there is no serious international body that, should they be attempted, would be able to enforce them. The Organisation for Economic Co-operation and Development (OECD), the International Labour Organisation (ILO) and the UN have all produced draft ideas about some tepid forms of regulation, but none of them can be taken seriously as a potential legal order.[5]

Of course traditional international organisations – subject as they are to national agreements and vetos – will offer no serious long-term threat to the global corporations. What is ideally needed is truly global authority with truly global accountability. David Held argues that 'if the history and practice of democracy has until now been centred on the idea of locality (the city state, the community, the nation), it is likely that in the future it will be centred on the international or global terrain'.[6]

Held's idea is to recast systems of political accountability to match the new global activities of economics, environment and communications. Edward Luce has advocated the same kind of global institutionalism – a new body, to replace or supplement the IMF, called the World Organisation of Finance (or WOOF), incorporating an international financial court with the power to regulate international markets and enforce minimum standards of commercial disclosure by both borrowers and lenders. It would arise, he argues, out of an international treaty following negotiations between sovereign states.[7]

A radical visionary outcome of this new cosmopolitan model of democracy – in a world of global interconnectedness – would of course be a global parliament with limited tax-raising powers.

Of course there is always a potential, no matter how limited, for existing international organisations to develop into the kind of global supranational authorities that the reformers seek. A – very weak – form of embryonic global governance already exists in the United Nations. Other global institutions are beginning slowly to test their strength. The World Trade Organisation – the successor to GATT – has organised some global collective policies; and there appears to be a degree of international acquiescence in the Bank for International Settlement's supervisory role on the capital adequacy of banks as they conduct business across boundaries. The World Bank and the International Monetary Fund are also embryonic global political institutions – yet they are still far from the ideal, as advocated by global financier George Soros in an article in the *Financial Times*, of an international authority to supervise capital markets and regulate the allocation of credit.[8]

The sad truth is that there will always be a strict limit to such global political responses to global financial or economic problems. Modern capitalism will simply run rings around any serious attempt to so constrict them. Companies will pressure governments not to agree to anything much more than the weakest, token, global authority – the kind of authority that will bail out risk capital but will not regulate it. And should some governments resist this pressure, there will still be no agreement at the global level to abolish vetos by the largest countries in order to set up a world economic government.

This great political inadequacy was clearly visible during the 1998 Asian financial instability, when even a coordinated political response (involving interest-rate policy in particular) was very difficult to organise. And anyway, coordination between governments – even at moments of acute crisis – is always fragile, and even if agreed, can always break down under the pressure of events and divergent interests. If a global consensus, let alone a global authority, for the non-proliferation of developing countries' weapons of mass destruction is impossible to secure (most of the limited action, as opposed to words, tends to be unilateral, by the US), then so too will any long-term attempt to regulate even bigger players such as global corporations.

The vision of a global political order with a serious legislative and executive function, maybe even including some redistribution function, remains just that – a vision. Such a supranational political order (with a large internal market) does, though, exist, or potentially exist, in the new region-states that, intriguingly, globalisation is bringing into being.

The case of the United States

Arguably there is one regional or super-state already in existence – the United States. It possesses all the necessary ingredients for domesticating mobile capital. It is large and rich, with an internal market of over 220 million citizens and a GNP of over US\$7 100 000 million; and it has a federal governmental structure with central economic management institutions. In a real sense the US is the governmental prototype – a continent-wide federal state – for other areas of the globe, particularly the European nations now integrating and federalising within the European Union and the single currency.

Yet the irony is that the one polity capable of negotiating with global capital is also disarmed. At the centre of American culture and ideology, in the very marrow of contemporary American bones, is an antistatist and antipolitical bias. The huge success of the postwar US economy, the weakness of US trade unions (particularly in the south and west), combined with the historical antigovernment and antisocialist impulses of many immigrant Americans, has entrenched almost as a national doctrine the idea that 'the business of America is business'. Although the American public is by no means in love with big business (it is fond of no big institutions, particularly big government), no serious political opposition to the rule of the large postwar US corporations has developed. And the US federal government, rather than leading the way in constraining them, has provided the main political springboard for globalised capital, for free-market and free-trade ideology.

For most of the postwar decades the people of the United States did very well out of the increasing multinational character of its corporations. After all these corporate behemoths created and serviced a new world-wide market for US goods and services. Also, they were in considerable part the providers of the postwar capital that fuelled the postwar boom throughout the West. Consequently, and rightly, they have become associated in the American (and Western) mind with prosperity and the pleasant life of the American dream. The very names – IBM, General Motors, Johnson & Johnson – created confidence. They are now, though, in the age of concern about the environment and downsizing, somewhat tarnished; even so the US resident transnationals – which after all are still fresh from seeing off socialism (domestic and foreign) and 'winning the Cold War' – are still seen as symbols of American pride. As is the globalised, free-market, free-trade system they so powerfully proclaim.

The fact that many of these corporations also come top of the world league for shifting capital – and jobs – to low-cost areas is not yet fully appreciated. There is a growing awareness of this deadly trek, not least amongst US trade unions and some Democratic politicians (such as, in 1999, presidential hopeful and house leader Richard Gephardt), but public concern will come too late. At the time of writing the US government looked set to remain for some time under the thrall of the imperatives of new global capitalism. Indeed it is likely to remain globalism's primary governmental cheerleader.

The European Union (and the coming collision with global capital)

Europe, on the other hand, presents new global capitalism with a serious problem. According to the globalist gospel, the living standards of the peoples of the European Union are far too high to be sustainable in the early twenty-first century. There is much truth in the view that the continent is simply uncompetitive. The institutions of Europe – trade unions, welfare states, maximalist governments with high levels of public expenditure and high tax rates and social costs – are outdated and unreconstructed. The kind of major 'modernising' change adopted in the US and Britain during the 1980s still needs to be wrought.

There were signs in the late 1990s that some European political leaders were trying to address this European competitive deficit by bringing European business somewhat more into line with that of the US and Britain and making them more globally competitive. The *International Herald Tribune* reported (under the puritanical heading 'European Companies Gain From The Pain') that, 'following the methods adopted by

US companies in the 1980's, many European firms have been shedding labor, closing or selling off what they consider nonessential businesses and streamlining management in a drive for greater profitability'. (Companies cited included MAN AG, the German machinery concern, which had 20 per cent of its business marked for closure, and MAN Roland, which makes printing presses and was laying off 10 per cent of its workforce.) Also, Morgan Stanley, drawing on data from the OECD, pointed to two trends for which Europe would get high marks from globalists: it estimated that between 1990 and 1996 the European manufacturing workforce shrank significantly – by 17.9 per cent in Britain, 17.6 per cent in Germany and 13.4 per cent in France – and that profits were up in some of the companies that had restructured.

Of course, according to the globalists' mantra, none of this will be enough – for competitiveness is a dynamic concept and needs regularly to be addressed. The price of competitiveness is constant vigilance. Bernd Pischetsrieder, chairman of Bayerische Motoren Werke AG, sang to this globalist hymn sheet when he reported on the restructuring of his company in the late 1990s, saying that 'yes, there has been progress...but not enough progress'. As Lars Stalberg, head of corporate relations at Ericsson, has said, 'we have to *continually* rationalise production to meet the price pressures'.[9]

Yet another truth – perhaps an even more profound one than the uncompetitiveness of Europe – is that the continent may find it almost impossible to exact the required change, except perhaps just at the margins. The fact is that the changes demanded by global forces are radical, indeed revolutionary. They will eventually entail the overthrow of the whole structure of the continental labour market and welfare society as a prelude to a significantly lower average living standard and a horrifying widening of inequalities. What is more, the timescale demanded by the forces of globalism – a global economy in which time seems to be speeding up – is very short.

Europe will simply not be able to adjust to lower living standards and sharply divided societies without considerable social upheaval – leading, as with all unstable polities, to unknown outcomes. In an age when European integration – based upon the single currency – will be the dominant political dynamic, these revolutionary upheavals could perhaps take the form of a break-up of the union and the emergence of extreme ethnic and nationalist regimes, or alternatively of Europe-wide extremist politics.

Of course globalists ask: why can't the EU simply follow the US and British example? If they can adjust to the global market, why can't the

EU? Such questions need answers. One answer is that the leading European economies, until very recently, did not need to adjust. For most of the postwar period German social market capitalism remained highly competitive, and the French were the beneficiaries of a host of official and unofficial protective measures, including the Common Agricultural Policy.

Now that the EU is increasingly globally uncompetitive, however, with the strain beginning to show in high unemployment numbers, it is facing what Britain faced in the 1970s and 1980s. Yet as a response to the Thatcherite process of adjustment to the global economy during the mid 1980s, Britain went through what amounted to serious social upheaval, with – during the miners' strike – revolutionary pitched battles between trade unions and police, a veritable, televised 'civil war' in which the outcome was by no means certain. It was, perhaps, Britain's elitist political structures (an executive-driven, centralised state with no Bill of Rights or Freedom of Information Act) and its deferential culture (the country still had, and has, a monarchy!) that during these fateful years allowed its established order to survive – just.

The US started to dismantle its inefficient, uncompetitive, social-democratic economy by stages following the defeat of LBJ's 'Great Society', and US-based corporations began to downsize their home plants and offices during the 1980s. But the key to the ability of the Americans to 'globalise without revolt' is the high level of inequality – including inner-city deprivation – that American society is willing to tolerate. The US free-enterprise ideology – unlike the EU's social market culture – sees inequality almost as a necessary by-product of a free and dynamic economy. And in the US – again, unlike in the EU – the non-corporate forces acting for 'égalité' are weaker: the trade unions are losing members and the government itself is constantly on the defensive against a deep, sometimes frightening public cynicism about politics, a malaise that has not yet spread to business, even big business.

In sum, by the late 1990s at least, both the US and British polities had survived the adjustment to globalism. Should the EU, though, choose to travel this same globalist road, there is no certainty that, subject to the same pressures, the EU nations would see a similar outcome.

Defending the EU's social-democratic model

So, it now seems inevitable that a great world drama is about to be played out. What *Time* magazine calls the EU's 'more caring but costly' social model – the genuine 'third way' – will, in order to survive, need to take on and beat the forces of 'ruthless capitalism' unleashed by globalisation.[10] The stakes in this contest are truly enormous. Should new global capitalism win, should its writ run through Europe as well as the rest of the world, then its average living standards will fall. One analyst has gone so far as to argue that 'if [Europe's] planners can't intervene successfully or are blocked by laissez-faire dogma, then the West deserves to see its living standards dragged down to the level of Bangladesh'.[11]

This contest will play itself out under the banner of 'free market' versus 'social democracy'; but it will also be about concrete interests – with the globalised super-rich (and their supporters and aspirants) and globalised corporations on the one side, and the European polity, and its political-cum-business class, on the other. It is no exaggeration to say that upon the outcome of this historic contest rests the way of life not only of the European peoples but of the West, including the US (where there are serious, though minority, social and political forces sympathetic to a return to social democracy), which will watch and await the outcome.

How does the EU stand on the eve of this great contest? The strength of Europe should not be underestimated. It has its huge single market, arguably the largest and most prosperous in the world, to which the global corporations seek access as a strategic priority; and in January 1999 many of the EU member states adopted the single currency, the euro. The leverage that the single market gives to Europe was on display in July 1997, when in a landmark contest the EU went head to head with the mighty global Boeing corporation over the social consequences of its merger with McDonnell Douglas. The EU threatened to fine the new giant 10 per cent of its revenues per year, and primarily because of its need for access to the European market, Boeing, after refusing, finally agreed to the EU's conditions.

Also, at the time of writing Europe seemed to be coping relatively well with the financial crisis that began to afflict the global economy in 1997. As American commentator Jim Hoagland has argued, 'the emergence of the much maligned welfare states of Europe as a zone of relative currency stability and a source of growth is a big economic change that official Washington is having trouble taking on board. It contradicts much of the conventional wisdom that developed about the global economy in the 1990s.' He also suggests that the way in which official Washington responds to this new Europe – to the idea that global free-market economics may have serious, potentially devastating consequences, and that there might be an alternative, less destructive model – 'will determine the course of world economic history for the next few decades'.[12]

Of course, under pressure from the forces of globalisation the EU's still powerful political-cum-business class could, theoretically at least, begin to buckle. Europe's business leaders – particularly those global corporate chiefs with businesses resident in the EU – are, of course, the most potentially footloose. Eurobusinesses, like businesses everywhere else, are looking for the highest profits and the lowest social costs. Yet – and here is the key to the potential resilience of the EU – big Eurobusinesses, like big extra-Eurobusinesses, may be footloose, but are still highly dependent upon selling in the internal European market, access to which is ultimately governed by the politicians of the European Union.

Yet the EU's political class – from French technocrats, Brussels civil servants and German politicians – seem in no mood to dismantle the social democratic model. Of course global pressure for low tax regimes and against protectionism in trade will be insistent; but, amongst Europe's political class at any rate, they will probably take second place to the need to protect employment and the welfare state, particularly health, educational and pensions provision. 'Making Europe competitive' may remain an acceptable political slogan, but it is only likely to be implemented at the margins.

The left-of-centre governments of Chancellor Schroeder in Germany and Prime Minister Lionel Jospin in France, elected in the late 1990s, provide a pivotal critical mass supporting this new twenty-first-century European ship of state. The French elite seem to have established a firm consensus against dismantling social democracy – even conservative President Jacques Chirac wants there to be 'no question of importing the UK social model into France'.[13] And although the German consensus remains relatively committed to the orthodox anti-inflation strategy of the globalists, since the abolition in 1999 of the Deutschmark it has had less of a say about monetary policy. Germany is likely to continue to support all the main features of the European social-democratic model – regulated labour markets, a role for trade unions, a capitalist–public mixed economy with levels of taxation (including social costs on business) set to meet the expenditure of established social provision.

The birth of the euro

The EU's coming battle with the global economy will take place on a number of fronts. One such is the currency. The first day of January 1999, when the euro came into being, was an historic milestone if there

174   *The Super-Rich*

ever was one. By replacing the mighty Deutschmark, as well ending the rule of the Bundesbank, the euro had arrived as a major world economic player – but so too had the EU political class, the increasingly integrated governing elite who had masterminded the process of monetary union.

Within days it was clear that the new currency would seriously challenge the dollar. Some informed American forecasters believed that although the use of the euro in trade transactions might be limited, its use in international financial transactions – arguably 40 times the volume of trade transactions – would be massive.[14] In 1996 the US dollar, the globe's 'vehicle currency', was used in 40 per cent of all foreign exchange transactions – on the basis of 14 per cent of world trade. In the same year the EU's world trade share was 16 per cent.[15] During 1999, as winter turned to spring, the euro was indeed becoming one of the world's two reserve currencies. As Janet Bush has argued, 'what we are beginning to witness is a battle for influence [between the dollar zone's economic model and that of the Euroland countries] truly worthy of the millennium'.[16]

A 'political' euro

Yet the euro project has always involved much more than a simple economic challenge to the dollar – it also represents a reemergence of politics alongside economics, of the state alongside the market. The mere act of creating a European single currency introduced a new political framework and reality into the world of markets as it dealt a blow to global capital's ability to divide and conquer the European nation-states through currency speculation. None other than the first president of the new European Central Bank, Wim Duisenberg, in an interview on the eve of the launch of the euro, agreed that 'the loss of sovereignty' caused by the euro 'was not for nations, but rather for the markets' – meaning the loss of speculative ability to buy and sell separate European currencies.[17]

This *political* character of the euro is hardly surprising. After all, the new single currency was conceived and created by politicians. The European Central Bank in Frankfurt is a *political* creation – constructed, against great opposition, by the public sector, by politicians and 'functionaires', and implemented by treaties and elected governments. Two of the early proponents of the single currency – French President Valéry Giscard-d'Estaing and German Chancellor Helmut Schmidt – both possessed a keen geopolitical understanding and motive, as did German Chancellor Helmut Kohl who, with the assistance along the way of

French President François Mitterrand and European Commission President Jacques Delors, guided the euro project to fruition.

From the start, for its founders, the euro project was about politics, about geopolitics – about the need to integrate Europe further, about the provision of a unifying symbol, about Europe's place in the world. No wonder that as early as 1996 French Foreign Minister Jean Arthuis suggested, at the European Finance Foundation meeting in Frankfurt, that the then projected euro could easily become the world's leading reserve currency and therefore a foreign policy instrument that would be more effective than import duties.[18]

The euro can also serve another political end. As the perceptive American commentator William Pfaff has provocatively argued, 'the new European currency has been established to protect the European social model, and European industrial and technological sovereignty, against American competitive pressures, and to protect the particular characteristics and values that set European society off from American society'.[19] A reserve currency status can certainly be used politically for social ends, and the euro will allow the EU some economic space to defend its different social model. The US has enjoyed the seignorage profits deriving from having a reserve currency – profits earned by its central bank and estimated to be between $5 billion and $10 billion a year. Also, 'a country with reserve status currency is able to accumulate external debt without having to increase the yield on its assets', and its currency can appreciate despite the accumulation of debt and low interest rates.[20]

Of course nothing is preordained. The EU social model might well be protected from the ravages of the global economy, but could also be up-ended from the inside. The euro will be administered by bankers – central bankers – most of whom possess ultraorthodox financial and economic attitudes, having learnt their trade during Volker's anti-inflationary counterrevolution in the 1970s. This conservative – and globalist – orthodoxy has been reinforced by the Maastricht Treaty, which set up the European Central Bank in Frankfurt and has created what Wolfgang Munchau has described as 'a shrine to conservative economic thinking. The primacy of price stability, the absolute independence of the central bank, and the prescription of fiscal austerity are more than just policy. They are constitutional law.'[21]

Also, the culture of the Bundesbank – inevitably a continuing influence within the European Central Bank – will act as a pressure for globalist financial ideology. Whereas the US Federal Reserve tends to respond both to deflation and inflation, German banking orthodoxy has been slow to reduce interest rates when unemployment is rising, but quick to put them up when inflation rises. It is this potential European 'bankers' regime' that led Robert Reich to suggest that 'the euro is a big step towards the Americanisation of the European economy'.[22] But whether bankers will run Europe's economy and erode from the inside its social democratic model, will, to a large extent, depend upon whether the French can secure allies in limiting the control of German banking instincts over the euro.[23]

Bankers are not, though, automatons – living in a protected world utterly oblivious to political pressure. One of the chief characteristics of successive chairmen of the Federal Reserve Board in Washington (rather like that other unelected US official, his Supreme Court opposite number) is a highly political, indeed social, sensibility. In a democratic age, unelected institutions in the EU, just as in the US, need, in order to survive, to adopt a 'political feel' alongside their technical competences. Should a sustained consensus amongst Europe's elected politicians develop in favour of a pan-European expansionary economic policy – more concern with growth and employment, less with inflation – then the Eurobankers will find it difficult to resist.

Such unorthodox 'growth' arguments can already be heard from Europe's political class. Even as the euro was being born, Germany's Social Democrat finance minister, Oskar Lafontaine, dubbed 'red Oskar' by the British proglobal press, was placing the cat amongst the pigeons by pioneering a political campaign for a return to a more social (less financial) economic order, one that would be concerned primarily with employment.[24]

Although in the initial years at least the bankers in Frankfurt will be in charge of the monetary side of the euro, the parallel political institution, the 'Euroland club' within the Council of Ministers (EcoFin) in Brussels, will over time become, in all but name, the economic government of Europe – able to act politically through both budgetary and exchange-rate policy. Bankers will be balanced by politicians.[25]

There are two ways in which the politicians, these ministers in Brussels, could gain a decisive victory over the bankers. One way would be to create – through the coordination and harmonisation of national budgets – a social-democratic fiscal policy that would compensate for any niggardly orthodox monetary regime. If monetary policy were to threaten social goals, then a pan-European fiscal policy could be used to compensate. In early 1999, just weeks after the arrival of the euro, moves to harmonise taxes and even spending programmes (and to reduce, even eliminate national vetos in economic policy) were already being proposed by German and French government officials.

Another way that the EU politicians could outwit the bankers was hinted at after the historic 1998 election of Chancellor Gerhard Schroeder's Social Democratic administration in Germany. The Maastricht Treaty gives to the politicians power over the exchange-rate policy of the euro, and the new German administration – again under the influence of Finance Minister Oskar Lafontaine – was attempting to introduce the idea of exchange-rate target zones. These target zones would aim to prevent the euro from overvaluing itself against the dollar, thereby damaging the EU's export industries and employment. In this way, in an idea proposed by leading French geo-economic stategists for some time, the euro would be 'managed' politically – become, like the dollar in Washington, an arm of governance rather than markets.

Thus such a 'political' euro would match the 'political' dollar in the great game of world finance and politics. But the game would be played for a reason: the objective of this political euro would be to protect from the ravages of the global economy the EU's employment levels, welfare societies and average standard of living.

Teething problems

Even as the euro began to establish itself during 1999, critics were still suggesting that the whole euro project – together with European integration and the EU's social-democratic model – might unravel. The sceptical thesis runs that the single currency area – Euroland – may not be an optimum currency area (where capital and labour mobility can even things out by substituting for devaluations, or revaluations). Loukas Tsoukalis has argued that 'the loss of the exchange rate instrument . . . - while labour mobility as well as wage and price flexibility remain too weak to act as effective substitute, could turn whole countries into depressed regions. This is what most of the economic argument [about the euro] boils down to.'[26]

In other words Euroland could simply reproduce, on a geographical basis, the kind of Anglo-American inequalities that the EU social model is supposed to avoid. These inequalities could build up serious popular resistance to Euroland (and the wider European Union) and reignite nationalist and separatist sentiment. In a world of increasing electoral volatility, an assertive media-dominated democratic culture and technological advance, antifederalist populist, chauvinist and extremist movements could spring up very quickly indeed. (The fact that at the turn of the millenium only sections of English opinion exhibited a traditionalist chauvinism towards European integration does not mean that such separatist instincts could not spread.)

The only way to preclude this potentially devastating unravelling would be to deepen, rather than weaken, the European federalist dynamic. An enlarged federal budget and, over time, perhaps even federal taxation, could stabilise (in the event of asymmetric shocks) by redistributing resources to the necessary regions. The experience of the federal dimension in the United States and Germany is instructive here – for both Washington and Bonn have played a key redistributive role in their respective societies, and there is no reason why the EU could not do the same.[27]

The Padoa–Schioppa Report (1987) recommended that automatic redistribution by net national contributions be related to national income per capita. And a year later, the Delors Report also argued for a strong redistributive element in the federal budget. It remains a fascinating projection that an EU budget accounting for 2–2.5 per cent (instead of 1.2 per cent in 1997) of total EU public spending, could, with progressive taxation and a heavy concentration on regional policies, result in 'a 10 per cent reduction in inter-regional disparities' inside the EU.[28]

The constraints on securing a higher federal budget would be considerable. In the absence of transfer payments, the only other way to alleviate asymmetric shocks would be to allow the troubled country or countries temporarily to increase their public expenditure, and therefore their budget deficits. At the time of writing (early 1999) Portugal, because of its links to the ailing economy of Brazil, was, potentially at any rate, about to experience the first asymmetric shock of the euro regime; thus possibly presenting the Euroland finance ministers – those in the Club X in EcoFin – with their first big test.

Political trade

The EU's social democratic model will not survive simply because a single currency exists. The single currency (like the single market out of which it grew) is a prerequisite, an enabling institution to allow the EU some leverage with corporations and capital as Europe intervenes in the global economy.

There is little doubt that 'the EU has a variety of policy instruments which can be used as means of influencing the allocation of resources between itself and the rest of the world'.[29] Amongst them is a comprehensive industrial policy – essentially the use of the state to strengthen Europe-based companies as they seek market share, as well as 'protectionist' trade policies. Even amidst the free-trade fashion, unfair trade practices and social dumping (where low or non-existent social costs mean that unfair trade practices can take place) are now legitimate areas for debate and action.

Resistance to the idea of a European strategy involving 'strategic' (or political) trade (protection) is weakening. Intellectually, 'free trade is not passe, but it is an idea which has irretrievably lost its innocence'. It will lose its innocence politically as well, as the imperatives of globalism bear down on the EU.[30] Also, Europe's regional self-sufficiency in trade is marked – in the mid 1990s three quarters of the average EU country's total trade took place within the EU; and this figure is likely to increase with the addition of Central European nations.[31] This crucial self-sufficiency, the fact that the EU can, at a pinch, 'go it alone', will mean that the EU will possess real bargaining power in future negotiations about the world trade regime.

All the traditional tools would be available to the EU in any strategic trade regime. They would include community preference, including variable import levies (calculated by the difference between threshold prices and the price offered by low-cost third-country, Third World, suppliers), export restitutions (covering the difference between EU and world prices), quantitative restrictions on low-cost traded products (such as the Multi-Fibre Agreements) and the encouragement of voluntary export restraints (which used to protect the European steel and car industries). A whole series of non-tariff barriers, particularly technical standards such as health and safety measures, are also available.

Of course, a European strategic trade policy does not necessarily mean unilateralism. Ideally the EU needs to protect its average living standards through trade agreements with the rest of the world, particularly the US. The forum already exists for such negotiations in the World Trade Organisation (WTO), the successor to GATT. The WTO is, though, still a only forum – the Uruguay Round, completed after 12 years of bargaining in Marrakesh in April 1994, was something of an elephant labouring to produce a mouse; and the WTO's global trade liberalisation programme is far more superficial, and therefore less effective, than European integration. In the race between world trade liberalisation and European integration, Europe is winning hands down.[32]

Looking to the future, the WTO will probably become an economic UN where regional trade groupings (the EU, NAFTA, and the Asian and Latin American groupings) will argue, negotiate and, hopefully, agree – but sometimes, as in the security area, unilateral action will no doubt occur from time to time.

Taxing mobile capital

As well as developing a trade strategy, the EU should not be shy about intervening in the mobile capital game – through taxes on capital transactions. Chile has already been operating a transaction tax, and requires investors to deposit 30 per cent of their funds with the central bank for one year. And little Chile has yet to be severely punished by the global economy.

The American economist James Tobin has suggested levying a tax of 1 per cent on all foreign currency transactions.[33] For some reformers his proposed tax may be too low – some suggest 2 per cent of outlay; but even at this level Paul Davidson argues that the tax is but a 'grain of sand in the wheels of international finance . . . when boulders are required'. He accepts that the tax might limit speculation when small exchange-rate changes are expected; but that when a fever sets in amidst the movement of huge sums, 'the Tobin Tax' and other transaction costs will become insignificant. Of course it all depends on the political will to impose as high a tax as is required.[34]

It is here that the EU could make its mark. Such is the power of the global economy that 'even if the G-7 countries all introduced a Tobin tax, the financial sector could formally switch its business to offshore branches from the Cayman Islands to Singapore'.[35] Yet, given the political will, it is not farfetched to see a future in which the EU could act alone. Professor Tobin himself, reentering the fray in 1995, suggested that individual polities could impose an additional tax on the lending of their currencies to foreign institutions and to foreign branches of their domestic banks. All the EU would need to do would be to tax the foreign customers – banks and individuals – of Europe's banks when they lent them euros.[36]

Reforming the corporation

Theoretically, however, a strong case can be made that as long as the EU protects itself against unfair competition from abroad, thus taming the external impact of globalism on Euroland, then the writ of Thatcherism (competition, labour market 'flexibility', indeed the whole free-market mantra) can run throughout Europe without seriously harming average living standards, at least in the medium term. In such circumstances 'Euro-Thatcherism' would remain an option.

However, such is the dynamic nature of modern capital that it will ultimately seek to break its bounds in the search for the wider horizons of low-cost centres. In any Euro-Thatcherite regime, capital and corporations would dominate the state (in the ways I tried to describe in the previous chapter) and would inevitably use their power to create an irresistible, internal European momentum for global capitalism, and the erosion of European living standards and the European social model.

Thus any serious social-democratic agenda for Europe must include the tricky and controversial task of tackling the vitals of modern global capitalism, of altering the domestic relationship between capital and government. This huge, revolutionary task needs to start in the engine room of modern capital where the fires of the global regime are stoked – the corporation itself.

A view is growing that there is something wrong with the very structure of the modern corporation. Some reformers see the problem as essentially financial, the use and abuse of corporations (and the imposition of short-term thinking) by the arms-length relationship of financiers and banks. What is needed, argues Will Hutton, is some link between ownership and committment to the enterprise. He suggests that 'groups of core institutional shareholders might be formed who would be represented on company and bank boards by non-executive directors with their own, information-gathering secretariats. Voting rights might be limited only to those shareholders who are represented on company boards, thus legally linking ownership with obligations to commitment.'[37]

Let us stand back for a moment. These business organisations, which are arguably becoming the most powerful institutions in the world and affecting the lives of everyone on the planet, are governed like medieval fiefdoms – by small groups of managers in the interests of small group of shareholders, with everyone (but everyone) else excluded from even the remotest connection with corporate governance. Reformers tend to focus on the impotence of the millions and millions of corporate employees, but the fact is that everyone (but everyone) else – public sector employees, retired people, students – are also excluded. An argument in favour of reforming trade unions used to be that millions and millions of people were not covered by them. This argument applies much more dramatically to corporations.

The management philosopher Charles Handy has argued that 'the current conception of the corporation is inadequate for modern times'. He suggests that 'the language of property and ownership no longer works . . . [the corporation] cannot divorce itself from the wider society in which it operates'. Instead, he argues, the public corporation should be regarded as a community, not as a piece of property, and that 'the language of political theory is ... more appropriate for describing it than the language of property'. He suggests that 'the idea of the corporation as the property of the current holders of its shares ... is an affront to natural justice in that it gives inadequate recognition to the people who work in the corporation and who are, increasingly, its principal assets'. He wants 'citizen corporations', corporations as political organisations bestowing rights on workers, and he argues that the form of corporate governance should be changed to reflect power coming 'from the operating units rather than from outside investors'.[38]

These ideas have not appeared from out of the blue. A form of employee participation was proposed in the Bullock Report in Britain in the late 1970s. It recommended a scheme whereby companies with 2000 or more employees should have four to seven shareholder directors, the same number of employee directors and three to five coopted directors; and a minority report recommended a scheme similar to the German version of codetermination.[39] Bullock's recommendations for industrial democracy fell foul of Britain's deeply adversarial, class-based, 'them and us' culture, where militant trade unions fought pitched battles with an upper-caste management. The less socially antagonistic and more economically successful continental European environment was able to persist with the idea of the company as a 'community' rather than a 'property' – and under the EU Social Chapter companies with 1000 or more employees in the EU as a whole and 150 or more in each of two member states must now have either a European Works Council or some other agreed 'information and consultation procedure'.

This idea that the ownership of the corporation should be transferred from shareholders to the people who work in it is the radical heart of the matter. Such a governance change, unlike state ownership, would not destroy the market. The profit motive would remain, competition (with other units) would remain, even the price mechanism would remain. The essential pluralism of contemporary capitalism would be retained, but business would become a community, or a series of communities, in which corporate decision making would become accountable not to shareholders but to employees. This 'citizen corporation' is not unlike the old idea of cooperatives (a concept floated as an option during the 1970s, but largely rejected by the left in favour of state ownership).

The sheer radicalism of this change, though, lies in the way in which it would play out in the game of global capitalism. The fact is that such a change in corporate governance would dramatically lessen the pressure to transfer capital, and jobs, to low-cost centres abroad, as the ownership of the corporation would have been transferred from shareholders (seeking performance and profits) to newly enfranchised employee governors who would themselves be at risk.

Reflecting the late-twentieth-century distaste for the state, Charles Handy wants his ideas about new forms of corporate governance to be enacted voluntarily, not through legislation. Shareholders, though, will resist, and stock markets are well-entrenched (Britain's stock market capitalisation was a staggering 175 per cent of GDP). The fact is that in today's US and British capitalism 'the idea of stakeholder capitalism has all but disappeared, to the benefit of stockholder and manager'.[40] So, such an historic change can only be wrought by the state. Changing the rules of corporate governance – particularly removing or weakening the rights of shareholders – is a huge uphill task for any government. So new-style 'citizen corporations' will remain a long-term goal only. However, should a political consensus build up for such a move, such a constitutional change would be more acceptable to modern corporations than state ownership or crippling levels of taxation.

A social-democratic agenda for Europe, however, must entail a major reform programme for government itself. As the federal EU state – the Council of Ministers, the Commission, the Parliament – will play a bigger economic role, it will need to be more representative of and sensitive to public opinion than it is at the moment. This 'democratic deficit' can only be filled by giving the European Parliament more power over the European executive (the Commission); and it would be no bad thing if the European Parliament actually used its 'nuclear' power to sack the whole Commission, as it nearly did in 1999 before it resigned. Such a flexing of the European Parliament's muscles might alter the still overly bureaucratic, executive-driven culture of Brussels.

Anglo-America

If the EU politicians use the euro intelligently and *politically*, and establish some kind of strategic trade policy (even if initially they cannot alter the balance between state and capital by reining in – or even reforming – the corporations), then they will stand some of chance of preserving the average EU living standards into the next millenium.

As Euroland begins to confront the global economy, however, Anglo-America (the globalised economies of the US and Britain), initially at any rate, are most likely to watch and wait. There will be a huge temptation in New York and London to believe that Euroland, with its expensive jobs and welfare provision, will become uncompetitive, its social content unsustainable. Indeed the globalisers in Anglo-America may turn out to be right. Yet, whilst Europe may be becoming less competitive, Anglo-America will continue to see growing inequality and real job losses, with its populations becoming more and more casualised, more and more insecure, less and less socially protected. And should China and India continue to establish themselves in the global economy, capital will flow out at an increasing rate – so much so that political support for the globalist economic strategy may collapse.

Social democracy

Should such support drain away, then social democracy will return to the Western agenda with a vengeance. As Anthony Giddens has argued, 'social democracy can not only survive, but prosper, on an ideological as well as practical level'.[41]

It is vitally important not to be too mealy-mouthed about the ideas of social democracy. Today it is often confused with the ambiguous and tentative 'third way' netherworld ideas popularised by the left-of-centre governments in the US and Britain in the 1990s. It should not be. To restore the balance of social democracy in the face of 'the manic logic' of global 'turbo-capitalism' will take serious political leadership and hard choices. But luckily, social democracy's core ideas – those which governed our lives for over three decades after the Second World War – are clear. In its contest with global capital there are two social-democratic imperatives, and they both go against the current grain.

First, *the state (albeit in a reformed form) will need to be reasserted against capital* – and we will need to learn that there is nothing wrong with the kind of role, reach and power of the state as it existed from the 1950s to 1970s, before the oil crisis exploded the postwar social-democratic consensus.

Also, as a matter of principle social democrats do not see economic organisation – whether by the state or the private sector – as an end in itself, but as a means to political and social ends: justice, equality of opportunity and the freedom of the individual. There is no moral content in the type of ownership. There is nothing inherently good (or inherently bad) about private or public ownership, about the state or the corporation. This idea was best expressed by Tony Crosland when, generating considerable controversy on the left, he argued that neither public nor private ownership was therefore an end in itself.

Those who fear any increase in the power of the state tend to appeal to the idea of freedom. Yet this idea of freedom can move European social democrats to tears just as much as it does American Republicans, and the social democrat sees the unconstrained private sector as being as much a threat to 'freedom' as the unconstrained state. For human beings, to be 'owned' by the corporation is as large an affront to individualism and human dignity as being 'owned' by the state.

Secondly, *the market, particularly the global market, will need to be constrained*. Why, social democrats might ask, should we not fear an over-mighty market as much as we worry about an overmighty state? Also, market ideologues argue that the free market is a more efficient mechanism for economic growth than what they call the 'sclerotic' social-democratic mixed economy of Europe – but if this were indeed true, then Germany would be far less productive than the US. The truth is that inefficiencies in the free-market economies and within corporations go largely unreported. Yet an unconstrained private sector entrenches the inefficiencies of inheritance, the wastefulness of corporate expense accounts and other 'social costs' such as the business class's health care and retirement packages.

Luttwak's dilemma

However the efficiency of the economic order is not necessarily a first priority. In the conclusion to his compelling *Turbo Capitalism*, Edward Luttwak produces the example of contemporary Venice and poses a dilemma about its future. Globalisation, he argues, will make this unique European city more efficient and competitive, and 'the overall balance of power between young and old [will] shift in favour of the former, increasing the sheer vitality of its now very staid society'. Yet at the same time he argues that global capitalism will increase the distance between employers and employees, 'sometimes to intercontinental proportions when the new employers are multinational corporations'; and he also suggests that old social-democratic Venice will lose much of its authenticity and charm.[42]

Luttwak's 'dilemma' is not really a dilemma at all. Social-democratic Venice is probably as good as it gets. Like social democracy itself, Venice has balance. It has its inefficiencies and rigidities (such as the uncompetitive licensing of gondolas and restrictive opening hours), but these are balanced out by the indubitable fact that Venice, like Paris, is a Western capitalist city existing in a Western capitalist system – all this and charm too.

Come back Marx: all is almost forgiven

Should Europe's social democrats begin to reassert their social heritage in the contest with raw global capitalism, an insistent question will emerge: will they need to swallow hard and accept some of the truths of Marxism? As one American commentator has argued, 'there has tended to be a total rejection of anything termed "Marxist" without any evaluation'.[43] It is not so much 'come back Marxism all is forgiven' as acceptance that some of the basic analyses of Marx may shed considerable light on this new type of capitalism.[44] Surely even a 'Cold War social democrat' – like this author – can accept that Marxism's analysis of capitalist production, of the crucial distinction between labour and capital, of increasing profits, of the increasing poverty of those who have only their labour to sell (for labour, read non-essential skills), retains, for this age, a gravamen of real truth?

The Marxist analysis of capitalism has been the victim of two historical epochs. The first was the epoch of Bolshevism – for the Bolsheviks, and later the Communist Party of the Soviet Union, by appropriating the ideology, allowed the opponents of Marxism to give life to the argument that oppression and compulsion lay at the heart if not of the Marxian analysis, then certainly of the Marxian prescription.

Much more devastating for Marxism, though, was the social-democratic age. Social democracy – or at least as propounded in the 1950s and 1960s in Britain by the likes of Anthony Crosland and John Strachey, and in the US by the likes of Daniel Patrick Moynihan and Sidney Hook – was based upon the simple proposition that capitalism had changed: that the raw nineteenth-century version had been tamed by trade unions, and the growth of government (indeed Crosland argued that in the postwar social-democratic consensus unions were too strong), and that consequently the Marxist approach was largely redundant. However, now that globalisation has eroded unions and governments and raw capitalism is back with a vengeance, social democrats should generously recognise the contribution that aspects of the original Marxist critique can make to current understanding.

As I have argued in this book, whilst capitalism was constrained by democratic nations (by taxation, unions and planning) then the dynamic of capitalism was harnessed for social progress – rather than, as in the Marxian prognosis, allowed to run free to dissolve in its contradictions, and in the process impoverish the majority.

We are still a long way from mass impoverishment, but the old social-democratic model of developing classlessness – in reality a growing middle class absorbing the upwardly mobile from below – is being replaced. In the globalised West we are now facing a fearsome new society, polarised and insecure. Already a global caste of super-rich families exists over and above a domestically rooted and seriously fragmented middle class, many of whom are, in turn, but one step from descending into what may soon emerge as a restive underclass (and a bulging prison population).

It would be the most foolish tragedy if globalisation, with all its promise of better times, of nothing less than 'the end of history', should, because we are fearful of taking the necessary corrective action, lead us to this fate.

Notes and References

1 The New World

1 The median income of US families was about $37 000 in 1993. US Census Bureau, Income and Poverty, CD-ROM, table 3F (1993). The median income of UK households was about $16 500 (The exchange rate used here is $1.6 to the pound) in 1990 at 1993 prices. See John Hills, *Income and Wealth*, vol. 2 (Joseph Rowntree Foundation, Feb. 1995).

2 Thomas J. Stanley and William D. Danko, *The Millionaire Next Door* (Atlanta, GA: 1997). Some scholars have suggested defining 'the rich' not in terms of millions but rather as those with a family income over nine times the poverty line – in US terms about $95 000 a year in 1987. See S. Danziger, P. Gottschalk and E. Smolensky, 'How The Rich Have Fared, 1973–87', *American Economic Review*, vol. 72, no. 2 (May, 1989), p. 312.

3 The US Finance House Merrill Lynch in conjunction with Gemini Consulting, 'World Wealth Report 1997' (London: Merrill Lynch, 1997).

4 Stanley and Danko, *The Millionaire Next Door*, op. cit., p. 12.

5 US figures for 1995 from Arthur B. Kennickell (board of governors of the Federal Reserve System) and R. Louise Woodburn, 'Consistent Weight Design for the 1989, 1992 and 1995 SCF's and the Distribution of Wealth', revised July, 1997 unpublished. The UK figures are for 1993–4. For the UK figures, which include pensions, see Hills, *Income and Wealth*, op. cit., ch. 7.

6 Merrill Lynch, 'World Wealth Report, 1997', op. cit.

7 The 'World Wealth Report, 1997' (Merrill Lynch, op. cit.) projected, before the late 1997 Asian economic decline, that in 2000 the division of high net worth assets by source region would be Europe 7.1, North America 5.8, Asia 6.1, Latin America 3.8, Middle East 1.2 and Africa 0.4.

8 Of these multimillionaire Americans, families of British (that is English, Scottish, Welsh and Irish) and German descent account for 41.3 per cent of the total.

9 *Newsweek*, 4 Aug. 1997 (source IRS).

10 The UN *Human Development Report* (1996) put the figure at 358, and *Forbes* magazine's 1997 wealth list put the figure at 447, up from 274 in 1991.

11 *Newsweek* 4 Aug. 1997 (source *Forbes*, op. cit.)

12 See also, Phillip Hall, *Royal Fortune: Tax, Money and The Monarchy* (London: 1992) for a systematic account of the mysteries of the royal finances. One fact about the Queen's money remains: since 1998 she has remained above the law as far as taxation is concerned as she is not treated in exactly the same way – with all tax laws applying to her – as every other British person.

13 See *Newsweek*, 'The New Rich', 4 Aug. 1997.

14 Hills, *Income and Wealth*, op. cit., p. 9. Hills suggests that 'If Britain's richest man, Soho millionaire Paul Raymond, receives a modest 3 per cent net real return on his reported £1.65 billion fortune' his income would be £1 million a week.

15 Figures from *Newsweek*, 4 Aug. 1997, reporting *Forbes* in June 1997. The figures for the Queen were for 1992 (as published in *The Sunday Times'* 'Rich List', 1997), and were subsequently revised downwards following a complaint to the Press Complaints Commission.

16 The World Bank's *World Atlas*, calculated the GNP of the USA as $7 100 007 000 000 and that of the Group of Seven as $17 948 000 000 000 (Washington, DC: World Bank, 1997). Calculations in US dollars and US computations of billion and trillion.

17 John Gray, 'Bill Rules the World – And I Don't Mean Clinton', *Daily Express*, 11 Sep. 1998.

18 UN, *Human Development Report*, (1966). Comparing wealth with income is highly problematic, but nonetheless serves to display the enormity of the comparison. These comparisons – between asset net worth and gross national product (GNP) are not of course comparing like with like, but are used in order to show the extent of the egregious financial and economic power of the high net worth individuals. The most reasonable method of comparison would be to compare the net worth of super-rich individuals and groups of super-rich individuals with the total net worth of each country (That is, each individual/family in the country). These figures are not available for more than a handful of countries.

19 'Billion' here and throughout the book is used in the US sense that is, nine noughts.

20 Wealth figures from *The Sunday Times'*, 1997 'Rich List', op. cit., population figures for 1995 from *World Development Report* (Washington, DC: World Bank, 1997).

21 The US figure is from *Forbes*, June 1977, and the European and British from *The Sunday Times*, 6 April, 1977. For GNP figures see World Bank, *The World Atlas*, op. cit.

22 *Guardian*, 23 Sep. 1997.

23 These estimates are based upon the net worth estimates cited in *Forbes* magazine, June 1977, and in 'The Wealth Register', compiled by Dr Richard Beresford for *The Sunday Times* (extracts published in *The Sunday Times*, 6 April, 1997), who also cites *Forbes* magazine. *The World Atlas*, op. cit.

24 As I argue throughout this book, the super-rich are in reality global; but they all need a passport, and we are talking here about US passport holders.

25 The percentage of net worth of the total marketable net worth of all British passport holders.

26 *The Sunday Times*, 6 April, 1997. This is the British billion, that is, 12 noughts as opposed to the US nine noughts.

27   Andrew Lycett, 'Who Really Owns London?', *The Times*, 17 Sep. 1997.
28   Alan Blinder, former vice chairman of the US Federal Reserve, quoted in *Newsweek*, 23 June 1997.
29   Figures from 'Consistent Weight Design for the 1989, 1992 and 1995 SCF's and the Distribution of Wealth' by Arthur Kennickell (Federal Reserve System) and R. Louise Woodburn (Ernst and Young), revised July 1997 (unpublished). Figures derived from the Survey of Consumer Finances sponsored by the US Federal Reserve System and the Statistics of Income Division of the IRS.
30   See Charles Feinstein, 'The Equalising of Wealth In Britain Since The Second World War', *Oxford Review of Economic Policy*, vol. 12, no. 1 (Spring 1996), p. 96 ff. In British estimates distinctions tend to be made between marketable wealth and total wealth – marketable wealth excludes state pensions, occupational pensions and tenancy rights.
31   All HNWI assessments from Merrill Lynch, 'World Health Report', op. cit. The assessment of the assets of world-wide HNWIs was conducted before the collapse of many Asian markets in 1998.
32   Merrill Lynch, 'World Health Report', op. cit.
33   1995 figures in Kennickell and Woodburn, 'Consistent Weight Design', op. cit., table 9.
34   For precise figures see Hills, *Income and Wealth*, op. cit., pp. 98–9.
35   John Scott, *Corporate Business and Capitalist Classes* (Oxford, 1997), p. 65; see idem p. 70 and table 12, p. 74, for assessments.
36   Edward Luttwak, *The Endangered American Dream* (New York: 1993), p. 175.
37   These categories from Scott, *Corporate Business*, op. cit., pp. 278–9.
38   M. Soref and M. Zeitlin, 'Finance Capital and the Internal Structure of the Capitalist Class in the United States', in Mizruchi and Schwartz (eds), *Intercorporate Relations: The Structural Analysis of Business*, (New York: 1988).
39   M. Zeitlin, cited in Scott, *Corporate Business*, op. cit., p. 300.
40   Categories detailed in Kennickell and Woodburn, 'Consistent Weight Design', op. cit.
41   1995 salaries from Denny Braun, *The Rich Get Richer: the Rise of Inequality in the United States and the World* (Chicago: 1997), pp. 32–3.
42   *Business Week*, 21 April, 1997.
43   Reported in *The Philadelphia Inquirer*, 26 May, 1991.
44   *Fortune Magazine*, 4 May, 1990.
45   Kevin Phillips, *Boiling Point: Republicans, Democrats and the Decline of Middle Class Prosperity* (New York: 1993), p. 190.
46   See Stanley and Danko, *The Millionaire Next Door*, op. cit., p. 143.
47   For discussion of twentieth-century capitalist wealth concentration see: K. Renner, *The Institutions of Private Law and their Social Function*, translation of 1928 revised edition (London: 1949); R. Hilferding, *Finance Capital* (London: 1981); A. A. Berle and G. C. Means, *Corporations and Private Property* (New York: 1947); C. A. R. Crosland, *The Future of Socialism* (London: 1956); and Scott, *Corporate Business*, op. cit.
48   Scott, *Corporate Business*, op. cit., p. 303.
49   See M. P. Allen, 'Continuity and Change Within the Core Corporate Elite', *Sociological Quarterly*, vol. 19.
50   See Scott, *Corporate Business*, op. cit., p. 303.

51 A. A. Berle, *The American Economic Republic* (London: 1963). See also J. Burnham, *The Managerial Revolution* (Harmondsworth: 1945); C. A. R. Crosland, *The Future of Socialism* (London: 1956); A. A. Berle and G. C. Means, *The Modern Corporation and Private Property* (New York: 1947, 1st edn 1932); A. A. Berle, *The Twentieth Century Capitalist Revolution* (London: 1955).
52 For an attempt to fuse Marxist and managerialist analyses, see P. A. Baran and P. M. Sweezy, *Monopoly Capital* (Harmondsworth: 1966). See also Scott, *Corporate Business*, op. cit., for a systematic analysis of Marxist and managerialist analyses.
53 Figures from Christopher Parkes, 'The Birth of Enclave Man', *Financial Times*, 20–21 Sep. 1997.
54 Thomas L. Friedman, *International Herald Tribune*, 24 June, 1997.
55 *New York Times*, 18 April, 1997.
56 The US Alternative Minimum Tax is levied on those who have substantial incomes but, because of their use of tax shelters and exemptions, submit a zero tax return.
57 See Hall, *Royal Fortune*, op. cit.
58 *Guardian*, 7 June, 1997.
59 IMF and Gibraltar figures in Hans-Peter Martin and Harald Schumann, *The Global Trap: Globalization and the Assault on Prosperity and Democracy* (London and New York: 1997), p. 63. Originally published in German under the title *Die Globalisierungsfalle: der Angriff auf Demokratie und Wohlstand* (Hamburg: 1997).
60 An inside story of the Mexican 'bail-out' is told in Martin and Schumann, *The Global Trap*, op. cit., pp. 40–5.

2 The Super-Rich Game

1 Cited in Hans-Peter Martin and Harald Schumann, *The Global Trap: Globalization and the Assault on Prosperity and Democracy* (London and New York: 1997), p. 163.
2 US figures from Kennickell and Woodburn, op. cit. in note 5 previous chapter. British figures from John Hills, *Income and Wealth* (Joseph Rowntree Foundation, Feb. 1995), p. 94.
3 It is impossible to provide reasonably accurate hourly wage rates for some countries, particularly China, but a measure of the huge discrepancy between living standards can be seen in per capita GNP figures (GNP per capita in 1992 US dollars): China $470, USA $23,240, UK $17,790, Japan $28,190, Germany $23,030, France $22,260. In the US the average hourly earnings of production and non-supervisory workers on private non-farm payrolls was $11.82 per hour for 34.4 hours per week in 1996. *World Bank Atlas* (Washington, DC: World Bank, 1995).
4 James Goldsmith, *The Trap* (London: 1994), p. 18.
5 The figures for 1994 were Germany 21.6, France 28.5 (1992 figure), Portugal 20.8, Netherlands 22.01, Sweden 27.5 and Britain 12.8. *Eurostat*, 1994.
6 Quoted in Robert Taylor, 'Global Claptrap', *Prospect*, Dec. 1997.
7 William Greider, *One World, Ready or Not: The Manic Logic of Global Capitalism* (New York: 1997), p. 11.
8 'One World', *The Economist*, Schools Brief, 18–24 Oct. 1997.

9   Ibid.
10 See E. Swyngedouw, 'Producing Futures: Global Finance as a geographical product', in P.W. Daniels, *The Global Economy in Transition* (London: 1966), p. 135.
11 See J. H. Dunning, *The Globalization of Business* (London and New York: 1993), p. 287.
12 Taylor, 'Global Claptrap', op. cit.
13 See *New Left Review*, Dec. 1997.
14 See H. Brar, *Imperialism* (London: 1997).
15 W. Sengenberger and F. Wilkinson, 'Globalization and Labour Standards', in J. Mitchie and J. G. Smith, *Managing The Global Economy* (Oxford and New York: 1995).
16 See 'One World', *The Economist*, op. cit. On the amount of FDI, see Paul Hirst and Grahame Thompson, *Globalisation in Question* (London: 1996).
17 See Ankie Hoogvelt, *Globalisation and the Post Colonial World: The New Political Economy of Development* (London), p 87. The author also argues that the data used for this analysis is pre-1990.
18 See Brar, *Imperialism*, op. cit., pp. 86–9. An UNCTAD analysis of the regional distribution of world FDI inflows is instructive – after a dip in the late 1980s FDI investment in non-Western countries rose from 18.3 per cent to 35.2 per cent.
19 See UN, *World Investment Report 1998* (New York: UN Publications Offices, 1998). Figures from this report were reported in the *Financial Times*, 11 Nov. 1998.
20 See Brar, *Imperialism*, op. cit.
21 *Financial Times*, 11 Nov. 1998.
22 See World Bank, *World Atlas*, op. cit., pp. 36–7.
23 Martin and Schumann, *The Global Trap*, op. cit., pp. 68–9.
24 See *Newsweek*, 3 Oct. 1994.
25 *The Economist*, 18 Oct. 1997.
26 Michael Lind, *The Next American Nation: The New Nationalism and the Fourth American Revolution* (New York: 1995), p. 203.
27 Yonghao Pu, 'Shelter From The Storm', *Financial Times*, 13 Jan. 1996.
28 Jeffrey Henderson, 'Market Stalinism Going to the Wall', *Guardian*, 13 Jan. 1998, extracted from Grahame Thompson (ed.), *Economic Integration in the Asia-Pacific* (London: 1998).
29 John Gray, 'Bill Rules the World – And I Don't Mean Clinton', *Daily Express*, 11 Sep. 1998, p. 190.
30 Robert Z. Lawrence, *Single World: Divided Nations: International Trade and OECD Labor Markets* (Paris: 1996), p. 128.
31 See Martin and Schumann, *The Global Trap*, op. cit., pp. 1–5.
32 See Tony Crosland, *The Future Of Socialism* (London: 1956).
33 Cited in Ralph Miliband, *The State in Capitalist Society: the Analysis of the Western System of Power* (London: 1973), p. 132.
34 Joe Rogaly, 'Forget governments – companies rule, OK', *Financial Times*, 8–9 Nov. 1997.
35 These estimates, based upon a Conference Board of New York report, are cited in Mathew Horsman, *After The Nation-State: Citizens, Tribalism and the New World Disorder* (London: 1994), p. 201.

36 Sarah Anderson and John Kavanagh, *International Herald Tribune*, 23 Oct. 1996.
37 Robert Reich, *The Work of Nations* (New York: 1991), p. 110.
38 Ibid., p. 113.
39 Gray, 'Bill Rules the World', op. cit., p. 82.
40 Ibid; Martin and Schumann, *The Global Trap*, op. cit., p. 111.
41 See David Greenway (ed.), *Current Issues in International Trade Theory and Policy* (New York: 1985), quotation from Ravi Batra, *The Myth of Free Trade* (New York: 1993), p. 157.
42 Report in *Le Monde*, 29 April, 1993, cited in Goldsmith, *The Trap*, op. cit., p. 20.
43 David Hale, 'How the Rise of Global Pension Funds will Change the Global Economy in the 21st century', prepared for the 1997 Bank Credit Analyst Bermuda Conference, May, 1997, unpublished, p. 10.
44 John Scott, *Corporate Business and Capitalist Classes* (Oxford: 1997), p. 86.
45 Hale, 'The Rise of Global Pension Funds', op. cit.
46 Ibid.

3   The Rest of Us

1   See Alan Greenspan's evidence to the House Banking Subcommittee, 23 July, 1997, particularly his exchanges with Representative Saunders of Vermont.
2   OECD figures from Anthony Atkinson, Lee Rainwater and Timothy Smeeding, 'Income Distribution in Advanced Economies: Evidence from the Luxembourg Income Study', working paper 120 (Syracuse, NY: 1995).
3   Ibid., pp. 36–7.
4   Anthony Atkinson, Lee Rainwater and Timothy Smeeding, *Income Distribution in OECD Countries* (Paris: OECD, 1995).
5   *New York Times*, 18 April, 1997.
6   In Britain the Gini index rose nine points – from 25 to 34 – between 1979 and 1991, far higher than in the Netherlands, France, West Germany, Ireland, Portugal and Italy. See A. B. Atkinson, 'The Distribution of Income', in John Hills (ed.), *New Inequalities: The Changing Distribution of Income and Wealth in the United Kingdom* (Cambridge: 1996), pp. 20–3. (The Gini coefficient is a commonly used index of income inequality. The index is zero if all the units – families or individuals – in a country have the same income and rises to a maximum of 100 if a single unit has all the income.) Atkinson warns his readers that these statistics are not comparable because they are derived differently in each country, but that they 'may serve to give an indication of the relative trends in different countries'. Also, the figures for France cease in 1984.
7   The Gini coefficient can be calculated in differing ways but all the methods show the trends of British inequality rising since the mid 1970s. One such Gini trend shows a dramatic rise of a third between 1977 and 1991. See Hills, *New Inequalities*, op. cit. On page 2 Hills sets out the differing methods of calculating the Gini coefficient: the CSO Blue Book method, the CSO Economic Trends method and the Institute for Fiscal Studies method. He also points out that the basis of the statistical assessment for the CSO Blue Book method alters. The financial year 1984–5 is the final date for data taken from the

194   *Notes and References*

analysis of post-tax income tax units – either married couples or singles – the
'Blue Book' of the Central Statistical Office (now the Office of National
Statistics). After 1984–5 a new measure took over, based on the CSO's 'Economic Trends', which adjusts households' total disposable income for size
and composition (for example children are assumed to consume less). That
adjustment is called 'equivalisation'. A Gini of 35 on the 'Blue Book' data for
1984–5 is reposted as 25 in 'Economic Trends'. In other words, equivalisation
acts to give a more egalitarian picture. On the new 'equivalised' scale, it then
rises to 36 in 1990, going back to 35 in 1993. The ratio of 25 to 35 is 1.4. The
inference may be valid; a ratio increase of 40 per cent, to restore the basis of
comparison, yields a parallel Gini for 1993 of 49 on the first measure used –
that is, 35 for 1984–5, its final date, raised by 40 per cent. Indeed if you add a
40 per cent ratio to get 49 for 1993 on the rerated scale, then the apt
regressive parallel, after 'unequalisation' since 1976, may go back not just
to 1938 but to 1913, which is 47–53 on the first measure. Under the impact of
globalisation Britain was returning to the social profile – in equality if not in
employment – of the 1930s. John Hills argues, in a Joseph Rowntree Trust
study, that 'the rise in inequality in Britain after 1978 . . . is more than large
enough to offset all the decline in inequality . . . between 1949 and 1976–7 –
and almost large enough to take it back to 1938'. John Hills, *Joseph Rowntree
Foundation Inquiry into Income and Wealth*, vol. 2 (York: Joseph Rowntree
Foundation, 1995, p. 25.)

8   See Hills, *New Inequalities* (Cambridge: 1996) p. 45. Figures taken from P.
Saunders, 'Rising on the Tasman Tide: Income Inequality in Australia and
New Zealand in the 1980's', discussion paper no. 49 (University of NSW:
1994).

9   A. B. Atkinson, 'Seeking to Explain the Distribution of Income', in Hills *New
Inequalities* p. 19.

10 Denny Braun, *The Rich Get Richer: The Rise of Inequality in the United States and
the World* (Chicago: 1997), p. 118.

11 From Current Population Survey, US Bureau of the Census for relevant years,
and from Summary Federal Tax Information By Income Group and Family
Type 1996. Projection Based Upon Congressional Budget Office's January
1995 Economic Forecast.

12 Kevin Phillips, *Boiling Point* (New York: 1993), Appendix A.

13 Summary Federal Tax Information by Income Group and Family Type projected for 1998 based upon the CBO's January 1997 forecast.

14 Reich, *The Work of Nations*, op. cit., p. 198.

15 The *New York Times* reported that 'in the first quarter of the year [1997] the
wages of full time adult workers in the bottom 10% of the wage spectrum rose
by 4.4% to $259 a week, or $6.48 an hour. By comparison the median weekly
wage rose by 3.5% to $536, or $13.40 an hour.' 'Caren Good, aged 34, slips
cheques into a whirring machine with her left hand, while her right records
the amounts on a keyboard . . . . For this she earns $7.10 (£4.43) an hour, her
highest wage in years.' (Reprinted from the *Guardian*, 27 May, 1997.) Caren
Good is in Robert Reich's 'routine production services' category.

16 From Arthur B. Kennickell and R. Louise Woodburn, 'Consistent weight
Design for the 1989, 1992 and 1995 SCF's and the Distribution of Wealth',
revised, July, 1997, unpublished. Table 9, p. 29.

17 Figures from ibid. The Federal Reserve paper reported 'a statistically significant increase in the share of household net worth held by the wealthiest half a percent of households from 1992 to 1995, driven in large part by a rise in their share of personal businesses'. Also, The Federal Reserve's Survey of Consumer Finances had earlier shown a 'dramatic increase in the concentration of wealth amongst the wealthiest half a percent of households from 1983 to 1989' (ibid., p. 31).

18 Figures from ibid. These Federal Reserve figures show the share of liabilities of the bottom 90 per cent of American households as having risen from 62 per cent in 1989 to 71 per cent in 1997, whereas the liabilities of the mega-rich (the top 500 000 families) fell over the same period from 12.5 per cent to 6.8 per cent of the total.

19 Ibid.

20 Figures from James Banks, Andrew Dilnot and Hamish Low, 'Patterns of Financial Wealth Holding in the United Kingdom', in Hills, *New Inequalities*, op. cit., p. 342.

21 Charles Feinstein, 'The Equalising of Wealth in Britain Since The Second World War', *Oxford Review of Economic Policy*, vol. 12, no. 1, (Spring, 1996), p. 96 ff. Feinstein argues that the key beneficiaries of the widening wealth ownership between 1911 and 1930 appear to have been 'the next 9%'. Gainers from reduction in wealth shares at the top seem to have extended outwards after that; the share of total wealth taken by the lower 75 per cent rose from a mere 3 per cent in 1930 (in England and Wales) to 43 per cent in 1980.

22 Ibid.

23 John Scott, *Who Rules Britain?* (Cambridge, UK: 1991), pp. 83–4.

24 Figures from D. Massey and A. Catalano, *Capital and Land* (London: 1978), p. 59.

25 Arthur Seldon, *Capitalism* (Oxford: 1990), p. 195

26 Jeff Gates, *The Ownership Solution* (London: 1998), p. 217.

27 Denny Braun, *The Rich Get Richer* (Chicago: 1997), p. 30.

28 Will Hutton, *The State We're In* (London: 1995), p. 172.

29 Ibid., pp. 172, 192. See ibid., ch. 7, for a general argument about equality.

30 See Braun, *The Rich Get Richer*, op. cit., p. 24.

31 Robert Nozicke, *Anarchy, State and Utopia* (London: 1904).

32 This is Anthony Crosland's thinking on the subject, as enunciated by Raymond Plant and quoted in Eric Shaw, 'Capitalism's Premature Mourner', *The Times Higher Education Supplement*, 3 Oct. 1997.

33 Robert Z. Lawrence, *Single World, Divided Nations? International Trade and OECD Labor Markets* (Paris: 1996), p. 16.

34 The figure was adjusted for inflation by the Commerce Department's price index. Report from chief economist at Merrill Lynch, *Washington Post*, 7 Aug. 1997.

35 US Bureau of Labor Statistics, Series Catalogue EEU00500006. Between 1987 and 1996 the average hourly earnings of production workers in the private sector rose from $8.98 to $11.81; and in the same period prices (the CPI) rose from 113.6 to 156.9. US Bureau of Labor Statistics data for National Employment Hours and Earnings, series id: EEUOO500006, derived from http://stats.bls.gov:80/cgi-bin/surveymost.

36   See exchanges between Alan Greenspan and Congressman Bernie Saunders, House Banking Sub-Committee, op. cit.

37   Alan B. Krueger, 'The Truth About Wages', *New York Times*, 31 July 1997. Emphasis added.

38   The Commerce Department's price index for PCE (personal consumption expenditure) rose less rapidly than the more widely known CPI (consumer price index) of the Labor department, and some economists were beginning to argue in 1997, as part of the reaction to the growing evidence of falling incomes, that the CPI was flawed and overstated inflation somewhat. Global capital's supporters also argue that this decline in real wage rates was in large part due to falling productivity per worker.

39   John M. Berry, *Washington Post*, 7 Aug. 1997.

40   Quotes from Lawrence, *Single World, Divided Nations?* op. cit., p. 16.

41   Stephen P. Jenkins, 'Recent Trends in the UK Income Distribution: What Happened and Why?', *Oxford Review of Economic Policy*, vol. 10, no. 1 (Spring, 1996).

42   The gross weekly and hourly earnings of full-time adult employees in Britain showed a changing picture between 1989 and 1995. For men, from 1992 to 1995 the lowest male decile's pay rose from £170.20 a week to £182 and that of the lower quartile rose from £219.30 to £237.10. Prices also rose over the three years. The lower quartile's gain of 8 per cent would have been more than cancelled out by a mix of inflation and indirect tax rises. The upper quartile's weekly gross earnings rose by 10 per cent from £401.9 to £442.7; the highest decile's by 10.5 per cent from £544.10 to £600.80. The upper quartile and the highest decile would also have had a much higher take in unearned investment income. The benefits upon which the less well-off relied only rose with prices. If we cross-compare gross hourly and gross weekly pay by group, we also discover that on average the lowest decile worked 43 a week and the highest decile 38.5 hours a week, a fall from 40 hours a week for the highest decile since 1989 and a rise from 41.5 for the lowest decile. For women, the lowest decile also lost out relatively in weekly pay increase terms compared with the higher groups. Data from New Earnings Survey, 01928 79 2077 (London: Central Statistical Office, 1996).

43   Figures and quotation from 'News From Labour', Labour Party Media Office, 29 Jan. 1997. The figures were derived from the Labour Force Survey, supplied by the Commons Library to the Labour Party.

44   See Braun, *The Rich Get Richer* op. cit., p. 245.

45   Bennett Harrison and Barry Bluestone, *The Great U-Turn: Corporate Re-Structuring and the Polarizing of America* (New York: 1988).

46   *New York Times*, 8 Aug. 1997.

47   Government bulletin, 'Labour Market Trends', January, 1997.

48   Paul Gregg and Jonathan Wadsworth, 'More Work In Fewer Households?', in Hills, *New Inequalities*, op. cit., p. 181 ff.

49   Hutton, *The State We're In*, op. cit., pp. 107–8.

50   Bureau of Labor Statistics, survey of contingent workers, 1995, cited in Braun, *The Rich Get Richer*, op. cit., p. 245.

51   *New York Times*, 8 Aug. 1997.

52   Harry Shutt, *The Trouble with Capitalism: An Enquiry into the Causes of Global Economic Failure* (London: 1998), p. 96.

53 Quoted in Martin and Schumann, *The Global Trap*, op. cit., p. 122.
54 Both quotes from Richard Sennett, 'Work Can Screw You Up', *Financial Times*, 17 Oct. 1998.
55 Braun, *The Rich Get Richer*, op. cit., p. 188.
56 *Wall Street Journal*, 17 July, 1997.
57 Paul Ryan, 'Factor Shares and Inequality in the UK', *Oxford Review of Economic Policy*, vol. 12, No. 1, Spring 1996, op. cit., table 3, p. 117.
58 Charles Handy, 'The Citizen Corporation', presented at The Sovereignty Seminar, Birkbeck College, London University, 23 April, 1997.
59 Banks *et al.*, 'Patterns of Financial Wealth Holding', op. cit., fig. 13.5.
60 Ibid., table 13.5. Figures from Inland Revenue Statistics and FRS.
61 Cited in Kevin Phillips, *Boiling Point: Republicans, Democrats and the Decline of Middle Class Prosperity* (New York: 1993), p. 191.
62 Ibid.
63 Monica Castillo, 'A Profile of the Working Poor', Report 896 (Bureau of Labor Statistics, Washington, DC, 1995), p. 1.
64 See John Hills, *Income and Wealth* (Joseph Rowntree Foundation, February 1995), vol. 2, p. 33.
65 Paul Gregg and Jonathan Wadsworth, 'More Work in Fewer Households?', in Hills, *New Inequalities*, op. cit., p. 181 ff. Quote from p. 204.

4 Super-Rich Capitalism

1 John Gray, *False Dawn* (London: 1998), ch. 4.
2 Jeff Gates, *The Ownership Solution* (London: 1998), p. 217.
3 Arthur Seldon, *Capitalism* (Oxford: 1990), p. 278.
4 *Guardian*, 7 June, 1997.
5 R. H. Tawney, *Religion and the Rise of Capitalism* (London: 1960), Max Weber, *The Protestant Ethic and the Spirit of Capitalism*, trans. Talcott Parsons (New York: 1958); H. Gutman, *Work, Culture and Society in Industrialising America* (Oxford: 1977).
6 Peter Saunders, *Capitalism: a Social Audit* (Buckingham: 1995), p. 17.
7 Michael Rose, *Re-working the Work Ethic* (London: 1985).
8 Tawney, *Religion*, op. clt., p. 207.
9 Will Hutton, *The State To Come* (London: 1997), p. 40.
10 Martin Wolf, 'Caging The Bankers', *Financial Times*, 20 Jan. 1998.
11 Edward Luce, 'Age of Uncertainty', *Prospect*, July, 1998, p. 27.
12 Reported by Larry Elliot, 'Sending Out an S.O.S.', *Guardian*, 12 Jan. 1998. See also Larry Elliott and Dan Atkinson, *The Age of Insecurity* (London: 1998). 'Chapter Eleven' allows a business in trouble to seek protection from its creditors without necessarily closing down.
13 Phillips, *Boiling Point: Republicans, Democrats and the Decline of Middle Class Prosperity* (New York: 1993), p. 191.
14 Ibid.
15 Thomas J. Stanley and William D. Danko, *The Millionaire Next Door* (Marietta, Georgia: 1996).
16 Woolf's projection and the quote are from Phillips, *Boiling Point*, op. cit., p. 192.
17 Frederich Von Hayek, *The Constitution of Liberty* (London: 1960), pp. 90–1.

18   Quoted by Irwin Seltzer in *The Sunday Times*, 1 June, 1997.
19   Stanley and Danko, *The Millionaire*, op. cit., p. 143.
20   Ibid., table 5–1, p. 145, from a survey of 222 millionaires with at least one adult child of 25 years of age or older.
21   Ibid., p. 91.
22   Ibid., p. 143.
23   Phillips, *Boiling Point*, op. cit., citing a *Boston Globe* report of 6 Oct. 1991, p. 190.
24   Stanley and Danko, *The Millionaire*, op. cit., p. 153.
25   Number of millionaire households: English 732 837 (21.1 per cent of millionaire household population); German 595 171 (17.3 per cent of millionaire household population); Irish 429 559 (12.5 per cent), Scottish 322 255 (9.3 per cent). Figures from Stanley and Danko, *The Millionaire*, op. cit., table 1–1, p. 17.
26   Hayek, *The Constitution of Liberty*, op. cit., p. 397.
27   Marc-Henri Glendening, 'Thatcherism and Libertarianism', in Arthur Seldon (ed.), *The New Right Enlightenment* (London: 1985), p. 127.
28   Karl Popper, *The Open Society and its Enemies* (London: 1962). For his views on the Thatcher government's strategy of social mobility see Norman Tebbit, *Upwardly Mobile* (London: 1988).
29   Quoted in William Greider *One World, Ready or Not: The Manic Logic of Global Capitalism* (New York: 1997), p. 288.
30   Weber, *The Protestant Ethic*, op. cit., p. 56.
31   Peter Singer, *How Are We To Live?* (Oxford: 1993). See George Gilder, *Wealth and Poverty* (New York: 1981).
32   Quoted in Adam Smith, *The Roaring Eighties* (New York: 1988), p. 209.
33   Seldon, *Capitalism*, op. cit., p. 311.
34   See Denny Braun, *The Rich Get Richer* (Chicago: 1997) pp. 32–6.
35   Gates, *The Ownership Solution*, op. cit., p. 217.
36   For the sums involved until 1991 see Stephen Haseler, *The Politics of Giving* (Washington, DC: 1991).
37   Figures from Howard Hurd and Mark Lattimer, 'The Millionaire Givers', quoted in the *Guardian*, 23 Sep. 1997.
38   Amartya Sen, *On Ethics and Economics* (New York: 1987).
39   Charles Handy 'The Citizen Corporation', paper presented to The Sovereignty Seminar, Birkbeck College, University of London: 23 April, 1997, unpublished.

5   A World without Politics

1   Peter Drucker, 'The Age of Social Transformation', *Atlantic Monthly*, Nov. 1994.
2   Arthur Seldon, *Capitalism* (Oxford: 1990), p. 111
3   Blair agreed to take a lower place on the bill that the popular singer Elton John on the Des O'Connor Show (LWT, July, 1998).
4   See: British Public Opinion, MORI polls, the newsletter of MORI, published every month, for regular polling information on the monarchy.
5   See particularly Julian Le Grand and Robert Goodin, *Not Only The Poor* (London: 1987).
6   For a comprehensive review of factors affecting turnout in Britain from 1945–89 see David Butler, *British General Elections Since 1945* (Oxford: 1989). For

details of US turnout until the 1990s see Philip John Davies, *Elections USA* (Manchester: 1992).

7 Quote from Joseph S. Nye, Jr, Philip D. Zelivok and David C. King (eds) *Why People Don't Trust Government* (Cambridge, Mass., 1997). This volume is part of The Kennedy School's 'multi- year research and outreach project that will consider and articulate visions of government for the twenty-first century.'

8 S. Mulhall and A. Swift, *Liberals and Communitarians* (Oxford: 1992), p. 67.

9 Alan S. Milward, *The European Rescue of the Nation State* (London: 1992).

10 Linda Colley, *Britons: Forging The Nation 1707–1837* (London: 1992), p. 291.

11 For a systematic account of how political and social values conditioned an imperial system see Correlli Barnett, *The Collapse of British Power* (London: 1972).

12 For the ideas of Herbert Spencer see W. H. Greenleaf, *The British Political Tradition, Vol 2: The Ideological Heritage* (London: 1983), p. 51.

13 William Pfaff, *International Herald Tribune*, 2 Dec. 1997.

14 Matthew Josephson, *The Robber Barons* (London: 1962), p. 316.

15 Quoted in ibid.

16 Alfred D. Chandler, Jr. *The Visible Hand: The Managerial Revolution in American Business* (Cambridge, Mass: 1977), p. 1.

17 Werner Sombart, 'Capitalism', in *The Encyclopaedia of the Social Sciences* (New York: 1930).

18 Chandler, *The Visible Hand*, op. cit., p. 10.

19 John Sheldrake, *Management Theory: From Taylorism to Japanization* (London: International Thomson Business Press, 1996). See also R. Gillespie, *Manufacturing Knowledge: A History of the Hawthorne Experiment* (Cambridge: 1991); David Hounshell, *From The American System To Mass Production 1800–1932; The Development of Manufacturing Technology in the USA* (Baltimore, MD: 1984).

20 F. M. L. Thompson, *The Rise of Respectable Society: A Social History of Victorian Britain 1830–1900* (London: 1988).

21 See Frederick W. Taylor, *Shop Management* (New York: 1911). The standard biography is Frank B. Copley, *Frederick W. Taylor, Father of Scientific Management*, 2 vols (New York: 1923).

22 Josephson, *The Robber Barons*, op. cit., p. 322.

23 See particularly Paul Hirst and Grahame Thompson, *Globalisation in Question* (London: 1996).

24 Quoted in Stephen Haseler, *The English Tribe* (Basingstoke, Hants: 1996), p. 56, from Stephanie Lewis, *The Times* Shopping Section, 23 April, 1994.

25 For a discussion of 'Englishness', see Haseler, *The English Tribe*, ch. 1, 'The Making of Englishness'.

26 Eric Shaw describing the views of British social democrat Anthony Crosland in 'Capitalism's Premature Mourner', *The Higher*, 3 Oct. 1997.

27 J. G. Ikenberry, 'Funk de Siecle: Impasses of Western Industrial Society at Century's End', *Millenium*, vol. 24, no. 1 (1995).

28 Richard Falk, 'Regionalism and World Order After the Cold War', *Australian Journal of International Affairs*, vol. 49, no. 1 (1995).

29 See Charles Levinson, *Vodka–Cola* (Horsham: 1980).

30 For a discussion of technology transfers by transnational corporations see Peter Dicken, *Global Shift* (London: 1992), ch. 12.

31   See D. D. Marshall, 'Understanding late Twentieth Century Capitalism: Reassessing the Globalisation Theme,' *Government and Opposition*, vol. 31, no. 2 (1996); also David Held, 'From City States to a Cosmopolitan Order?' in *Prospects for Democracy*, ed. David Held (Oxford: 1992), and Kenichi Ohmae *The End of the Nation-State* (New York: 1995).

32   Robert Reich, *The Work of Nations* (New York: 1991), p. 8.

33   R. W. Cox, 'Globalisation, Multilateralism and Democracy', in Robert W. Cox and Robert Warburton, *Approaches To World Order* (Cambridge: 1996).

34   Ian Clark, *Globalisation and Fragmentation: International Relations in the Twentieth Century* (Oxford: 1997), p. 195. For a similar analysis see M. Kaldor, 'Europe, Nation States and Nationalism', in D. Archibugi and D. Held (eds), *Cosmopolitan Democracy: An Agenda For a New World Order* (Oxford: 1995).

35   F. A. Hinsley, *Sovereignty* (Cambridge: 1986), p. 142.

36   Quotation from J. C. D. Clarke in Jack G. Greene, 'Why did they Rebel?' *The Times Literary Supplement*, 10 June, 1994.

37   Quotation from Hinsley, op. cit., pp. 208–9.

38   Harold Laski, *The Grammar of Politics* (1941), cited in Hinsley, op. cit., p. 216.

39   Matthew Horsman and Andrew Marshall, *After the Nation-State: Citizens, Tribalism and the New World Disorder* (London: 1994), p. 49.

40   Anthony Sampson, *The Independent*, 16 November, 1994.

41   Neal Ascherson, 5th Sovereignty Lecture, 'Local Government and the Myth of Sovereignty', given to Charter 88 on 25 February 1994, reprinted in *The New Statesman*, 11 March, 1994.

42   Joseph A. Camilleri and Jim Falk, *The End of Sovereignty* (Aldershot: 1992).

43   S. Mulhall and A. Swift, *Liberals and Communitarians* (Oxford: 1992), p. 67.

44   Alan S. Milward, *The European Rescue of the Nation-State* (London: 1992).

45   Horsman and Marshall, *After the Nation-State*, op. cit., p. 253.

46   Quoted in Newman, *The Rise of English Nationalism, 1740–1830* (New York: 1987), p. 253.

47   Quoted in W. H. Greenleaf, *The British Political Tradition* (London: 1983), p. 257.

48   Quoted in Newman, *The Rise of English Nationalism*, op. cit., p. 49.

49   Quoted in Anthony Sampson, *Independent*, 16 Nov. 1994.

50   Quoted in J. R. Dinwiddy, 'Parliamentary Reform as an issue in English politics, 1800–1810', London University PhD dissertation, 1971.

51   Neil Ascherson, 5th Sovereignty Lecture, given to Charter 88, 25 February, 1994, reprinted in *The New Statesman*, 11 March, 1994.

52   Quoted from John Plamenatz, 'Two Types of Nationalism', in Eugene Kamenka (ed.), *Nationalism: The Nature and Evolution of an Idea* (Canberra: 1973), p. 23.

53   Kenneth Minogue, *Nationalism* (London: 1969), pp. 23–4.

54   Ernest Gellner, *Nations and Nationalism* (London: 1983).

55   Gerald Newman, *The Rise of English Nationalism, 1740–1830* (New York: 1987), p. 199.

56   Ibid, p. 87.

57   Minogue, *Nationalism*, op. cit.

6 A World without Democracy?

1 J. M. Buchanan, *The Economics of Politics* (London: Institute of Economic Affairs, 1978), p. 18.
2 George Soros, 'The Capitalist Threat', *The Atlantic Monthly*, Feb. 1997. Emphasis added.
3 See Maurice Cranston, *Freedom: A New Analysis*, 2nd edn (London: 1955).
4 Kenneth Minogue, *Politics: A Very Short Introduction* (Oxford: 1995), ch. 1.
5 Maurice Duverger, *The Study of Politics* (Walton on Thames: 1972).
6 See Bernard Crick, Henry Fairlie and Peter Harris, *Foundations of Political Science* 2nd edn (London: 1986), ch. 1.
7 From George Soros, 'Global Meltdown', *The Times*, 30 Nov. 1998. Extracted from George Soros, *The Crisis of Global Capitalism* (New York: 1998).
8 Seldon, *Capitalism* (Oxford: 1990), p. 98.
9 Charles Handy, 'The Citizen Corporation', lecture delivered at The Sovereignty Seminar, Birkbeck College, London University, 23 April, 1997.
10 D. Miller, *Market, State and Community: Theoretical Foundations of Market Socialism* (Oxford: 1989).
11 Anthony Giddens, *The Third Way: The Renewal of Social Democracy* (London: 1998), pp. 70–8.
12 Seldon, *Capitalism*, op. cit., p. 99.
13 Christopher Pierson, 'Democracy, Markets and Capital', in David Held (ed.), *Prospects for Democracy* (Oxford: 1992).

7 The Next Phase

1 'Global Capitalism, Once Triumphant, is in Full Retreat', *International Herald Tribune*, 10 Sep. 1998.
2 See Francis Fukuyama, *The End of History and the Last Man* (London: 1992).
3 George Soros, *The Crisis Of Global Capitalism*, extract in *The Times*, 30 Nov. 1998.
4 William Greider, *One World, Ready or Not* (New York: 1997), p. 473; Edward Luttwak, *Turbo Capitalism: Winners and Losers in the Global Economy* (London: 1998), p. 187.
5 Martin. J. Anderson, 'In Defence of Chaos', in Arthur Seldon (ed.), *The New Right Enlightenment* (London: 1985).
6 Seldon, *The New Right Enlightenment*, op. cit., p. 250.
7 E. G. West, *Education: A Framework for Choice* (London: 1967); Charles Hanson, 'Welfare before the Welfare State', in *The Long Debate On Poverty* (London: 1972); F. G. Pennance, *Choice in Housing* (London: 1968); Arthur Seldon, *Wither the Welfare State* (London: 1981); David Green, *Working Class Patients and the Medical Establishment* (London: 1985.)
8 See John Gray, *Limited Government: A Positive Agenda* (London: 1989). The quotations are from Seldon *Capitalism*, p. 236, and are Seldon's interpretation of Gray's 1989 analysis.
9 Quotes and examples from Hans-Peter Martin and Harald Schumann *The Global Trap* (London: 1997), p. 201.
10 Will Hutton, *The State We're In* (London: 1995), p. 306.
11 For the full development of this argument see Seldon, *Capitalism*, op. cit., chs 10 and 11.

12 'Will Europe Face up to Coming Reality?', *International Herald Tribune*, 20–1 Sept. 1997.
13 Ibid.
14 George Stigler, *The Citizen and the State* (Chicago, Ill., 1975).
15 Hutton, *The State We're In*, op. cit., p. 292. For a positive account of regulation see Ian Ayres and John Braithwaite, *Responsive Regulation* (Oxford: 1992).
16 See J. W. Burton, *World Society* (Cambridge, 1972); John Vogler, 'The Structures of Global Politics' in Charlotte Bretherton and Geoffrey Ponton (eds), *Global Politics* (Oxford: 1996).
17 Joel Kotkin, *Tribes* (New York: 1992).
18 John Eatwell, 'The International Origins of Unemployment', in John Eatwell (ed) *Coping with Global Unemployment*, (New York: 1995) See also Susan Strange, *Casino Capitalism* (London: 1997).
19 Ravi Batra, *The Myth of Free-Trade: The Pooring of America* (New York: 1993), p. 1.
20 US Department of Labor, Bureau of Labor Statistics, Employment and Earnings (Washington, DC: Government Printing Office, January, 1987).
21 Edward Luttwak, *Turbo Capitalism*, op. cit., pp. 182–3.
22 James Goldsmith, *The Response* (London: 1995), pp. 177–8.
23 Ravi Batra, *The Myth of Free Trade*, op. cit., p. 156.
24 William Greider, *Who Will Tell The People?* (New York: 1995), p. 393.
25 See S. Gill, 'Structural Change and Global Political Economy: Globalizing Elites and the Emerging World Order', in Yoshikazu Sakamoto (ed.) *Global Transformation: Challenges to the State System* (Tokyo: UN University Press, 1994), p. 178.
26 Bob Herbert 'How the Labor Game is Rigged', *International Herald Tribune*, 21 Nov. 1997.
27 Greider, *One World, Ready Or Not*, p. 297.
28 Roger Bootle, *The Death of Inflation* (London: 1996).
29 See Erica Goshen and Mark Schweitzer, 'Identifying inflation's grease and sand effects in the labour market', NBER Working Paper 6061 (Cambridge, Mass.: NBER, June, 1997).
30 For economists who argue that a small amount of inflation helps 'grease the wheels' and keep up employment levels, see George Akerlof and William Dickens, 'The Macroeconomics of low inflation', *Brookings Papers on Economic Activity*, 1 (Washington, DC, 1996).
31 'Leisurely Steps Towards EMU', letter by Lord Barnett and Lord Haslam in the *Financial Times*, 8–9 Nov. 1997.
32 Edward Luttwak, 'Central Bankism: A New Religion', *London Review of Books*, 14 Nov. 1996.
33 See *Financial Times*, 27 Jan. 1992.
34 Robert Z. Lawrence, *Single World, Divided Nations: International Trade and OECD Labor Markets* (Paris: 1996), p. 8.
35 Gregory Clark, 'For East Asia the Western Myth of Free Trade is a Good Joke', *International Herald Tribune*, 15 Aug. 1996.
36 Lawrence, *Single World*, op. cit., p. 129.
37 See Carles Calomiris, 'The IMF's Imprudent Role as Lender of Last Resort', *Cato Journal*, Winter 1998; Robert Wade, 'The Asian Crisis: Debt Deflation, Vulnerabilities, Moral Hazard or Panic'. Wade@rsage. org.

38 *International Herald Tribune*, 2 Feb. 1995.
39 See Richard E. Ratcliff, Mary Elizabeth Gallaher and Antony C. Kouzi, 'Political Money and Partisan Clusters in the Capitalist Class', *Research in Politics and Society*, vol. 4 (1992), p. 76, who show that business is more generous to Republican than to Democratic candidates. For the role of PACS see Dan Clawson, Alan Neustadtl and Denise Scott, *Money Talks: Corporate PACS and Political Influence* (New York: 1992).

8 The Hope of Europe

1 Larry Elliott, 'Quaint Relic is Exposed As a Lie', *Guardian*, 23 March, 1998.
2 From Stephanie Flanders, 'Portrait of Robert Reich', *Prospect*, June, 1997.
3 'UK government Should Show Leadership on Regulating Power of Multinationals', letter by Glenys Kinnock, MEP, and Harriet Lamb of the World Development Movement in the *Financial Times*, 9 March, 1998.
4 Nawal el Saadawi on BBC Radio 3's 'Sounding the Century' series, 28 Feb. 1998. Printed in the *Observer*, Sunday 22 Feb.
5 See Peter Dicken, *Global Shift: Transforming The World Economy*, 3rd edn (New York: 1998), p. 416 ff.
6 David Held, 'From City States to a Cosmopolitan Order?', in David Held (ed.), *Prospects for Democracy* (Oxford: 1993), pp. 45–6.
7 See *Prospect* magazine, July, 1998.
8 *Financial Times*, 31 Dec. 1997.
9 For the quotes and data see *International Herald Tribune*, 17 Nov. 1997 (emphasis added).
10 'The Right Track', *Time*, 8 Dec. 1997.
11 Gregory Clark in the *International Herald Tribune*, 15 Aug. 1996.
12 Jim Hoagland, 'Needed, a Cooperation Agenda for America, Europe and Japan', *International Herald Tribune* 12 Oct. 1998.
13 *Financial Times* 8–9 Nov. 1997.
14 William McDonough, president of the New York Federal Reserve Bank, suggests that because of this projected role for the euro 'the current role of the dollar should not be taken for granted'. See *Financial Times*, 18 Nov. 1997.
15 Richard Adams, 'Taking on the Dollar', *Financial Times*, 21 Nov. 1997.
16 *The Times*, 25 Sep. 1998.
17 Interview for CNN, World Business Today, 11 Nov. 1998.
18 *Frankfurter Allgemeine Zeitung*, 2 Sep. 1996.
19 *International Herald Tribune*, 7 Jan. 1998.
20 See Adams, 'Taking on the Dollar', op. cit. For a discussion of the advantages of seignorage see Christopher Johnson, *In with the Euro, Out with the Pound*, (London: 1996), pp. 17–18, 164–5.
21 Wolfgang Munchau, 'Return to Keynes', *Financial Times*, 26 Oct. 1998.
22 Quoted in the *International Herald Tribune*, 7 Jan. 1998.
23 See David Soskice, 'To the Core', *Prospect*, June, 1997, who argued for Britain to join France in breaking the German, and the bankers', control of what was then a putative single currency.
24 For an argument that the EU monetary authorities ought to be sensitive to unemployment in an age in which inflation is no longer a serious problem,

see Oskar Lafontaine and Christa Muller, *Keine vor der Globalisierung* (Bonn: Dietz Verlag, 1998).

25   For a survey of the powers of EcoFin see Tsoukalis *The New European Economy Revisited* (Oxford: 1997), pp. 168–70.

26   Ibid. However William McDonough, president of the Federal Reserve Bank of New York has argued that he 'does not support' the view that Europe is ... vulnerable to country specific shocks'; an alternative view is outlined in the *Financial Times*, 18 Nov. 1997.

27   See Barry Eichengreen, 'One Money For Europe; Lessons from the US Currency Union', *Economic Policy*, 10 April, 1990; Xavier Sala-i-Martin and Jeffrey, Sachs, 'Fiscal Federalism and Optimum Currency Areas: Evidence For Europe From the United States', in M. Canzoneri, V. Grilli and P. Masson (eds), *Establishing a Central Bank: Issues in Europe and Lessons From the US* (Cambridge: 1992).

28   Tsoukalis, *The New European Economy*, op. cit. p. 221.

29   Ibid., p. 234.

30   Paul Krugman, 'Introduction: New Thinking About Trade Policy', in Paul Krugman (ed.) *Strategic Trade Policy and the New International Economics* (Cambridge, Mass: 1986). For theoretical support for strategic trade see Batra, *The Myth of Free Trade*, op cit., and Luttwak, *Turbo Capitalism*, op. cit., see also Lester Thurow, *Head To Head* (New York: 1992); Laura d'Andrea, *Who's Bashing Whom: Trade Conflict in High Technology Industries* (Washington, DC: Institute For International Economics, 1992).

31   See Krugman, 'Introduction', op. cit., pp. 227–8 and table 10.1.

32   For the liberalisation measures achieved in the Uraguay Round see William Cline, 'Evaluating the Uraguay Round', *The World Economy*, vol. 18 (1995).

33   James Tobin, 'A Proposal For International Monetary Reform', *Eastern Economic Journal*, nos 3–4 (July–Oct. 1978).

34   Paul Davidson, 'Are Grains of Sand in the wheels of international finance sufficient to do the job where boulders are often required?', *The Economic Journal* vol. 107, No. 442, (May: 1997). For an argument that the tax should be higher than 1 per cent see Hans-Peter Martin and Harald Schumann, *The Global Trap* (London: 1998), pp. 82–5.

35   Martin and Schumann, ibid., p. 83.

36   Barry Eichengreen, James Tobin and Charles Wyplosz, 'Two Cases for Sand in the Wheels of International Finance', *Economic Journal*, no. 105 (1995).

37   Will Hutton, *The State We're In* (London: 1995), p. 302. Other books on this subject include A. de Geus, *The Living Company* (Cambridge, Mass., USA: 1997), and George Goyder, *The Just Enterprise* (New York: 1996).

38   Quotes from Charles Handy, 'The Citizen Corporation', lecture delivered at the Sovereignty Seminar at Birkbeck College, University of London: 23 April, 1997.

39   *Bullock Report on Industrial Democracy* (London: HMSO, 1977).

40   William Pfaff, 'To Each National Culture Its Own Form of Capitalism', *International Herald Tribune*, 2 Dec. 1997.

41   Anthony Giddens, *The Third Way: The Renewal of Social Democracy* (London: 1998), p. vii.

42   Luttwak, *Turbo Capitalism: Winners and Losers in the Global Economy* (London: 1998), p. 221.

43 Denny Braun, *The Rich Get Richer* (Chicago: 1997), p. 39.
44 Ralph Miliband's *The State in Capitalist Society: The Analysis of the Western System of Power* (London: 1973), is still one of the clearest expositions of the Marxist case, as it applied to social democratic capitalism in the Cold War era.

Index

1488